Pom's Odyssey

JOHN C HOLMAN

This book is a true story,
but some of the names, places and timelines
have been changed for dramatic effect.

DEDICATION

This book is dedicated to the memory of Noel and Enid Eliot.

PART ONE: THE DRUMMER

If a man does not keep pace with his companions, perhaps it is because he hears a different drummer. Let him step to the music that he hears, however measured or far away.

Henry David Thoreau,
Walden, Conclusion, 1854

.

TOWARD AUSTRALIA

I did not want to go to Australia. I did for most of my eighteen years but now on the brink of departure for a new life Down Under, I did not. I stood on the crowded foredeck of the *SS Australis* about to embark on the longest journey of my life; a participant in the largest planned migration of the twentieth century, and one of the million or so Britons who migrated to Australia during the twenty-five years that followed the Second World War. The date – November 20, 1969 – had been seared in my consciousness for weeks. Now the day had arrived and my mother stood at the dockside between my father and brothers, her face wet with tears, straining for a last glimpse of her oldest son as he waved goodbye. Trying to remember I was British, I stoically held back until the brass band played *Auld Langs Ayne* and my tears began to flow.

Had I known then that I would spend most of my life away from England, I think I would have jumped overboard, but the ship pulled away from the Southampton dock and my family became specks in the distance, leaving me alone among five thousand strangers on the biggest one class liner in the world.

How had I gotten myself into this predicament? What propelled me toward Australia?

It seemed I had been stumbling toward that far-off land most of my life. In 1961, when I was ten years old, my grandmother started to receive the *Australian Womens Weekly* from friends Down Under. Deep in the midst of an English winter, I was entranced by pictures of sweeping plains, wide rivers, blue skies and bright sandy beaches with suntanned surfers. It seemed so exciting in comparison with the gloomy grey skies, constant rain and damp of England. At school I created a geography project on Australia, filling a large scrapbook with glossy pictures from the aforementioned *Women's Weekly*.

The following year, we had a visit from those Aussie friends. Noel Eliot was tall, tanned and ruggedly handsome; his wife Enid, trim and athletic-looking. They certainly fit the stereotypical image of Australians and this combined with their open and easygoing manner left a strong impression on my young mind, inspiring me to compile Australia II, covering all the bits I had missed in my earlier project.

Mr. Tittensor, the headmaster of *St. Andrew's Church of England Primary*, wandered down the aisle between rows of wooden desks, lowering his white-haired head to look at Peter Parson's book filled with dinosaurs that popped-up from the page into three-dimensional figures, then to gaze admiringly at Johnnie Tudhope's beautiful handwriting and drawings of *Birds of the Hedgerow*.

"Wonderful work Tudhope. You have captured the impudence of the Blue Tit perfectly. Full marks, old chap... and the lesser spotted corn-cruncher is magnificent!"

While he fingered through Tudhope's workbook, I smoothed down the picture of Ayers Rock on the cover of mine. Little rivulets of white glue appeared from the base of the rock, like lava flowing from a volcano. I wiped them off with the end of my red tie – the only dash of color in an otherwise all-gray uniform.

At my side, Mr.Tittensor tilted his head awkwardly. A German bomb had fallen on Mr. T's house during the war and the injuries he'd sustained made it difficult for him to bend from the waist, forcing him to lower his lanky frame onto the small wooden chair next to me, his long legs sprawling out the side of the desk.

"What have we here, Holman?"

Mr. T ran his fingertips along the outline of Ayers Rock. A speck of glue splashed onto his index finger – the glossy picture lifted from the surface, leaving a small, bare patch on the rock and a red stain on his finger, which he wiped off with a handkerchief.

"Messy, Holman, messy. You need to plan ahead more."

"I know sir but we ran out of glue at home."

Ignoring my response, he flipped through the scrapbook with its pictures of the Snowy Mountains Scheme, dead cattle and sheep from the drought in western New South Wales, and the bold plans for a new Sydney Opera House. Inhaling deeply, he held his breath for a few seconds then exhaled a veritable tornado of air that rustled the leaves of the sugar cane plantations in Northern Queensland and steamed up his wire-rimmed National Health specs.

"This is commendable, Holman, but shows a decided lack of imagination."

"Yes, sir."

He removed the specs and rubbed the lenses with the ink-stained handkerchief. "Remember to plan ahead next time, Holman. Planning is everything." He replaced the specs and squinted at Ayers Rock through a thin veneer of red ink. "And I don't want to see an Australia III next year, understand?"

I understood but felt much happier at tea time, when from the comfort of my mother's chintz-covered sofa, Enid Eliot sipped a cup of Macleods finest blend and offered an entirely different opinion of my project.

"This is excellent, John! Deserves an A as far as I'm concerned. I'm so glad those old Women's Weeklies came to good use." Enid was a teacher who instantly I surmised was a woman at the very pinnacle of her profession. "What do you think, Noel?"

"I think John will have to come Down Under and pay us a visit one day," her husband replied, juggling a slice of Mum's coffee cake in one hand and a full cup of tea in the other.

"Yes, I would love to! When can I come?"

I sprang up from the sofa and upset Noel's equilibrium, causing hot tea to slosh out of his cup.

"When you've finished your education, John," Enid replied, rescuing the wobbly coffee cake from Noel's other hand. "I think it would be marvelous for you to come then."

The end of school seemed a long way off but that seemingly innocuous conversation over a cup of tea on a spring day in 1962 predetermined the course of my life. (Although, in many ways, it had been predetermined on a spring night in 1944, eleven thousand feet above France, when two German Fokker Wolfe 190s flashed out of the blackness and opened fire on an RAF Stirling bomber. The bomber spiraled downward, disintegrating in flames on the ground. Four men dangling from parachutes drifted silently toward safety in the fields of northern France but Johnny Grantham, the tail-gunner was not among them. My mother's youngest brother, the man for whom I was later named, died in his turret in a hail of bullets. The French Resistance rescued the four parachutists. When repatriated to Britain after D-Day, Noel Eliot, the pilot of that plane, confirmed to my grandparents that their youngest son had been killed and thus in the wake of tragedy the Australian connection with my family had been forged.)

By all accounts, my personality and disposition were similar to Uncle Johnny's, but that's where the comparisons end, at least in my own mind. He had been good-looking, a talented artist, and a superb horseman with a promising future as a jockey. I grew up in a similar environment to that of Uncle Johnny, on my grandfather's West Sussex farm with my mother, father, two brothers and a succession of rambunctious Jack Russell terriers in a world filled with horses and horse people. My family were not rich and not poor; we fell somewhere in the middle of the middle.

My grandfather, who we called Grampy, was a tough no-nonsense horse dealer. I loved him dearly but he never wasted an opportunity to remind me of my position in society.

When he learned that the local blacksmith had attended the

annual hunt ball, his face turned purple, and he banged the dinner table with his cane. "In my day, neither you nor the blacksmith would have been allowed to look in the window."

"Well. Thank goodness timed have changed," the teenage me replied.

Grampy glared, banged the table again and limped from the room. He knew his place in the social order but his grandson did not.

The Eliots had been a breath of fresh air, seemingly devoid of the constrictions of class that riddled rural Sussex. When they came to stay, I was the same age as their daughter Lindy, a tomboy with long pigtails and a mass of freckles. I took her into the wood next to our house, where my brothers and I had built a tree house in the fork of an oak tree from which a rope ladder dangled – a ladder that only a few dared climb.

Lindy was one of the few. She scampered up the ladder, her feet barely touching the rungs. My brothers and I stood at the bottom, our mouths agape as she climbed beyond the tree house to the top branches of the tree in seconds flat. She could care less about my brothers or me, which made it worse because Lindy seemed capable of doing most things better than us. I had never seen a girl like this. I decided there and then that I would go to Australia one day, if for no other reason than to marry Lindy!

But just as I began to take a vague interest in girls in general, I left the safe and comfortable environment that Mr. and Mrs. Tittensor provided at the co-ed village primary school to attend the boys-only *St. John's College*, an establishment on the lower echelons of the English public school ladder. I was enrolled as a day-boy but most *St. John's* students were boarders – sons of diplomats, ex-pats and British corporation executives from what remained of the empire. *St. John's* was well advertised in the *Hong Kong Times* or the *Lagos Gazette* or some such clarion of the realm. Promising a first-class English education to sons of empire at a bargain basement price, the reality was far removed from the promise.

I vividly remember the day when I began to think again

about Australia because pain etches itself on the memory. It was my second day at *St. John's* and I wandered nervously up the rhododendron-lined driveway toward the gothic revival pile that housed the senior school when…

"Whoop! Whoop! Whoop!"

Dashwood leaped from his cover in the rhododendron bushes and sprinted onto the gravel driveway, hollering like a demented Apache, surrounded by a small tribe of followers.

"Here he is, boys!"

Dashwood hated me, but he hated everyone at school so I didn't take it personally. During the two preceding years at the junior school, for a short time he and I had shared the same designated lunch table. If the canteen served a meal he did not like – such as creamed beetroot, braised liver or sheep brains – Dashwood would demand that one of the younger boys eat it for him. Memories of food rationing were not too distant, so we were not allowed to waste food. The punishment for failing to eat all of your lunch was the dreaded Saturday morning detention where one would have to write a thousand lines: *I must not waste food when millions in China are starving.*

"Holman, this is disgusting. You eat it."

Dashwood, his face a picture of revulsion, shoved his bowl of stewed prunes across the long wooden table. Watery custard slopped out.

"No! I won't." I shoved it back leaving streaks of the sickly looking sauce to fill the grimy initials that former pupils had scored into the tabletop.

Dashwood pushed it back toward me. There was little custard left at this point. Dashwood's eyes shone, his cheeks turned red, his muscles tautened. Mine tautened too when I felt a severe pain in the shins as the points of his winkle-picker shoes jabbed me under the table. Too young to psychoanalyze Dashwood, nor to even contemplate what kind of home he must have come from to turn him into such a horrible human being, I kicked back. I did not give in and he did not bother me again… until two years later when I joined him at the senior school.

Back on the gravel driveway, Dashwood slid to a halt, the friction from the smooth leather soles of his winkle-picker Chelsea boots caused sparks to fly. With his cap pushed back nonchalantly, horns sprouted above his pointed ears and a dollop of yellow-green snot hung from his aquiline nose.

"So we meet again, Horse Features… thought you could escape, did you?"

"Well, I was hoping that might be the case!"

I tried to sound calm. I wasn't trying to hide. I knew I had to face the music. I thought I had dodged a bullet when they did not come for me on the first day of school but they had just run out of time.

Dashwood wiped the snot with his finger and smeared it onto the front of my brand-new maroon blazer so it looked like an energetic snail had blazed a trail up to the breast pocket where the words *Spes Sibi Quisque* stood boldly imprinted in gold lettering. Loosely translated it meant *to have faith in oneself.* That was about all one could have faith in at *St. John's.*

Dashwood shoved me on the chest. I didn't see the boy on all-fours behind me, but I fell over him and landed bum-first on the hard driveway. Dashwood gripped one of my arms; someone grasped the other and started to pull me. Gravel grazed my buttocks through thin woolen trousers as reinforcements arrived to haul me through the park-like grounds, adorned with gargoyles and weird statues designed to ward off the devil. But the devil was in his element at *St. John's.* Ghosts haunted the place: the old Grey Lady who wandered the corridors at night, and a statue with no arms that came to life at full moon. I suspected that Miss Parker, the geriatric school nurse morphed herself into the Grey Lady, but I could never prove it. Miss Parker lived in a space at the top of the clock tower and was half deaf, presumably from sleeping with the bells.

We soon reached the bottom of the garden where a crowd of yesterday's victims had gathered to gloat over new victims being tossed from a great height into the Ha Ha, a bramble-festooned waterless moat.

"Get his legs. Get his fucking legs, you blokes." Dashwood yelled. I shut my eyes as hands grabbed the sleeves of my blazer and the legs of my trousers. I felt them lifting me off the ground… swinging me back and forth… higher and higher, until they let go. When I opened my eyes, I could see they had put too much effort into it. Describing a perfect parabolic arc, I soared over the brambles to land in a patch of nettles where I lay stunned and winded, the nettles stinging me through my clothing. I rolled away, my hands scratching feverishly at the mass of welts appearing on my skin. I sought out the spear-shaped reddish leaves of the dock plant that always grows conveniently near stinging nettles, plucked one, spat on it, then rubbed nature's remedy onto the spreading rash. It provided an instant relief. Looking up, I saw another victim standing on the brink of the Ha Ha. I knew Roger Durling from the junior school – he was Australian.

Dashwood put his skinny nose an inch from Durling's face. "Come on, chaps, let's see what the Wild Colonial Boy is made of."

Durling eyed his would-be torturer calmly. Dashwood took a step backward. Durling took a step forward. He had presence. You could feel it. The other boys could feel it. They retreated into the shadows.

"Alright, you cretins, let's show him who his masters are," Dashwood screamed, his annoying high-pitched nasal voice falling on deaf ears.

Durling just shook his head in silent defiance.

Dashwood's nostrils flared like a thoroughbred racehorse. He beckoned the boys to come over. They didn't. But Dashwood persisted.

"You bastard… you're going in like all the other newbies."

Durling stood tall with a smile on his face, which further angered Dashwood. He lashed out with his winkle-picker boots, but in one swift movement Durling caught his leg, swung him off the ground and out over the edge of the Ha Ha and let go. Dashwood landed square in the middle of the bramble patch and lay there spread-eagled like da Vinci's drawing of the Vitruvian Man… except Dashwood's plaintive squeals sounded more like a pig than the perfect human being.

While I stared in disbelief, Durling shrugged, dusted his hands, turned and walked away from the Ha Ha – and away from the school. His diplomat father was posted to Beirut so Durling was gone. I hardly knew him, but I have never forgotten him. His lack of deference to the bully boys and his confidence in standing up to them became another piece of the Australian puzzle.

In the summer of 1968 I happily bid adieu to *St. John's* with a handful of General Certificate of Education O-Levels and little clue as to what I was going to do with my life, but I was free – or at least I thought I was. I had no money and no skills, so I applied for a job that might pay well, given my limited talent.

The tobacco company, WD & HO Wills, had advertisements everywhere as they sponsored everything from show jumping to golf tournaments to motor sport. My father, who worked in the hotel trade thought it might be a good company to work for. But one step through the front door of their London office put that notion to rest. I waited in the lobby, listening to the clattering of typewriters and the shuffling of paper, until a pretty mini-skirted secretary beckoned me to follow her through the main office, past row upon row of desks manned by pasty-faced clerks filing documents and typing letters. I was ushered into a large office by a British Raj type wearing a red cravat and a waxed moustache that curled up at the ends. The sunny posters of tobacco plantations on the walls were a stark contrast to the bleak, grey "summer" weather outside the window. I squirmed in a chair. This was my first interview and unlike my father, who was a natural raconteur – I found it difficult to speak about myself. Luckily, the moustache did all the talking so I just nodded occasionally; he seemed more intent on telling me his life story than finding out about me. Abruptly the interview ended with "So, young man, when can you start…eh what?"

I already knew I did not want to start there…eh what, so I

mumbled something like, "I'm not sure…I will let you know," and shot out the door faster than a scalded cat.

I wandered down the Strand toward Trafalgar Square. Passing the office of the New South Wales Tourist Commission, I spied a poster in the window which said: *£10 can take you to Australia. Australia offers you a new life. Big opportunities with space to live. Higher wages, lower taxes.* The picture in the background was of a sun-drenched beach swarming with bikini-clad girls. I jammed into an overcrowded carriage during the height of rush hour. Peering out at the grimy, rainy suburbs of London sliding by, I thought… *this is not for me*, but that poster certainly helped me figure out *what was for me* – and it did not include office work in London.

I spent the rest of the summer of '68 following the Australian cricket team on my dilapidated Lambretta Cento motor scooter. In the green, pleasant grounds of Arundel Castle I watched them play the first game of the Ashes tour against a Sussex XI. Having never attended a professional cricket match, I marveled at Johnny Gleeson's ability to spin the ball with his patented flipper action, courtesy of a bent middle finger, which he tucked under the ball to impart extra turn. Ashley Mallet and Ian Redpath were superb fielders who flew horizontally above the turf in order to take catches that I would have thought impossible to even attempt; batsmen Ian Chappell and Bill Lawry were masters of movement, velocity and location. The quiet intensity with which these players approached the game was light years from the game we played at *St. John's*. Bill Lawry had a nose Cyrano de Bergerac would have been proud of, yet it did not seem to bother him – he was captain of the Australian cricket team, for God's sake.

Something about those players – their fitness, their supreme sporting confidence and their tough-yet-easygoing manner – sat well with a young man who had little confidence in himself and my latent feelings about Australia began to revive.

My father gave them a not-so-gentle push one chilly morning when he and I were out on exercise detail for Uncle Tony, who had inherited the farm after my grandfather died. I rode several yards in front of my father, straining to keep the grip on the reins of a feisty black mare that had just arrived, barely broken, from Ireland.

"Have you given any more thought to what you want to do, now that you've been out of school awhile?" my father shouted.

"Well… not a lot…"

I pulled back on the reins, which had no effect on the mare except to make her more jumpy. I held the reins tightly and she danced beneath me, her steel-shod hooves clattering on the granite roadway. I knew what Dad was angling at: I had finished school in May 1968. The job at WD and HO Wills had not worked out and it was now January 1969. I had been drifting. My only other real job, at a local wine merchant, had not lasted long. So I sat astride that jumpy black mare awaiting a lecture from my father.

"You've always been interested in Australia. I think you should go!" He yelled.

I gasped, "What? When?" The horse lowered her head and bucked.

"It's up to you. But, I think it'll be good for you to go away and live on your own for a couple of years…seeing as you have no definite plans for a career or university."

"Well…that's great…" The idea of further education had about as much appeal as rancid butter on a stale croissant.

I heard a tractor coming round the bend and I saw the black mare's ears go back.

Oblivious to my predicament, Dad shouted, "We'll write to Noel Eliot and see if you could stay with him until you get on your feet. How does that sound?"

The tractor appeared, slowed down and then backfired. The black mare's nostrils snorted steam. She rocked back on her hind legs and reared. I hung onto her thick mane and before her flailing forelegs had even touched the ground, she was careening full-tilt down the road toward the village of Maplehurst.

"Whoa…whoa…slow down!

I tugged on the reins but the mare galloped faster. The words of Uncle Tony ran through my head: *If the horse runs away with you, keep turning her in tighter and tighter circles and she'll eventually run out of real estate.* That theory proved a bit hard to put to the test on a narrow icy lane, but with steam rising from her rump and frothy white sweat dripping from her withers, the black mare gradually ran out of energy. She huffed and puffed to a halt next to the White Horse pub.

I heard my father's cob clattering along the road behind me. Then it cantered upsides. "Are you alright, Beak?"

My father had nicknamed me Beak when my lower jaw grew out of proportion to my upper jaw. My dentist called it a class three jaw. I called it the bane of my existence.

"Yes, Dad – it sounds great. I would love to go to Australia!"

And so the die was cast. Time to get my act together.

SECOND THOUGHTS

In the 1960s, the Australian government targeted Britain with an advertising campaign that promised an always-sunny paradise, a place to start anew or to find adventure. They needed immigrants and the price was right: ten pounds.

After I diligently filled out the application form for the assisted passage scheme, I decided to hand-deliver it to Australia House. Dressed smartly in a tweed jacket, red tie, white shirt, cavalry twill trousers and shiny brown shoes, I stood in drizzle at the top of the leafy lane that ran alongside the farm, rain trickling down my neck. I thrust out my thumb and watched car after car speed by along the A272 until a smoky truck pulled up and from the cab emerged a pasty face smeared with soot, looking like Al Jolson on a bad night. It was Eddie Searles, our local coal delivery man.

"Good mornin', John. I'm going as far as Horsham," he informed me.

"Great, thanks. I can catch a train from there."

I had one foot on the running board and one on the tarmac when Eddie nodded back toward the lane. I turned to see a grey Rolls Royce gliding to a halt. The rear smoked-glass window slid down silently to reveal the attractive face of Sally, my aunt by marriage to Uncle Tony.

"Where are you going, John?"

I took my foot off the running board.

"I'm trying to get to London – to Australia House, actually," I told her.

"Jump in. We're going to London. You don't mind dropping John off at Australia House, do you Bates?"

Mr. Bates, in full chauffeur livery, replied, "Of course not, madam."

I glanced at Eddie, then at Sally. No contest. Mr. Bates swung open the rear door and I sank into the plush leather seat. Sally's father, a bigwig at General Electric, had sent the company Rolls Royce to transport Sally on a shopping spree to Harrods. This was my lucky day.

At least I thought it was, until the sleek Silver Ghost pulled up in front of the massive Victorian edifice known as Australia House. A doorman watched intently as Mr. Bates stepped out and opened the passenger door for me.

"See you at three o'clock, Sir?" Mr. Bates asked deferentially.

"Er… thanks. That'll be fine."

I walked toward the building, where the doorman had swung open the big solid door. I nodded politely in acknowledgement and waved a thin folder in the air.

"Good morning. Could you tell me where I take my application for the assisted passage scheme?"

The doorman raised an eyebrow, scrutinizing me "Straight ahead. You can't miss it, but…"

"But what?"

"Well, it's none of my business, sir, but the assisted passage scheme is for them that can't afford it." Ready to show me the door before I had actually gone through it, he winked, "Know what I mean?"

"I know what you mean… and I can't afford it."

Leaving the doorman mystified, I proceeded through and approached a counter where a blonde woman in a blouse dotted with blue koalas was waiting. I pushed the manila folder toward her.

"I've filled out my application. Just dropping it off. How long does it take to…?"

She put up a hand. "How old are you, mate?"

I leaned against the counter.

"I'm 17 – but I'll be 18 in a couple of months!"

"Well then, you're too young. If you'd read the pamphlet that accompanies the form, you would have seen that you need to be 19 or older."

I had read the pamphlet but apparently missed that bit.

My long face grew even longer as she continued, "I'm sorry but the Australian Government considers you to be a minor and too young to emigrate on your own…"

I looked down at my feet. I looked up and our eyes met.

She softened. "Look, there is a way. If you can find an Australian who would be willing to act as your guardian for a couple of years and they write us a letter of intent, agreeing to be your sponsor, then you have a good chance of being accepted!"

Retrieving my folder from the desk, I walked past the judgmental doorman and down the Strand in a sort of daze.

My sullen mood had not improved much by the time Mr. Bates deposited me outside the gate at the bottom of our garden. My mother was sauntering along a row of runner beans with a wooden trug basket tucked under one arm; she read my body language.

"What's the matter, Duck?"

Mum called me Duck. Dad called me Beak. What hope was there!

With the scent of fresh chives and rosemary filling my nostrils, I picked up another trug basket and began to harvest along the other side of the row. The beans were ripe on the vine, threatening to bring down the flimsy row of crossed hazelwood poles erected to support the vigorous climbing plant.

"They say I'm too young to emigrate on my own."

"Well… you are only 17."

I peered at her through a small gap in the tangled foliage. "I know. They say I need an Australian citizen to sponsor me. I really want to go, Mum."

She put her hands through the gap and widened it, her dark hair covered by a silk scarf, attractive face framed by the leaves. "Well, why don't you write to Noel again, see if he might be willing to help?"

"Do you think he would?"

"You'll never know if you don't try."

Anxious weeks dragged by with no response to my letter. I began to think I should sign up for technical college to learn a trade but regardless I needed to make some money.

Money came in the shape of Southwater Brickworks, an old Victorian "dark satanic mill" that turned out hundreds of thousands of bricks a day. Surrounded by deep clay quarries, three tall chimney-stacks belched smoke above two grimy brick buildings, one housing row-upon-row of noisy brick-making machines; the other, red-hot kilns where shirtless men sweated from dawn to dusk.

My first assignment was in the dust room, a large loft where the clay rolled in from the quarries on a conveyor belt, piled up, then sat there to dry. I worked alongside Jock, a short, wiry Scotsman who had already spent a quarter-century of hard labor in the dust room. Jock and I toiled all day shoveling dirt onto another conveyor belt that fed into dozens of brick-making machines below us. The heat from these machines filtered through the wooden floors of the dust room so it felt like the Black Hole of Calcutta – in an attic. Jock had a persistent cough and continually spat globules of brown-colored phlegm into the pile of dirt at our feet.

"What's a lad like you doing working in a God-forsaken place like this?" he asked me.

"I'm planning to migrate to Australia and I need to make some quick money." Although I tried to sound confident it was going to happen, I was far from it, but I did not want anyone to think I could possibly see working at the brickworks as part of my career plan. That arrogance would get me into trouble.

"I'm happy for you, laddie. Always wanted to go there

meself, but…" Jock coughed, a deep wracking wheeze that made his eyes water, then pulled a stained handkerchief from his trouser pocket and spat into it. "Never could persuade the wife. She dinna want to leave the family."

"That's too bad."

"Aye, lad. If she'd had to work in this hell hole for twenty-five years, she mighta changed her mind."

Time was running out for Jock. He had contracted black lung disease and the doctors had given him two years at the most. Graduating from the dust room, I moved directly below to the brick-making room, where the dirt from Jock's attic funneled. The noise and heat from the brick-making machine's powerful engine, laced with the odor of sweat, wet clay and diesel oil, was almost overwhelming. My mentor, Bert, taught me how to grab the solid but still pliable bricks as they emerged from the machine – about one per second – and stack them onto a trolley. Hesitate and you were lost… another brick joined the messy glop at our feet.

Each trolley held five hundred bricks. When we finished loading one trolley, a worker appeared to shove it along rails to the kilns and an empty trolley appeared in its place. Brick after brick, trolley after trolley, eight hours a day, five days a week. Bert had been doing the job for forty years. How many bricks had he stacked in that time? Enough to build a small city, I imagine. I couldn't help noticing that his head had a distinctly rectangular shape.

Ted worked the machine next to ours. Ted had once been to the Isle of Wight but Bert had never been anywhere but Southwater. Ted's work outfit was identical to Bert and Jock's: neck bandana, dark woolen jacket, long-sleeved collarless woolen shirt, waistcoat, brown breeches and black leather hobnail boots. Unmarried Bert had a crush on unmarried Ted, a tiny man who had worked at the brickworks almost as long as him, and never missed an opportunity to grab Ted's balls or pinch his bottom. "Fuck" was the most heavily used word in Bert's vocabulary; I have never heard so many variants of one word.

"For fuck's sake, in '38 we told the fucking fuckers to go and get fucked and we fuckin' walked off the fuckin' job till they fuckin' gave us what we fuckin' wanted… you fuckin' understand?"

Loosely translated, this meant that in 1938 Ted and Bert had gone on strike with the other workers over poor conditions and slave wages. Thirty years later, we were on good money – or at least it seemed that way to me: I made twenty pounds a week.

The job and the waiting to hear from Noel Eliot were hard enough without the impact of a pale individual with pudding bowl haircut. Percy and I were the same age, but he did odd jobs around the factory floor, helping out when and where needed.

"Left school at 15 and come to work 'ere," he told me as we played darts in the break room.

"Are you going to stay?" I asked casually.

He threw his dart. It missed the board and clattered across the concrete floor. "What yer mean?"

"Well… do you have any other dreams or ambitions?"

He hooked his thumbs into the two waist pockets of his boiler suit and cocked his head to one side, his face reflecting total bemusement. Instantly I realized I had said the wrong thing. This was his lot in life and he had thought of nothing else.

"Why'd you come to work here then?" He asked me, his eyes mere slits.

"Oh… er…just to earn some money before I… I go to Australia!" I replied, sincerely hoping I *would* be going to Australia; the thought of spending any more time than I had to with Ted, Bert and Percy did not thrill me.

Percy looked me up and down, then tossed his three darts in quick succession, not caring where they landed. He walked away and never spoke to me again.

Stacking the trolley one morning, I noticed a clod of dry clay land a few feet away and shatter into dust. Then another clod landed a little closer. I looked up toward the balcony of the dust room and saw Percy leaning over the rail making faces at me.

Bert said, "Just ignore the fucker… bugger's a bit touched. He's a fuckin' gippo and lives in a caravan on the edge of the village. His old man does a bit of farm laborin' but spends more time having kids. He's got a fuckin' football team."

Percy threw another clod. I tried to jump out of the way, but it landed on my shoulder. He put his thumb to his nose, wiggled his fingers and stuck out his tongue. I stepped away from the machine, which kept running so the bricks plopped onto the floor. I did not care.

"You've had it now!" I shouted, suddenly realizing I was going to have to confront Percy. I did not want to confront him but I slowly climbed the wooden stairs to the balcony. As my head reached the top of the stairs, a clump of dirt whistled past it. I kept going until we stood facing each other on the balcony like two gunslingers. I picked up a lump of clay and took aim. He picked up a bigger piece and threw it; I ducked. Just as I was about to release my clod, Jock stepped out of the dust room and clipped the side of Percy's head with the back of his hand.

"Owwww!" Percy put his hand to his ear. "Owww… that hurt!"

"Of course it did, laddie! Of course it did and it'll hurt again if you dinna leave Johnny alone."

I lay in bed that night fretting that either Noel had not received my letter or he was not willing to sponsor me. As another day at the brickworks dragged by and I stacked bricks endlessly onto countless trolleys, the thought struck me that I might have to work in this awful place for at least another year, until I reached nineteen and could apply again for assisted passage.

The following evening, when I hopped off the bus and proceeded down the lane toward the bungalow, a red post office van pulled out of our driveway and proceeded up the lanc toward me. Ray Stevens wound down the window and grinned at me from under his blue peaked cap.

"Evening, John. I just delivered your Mum a letter from Australia! It had some nice stamps on it with sheep and sugar cane. Hope I've brought you some good news." Ray the post knew everything about everyone in the village.

"Thanks, Ray. I hope so too!"

I sprinted past my grandmother's old cottage and up our garden path flanked on one side by my mother's vegetable patch and on the other by her flower borders. I burst through the back door of the red brick bungalow and into the kitchen. My mother sat at a little green Formica-topped table with a pile of bills in front of her. One blue air mail envelope with stamps representing Australia's primary industries was set to one side.

She smiled at me and said, "It's from Noel, Duck!"

I began to rip open the letter.

"Careful, save those stamps for Nick!" My brother Nick was an avid stamp collector with a temper, so there would be hell to pay if he found out that in my haste I had ripped the stamps to shreds. My mother handed me a kitchen knife and I carefully pried open the prized letter, then read every word aloud:

23rd April, 1969   *Cambrey Farm*
                                                              Pialligo,
                                                       ACT, Australia

Dear John,

Thank you for your letter. Sorry about the delay. It took some time to get the necessary forms but just to let you know that Enid and I are happy to sponsor you. We have filled them out and sent them on to Australia House. You are welcome to stay with us as long as you like. Lindy is happy that you are coming too and will be writing soon...

Fondest Regards,
Noel

"Whoopee!" I tossed the missive in the air and did a little war dance. Then I saw my mother's half-happy, half-sad face and the reality struck that I was really going.

At an interview with an Australian immigration official in the nearby town of Crawley, I was informed that one of the benefits of being a minor meant that the Australian Government waived the £10 fee so I paid nothing. I had a choice of travelling by sea or air; I chose sea. *What a deal!*

Southwater Brickworks and I parted company after another four months. I had saved nowhere near enough to support myself for more than a limited period but, hey, Australia was the land of milk and honey. What did I need money for?

Plan ahead, Holman. Planning is everything. My life might have been a lot easier, had I listened to Mr. Tittensor's words of wisdom.

Words of encouragement came from my father's sister, a positive, free-spirited lady, auntie Doreen had never owned a car, a house or a television, but she exuded warmth and humor and became a great mentor to me. A couple of months before my departure I spent a weekend at her apartment in London, where I noticed a boomerang hanging on the wall of her kitchen. A label read: *Made with genuine Australian mulga wood.*

"Where did you get that?" I asked her at breakfast.

"Your great aunt Mary sent it from Australia."

Well, that was news to me. I did not know I had a great aunt Mary anywhere, let alone Australia.

"She's your grandmother's sister." Doreen tossed some lard into a frying pan and prodded it with a spatula. "Since your grandmother died, I've been corresponding with great aunt Mary – you know Christmas cards, birthday cards, that sort of thing."

"Why did she go to Australia?"

After an uncomfortable pause, Doreen confided, "There was a family scandal, John."

I waited for auntie Doreen to continue. Meanwhile, the overheated lard started to splutter. She ignored it and stared at a spot on the wall behind the stove.

"So... what happened?" I prodded.

She started very slowly, "During the First World War Mary had... she had... an affair with Samuel, your grandfather" then finished very fast, "Your grandmother found them in bed together."

How could I have lived for 18 years and not known this?

She broke a couple of eggs into the pan; they sizzled on contact with the lard.

"Your Dad and I paid the price."

"Why? How?"

She tapped the edge of the frying pan a few times with the spatula, then turned to face me.

"Because your grandmother walked out on us, never to return. Your grandfather simply packed Dad and me off to boarding schools. Your father was only five! He never knew a proper family life after that... well... not until he married your mother."

Auntie Doreen turned her attention back to the pan and flipped the eggs.

"I knew he had been sent to boarding school but I didn't know why...until now...but what happened to great aunt Mary?"

The eggs began to hiss and pop. She ignored them and sat down opposite me at a small table which folded out from the wall. She seemed relieved to have gotten this off her chest.

"Mary moved to Australia. I didn't know much about her because I was only three when it happened and for years her name was never mentioned; it was as though she did not exist... but just before my mother died the two of them patched up relations. They'd been estranged for forty years."

I found it hard to imagine how someone could bear a grudge for so long. My thoughts were broken by the sound of hissing fat splattering against the wall behind the stove. I noted that the eggs had taken on a solid appearance and the crinkly brownness round the edges was creeping toward the middle. Auntie Doreen remained at the table.

"I'd like to meet her."

"I'll give you her address, John. You can write to her."

With that sentence the last piece of the Australian puzzle fell into place. Little did I know that half a century after she fled to Australia, haunted by the scandal and the affects it had on our family, great aunt Mary would play a significant role in my life.

My room had played a significant role in my life too. It had always been a place of refuge and now, on the last night before life as I had known it would end, I did not want to be there.

I wanted to curl up near my mother and father, to hold them in an embrace and never let them go. They were my rock, my crutch, my sounding board. I defined myself by their achievements, their social standing. They had provided the good things in life: a nice home, an education, three square meals a day, love and security – but none of this necessarily prepared me for what lay ahead. I was always aware I had to make my own way in life to follow a different path, but I could not have envisaged how different that path would be.

I lay in bed with the lights on. My father's snoring sent shockwaves through the house; between his snores I heard the bed creaking, my mother tossing and turning, no doubt worried about losing her oldest son. I struggled not to fall asleep in a vain attempt to hold back the inevitable dawn. I felt my childhood slipping away. The tangible reminders were still there in my room: the Matchbox car collection, the precious Hornby 00 train set, the coin collection, and my favorite possession: a Grundig reel-to-reel tape recorder sitting on top of the cabinet next to my bed, which I used to record pop music off the radio. I turned on the reel-to-reel and shivered under the blankets as *California Girls* wafted through the chill November air.

I loved the Beatles, the Stones, and the Kinks, but it was the Beach Boys and the California surf sound that I really went crazy for. How could I have ever imagined Mike Love, Bruce Johnson and Al Jardine would be neighbors of mine one day. That one day was far, far in my future.

But, two hours earlier, I had kissed my girlfriend Delia

goodbye in the back seat of my mother's Mini-Cooper.

"I'm going to miss you, you know that, don't you?" she'd whispered in my ear.

I was going to miss her too. The fact I had a girlfriend at all was something of a revelation. Attending an all-boys school and living in a small village had not exactly been conducive to meeting girls, but two months before I was due to leave for Australia, Delia had come into my life. She seemed to connect with me on most levels and my jaw was never an issue. (In truth, it never was with any girls. It was all inside my head, a manifestation of my self-consciousness, but nevertheless it was there.) Delia shared a love of horses without being "horsey" and she laughed at my jokes, a good start to a relationship that was doomed from the beginning. We had a tender, almost non-physical relationship, as the idea of sex never entered my head; I was just happy she allowed me to kiss her.

My father must have thought I had learned all I needed to know about sex at *St. John's* because he never got around to giving me the old birds-and-bees speech. About the time my voice started to go up and down like Tiny Tim on helium, and hair started to grow in places it had never grown before, someone at school lent me a book called *Mandingo*. At night, under the covers with a flashlight, I started reading about love and lust among the slave population of the antebellum south. Reading a particularly steamy passage, I became aware of a swelling feeling in my loins. The more I read, the bigger the recalcitrant tonk grew, causing the bedcovers to rise up like a Bedouin's tent. I broke out in a cold sweat. *What was going on?*

The door squeaked but I kept reading... *He held her in his arms and she drew him into her...tighter...tighter...*

"Hrrummm... Hrrrummm..."

I looked up. My mother stood in the doorway, hands on hips. I pushed down on the lump in the bedcovers with my elbows while raising the book with my hands in order to hide my reddening face. A big mistake. Her eyes blazed as she took in the picture on the cover: a tall, handsome black slave with rippling muscles being fawned over by a beautiful white woman.

With one swift movement, she stepped toward the bed, calmly ripped the book from my hands. "That will be enough of that, young man!"

I feigned a modicum of outrage "What Mum, do you expect me to read Biggles for the rest of my life?"

She deigned not to answer, then was gone.

Now, Delia was gone, too. It seemed like the worst moment of my life, knowing it would be years before I saw her again. I drove home from Delia's in a daze.

My mother lent a sympathetic ear.

"I don't want you to go either, dear, but..." *I know. The passage is booked. There is no going back.* "... I understand how much Delia means to you, but try and enjoy Australia. The time will go much quicker if you do."

At that moment though, I confess I would have given up Delia to remain the son of a doting mother for the rest of my life... having my laundry done, my meals cooked, my bills paid, my bed made in perpetuity. I could easily have ended up a 55-year-old virgin living happily with his 85-year-old mother but instead my 49-year-old mother helped me finish packing my new lightweight suitcase, an 18th birthday present. As I stuffed it full of clothes it became clear I was trying to put in more than it was physically capable of holding. When I sat on the lid to force it shut, the hinges snapped off and it became useless. We were in crisis mode until Dad appeared with a large, thick, leather suitcase with unbreakable brass hinges vintage 1901; my paternal grandfather, Samuel Holman, had used it during the Boer War. Old Union Castle shipping-line stickers were plastered all over the exterior. It was a heavy case and I could barely lift it empty.

My father said with his usual aplomb, "It's an old campaign case. Your grandfather took it all over the world. They don't make 'em like this anymore, old boy."

There was no arguing with that, since we seemed to have a shortage of suitcases manufactured after 1910.

I stared into the bedroom mirror, placed my hands over my eyes then lowered them slowly as if the action might persuade the mirror to make me look different. It didn't so I switched off the bedside lamp and let the darkness envelop me.

PART TWO: THE VOYAGE

Australia is a large country with a small population, far from the rest of the world. No one goes there by chance, for it is not on the way to anywhere else.

Ian Bevan

GOING SOUTH BY GOING NORTH

A blast of Arctic air whipped across the English Channel. The salt spray stung my eyes, so I went in search of my cabin. A map on a bulkhead wall would have put Magellan to the test. Not knowing whether I faced aft or for'ard, I climbed numerous stairs, bolted along corridors, and rode up and down in elevators until I finally found the last cabin on the lowest deck – Z deck. I know it was the lowest deck because I could hear the propeller shaft rotating beneath my bunk.

I had expected to have a couple of cabin mates, but was startled to find I was to share with five men! They were: Hugh Francis and his two strapping teenage sons, Ian and Chris; Tom Heapy, a skinny bespectacled Yorkshireman in his late sixties, recently widowed and on his way to Australia to "live with me sister in Sydney"; and Jeff, who they were all huddled around as he sat head bowed, wringing his hands on a lower bunk.

"They never told me this would happen at immigration interviews!" he mumbled.

"They never told us either," responded Hugh, "but we have to make the best of it."

"Make the best of what?" I asked.

Jeff cracked his knuckles, and his head swayed from side to side. "We said goodbye to our families in Preston yesterday, like, and come down on train to Southampton. That were bad enough… not knowing when we'll see 'em all again… and… and now this!"

"Now what?" I said.

Hugh Francis put a fatherly hand on Jeff's shoulder. "Listen mate… you let us know when you two want some time together."

Jeff slumped over so his chin connected with his chest.

Tom Heapy drew me aside. "Jeff decided he'd use the £10 cruise to Australia as his honeymoon… except his new missus is exiled to a cabin full of nurses somewhere on Y deck!"

Tom rummaged in his portmanteau, pulled out a notepad, and wrote in bold letters: *DO NOT DISTURB*. He handed the sign to Jeff.

"Just tape this on door, lad. We'll give you and Vicky as much space as you need."

Jeff raised his head and a wisp of a smile appeared. "Thanks, fellers."

"The migrant decks are segregated into male and female cabins, John," Hugh explained. "The rest of my family… my wife, Susan, and my daughters, Cheryl and Julie – are on another deck, a day's climb away!"

I lay in the narrow bunk that night, listening to the snores of my cabin mates, punctuated by the varied creaks and echoes from the bowels of the ship when the realization hit me that I'd never shared a room, I didn't know how to cook or manage my finances, I'd never had to earn a living to support myself, never done my own laundry, never had to find a place to live. My emotions swung wildly from panic to sheer panic.

Perhaps I should have warned my cabin mates that I was prone to nightmares when under stress because in the early hours, I leapt from my bunk.

"The ship's sinking! The ship's sinking! Man the lifeboats… tell the Captain the ship's sinking," I screamed – or at least that's what my cabin mates told me I screamed – as I shot through the narrow passageway between the bunks and opened a door – BAM – my head connected with a wall and I collapsed in a heap. A bright light illuminated the darkness and

I woke to see Hugh gently patting my face and the bleary eyes of my other cabin mates staring down from their bunk beds. I lay half in and half out of the wardrobe.

"John, we're still afloat, lad. You can go back to sleep."

This was not an auspicious start to our four weeks together aboard *SS Australis*. My epic nightmares would have given Sigmund Freud a run for his money, but the damage was done, each night someone invariably would tease: *Do we have to man the lifeboats tonight, John? Is the ship going to sink, mate? Should we let the captain know? If you sleepwalk, lad, remember the door's that way!* And so on. At least they could see the funny side.

Next morning, the ship lay anchor in Rotterdam to fill with Dutch migrants; the morning after that, it was the port of Bremerhaven, to fill the remaining berths with scores of German and Yugoslavian migrants. The thing I remember most about Rotterdam and Bremerhaven is that we were there at all. I had not paid attention to the ship's routing that I had been given by the immigration people, so I'd expected the ship to be heading south toward Africa and warmer climes.

Three cold days out of Southampton, I sat in a blue and white striped canvas deckchair, wrapped in a blanket, staring at the rise and fall of the waves. The strong smell of linseed from the freshly oiled decks made me feel nauseous. I wondered what Mum and Dad were doing. It was around 4:00 pm – tea time, so they would probably be sitting in front of a warm log fire, tucking into a slice of Mum's nice coffee cake. Mum would be sewing or reading the paper while Dad would be sitting in his armchair, still groggy from his Sunday afternoon nap, trying to watch the football on the telly.

An old man lounging on the next deckchair rose up and pointed. "The White Cliffs of Dover. Them's the White Cliffs of Dover!"

It couldn't be. By my wayward calculations we should have been heading out of the English Channel into the Atlantic. Soon, all those around me were standing and staring. I stood too, and between breaks in the light misty rain I could clearly see the chalky white cliffs.

Just to confirm this was not some kind of mirage conjured up by my homesick psyche, a cross-channel ferry with the words *P & O Dover – Calais* emblazoned on its bow emerged from the mist and ploughed through the swell toward France.

I gazed at those white cliffs, feeling sorry for myself. I missed my family and I missed Delia. It did not help knowing that they were only fifty miles away. I felt so alone I would have jumped ship, given the opportunity, but darkness fell, the coast melted away, and I went below decks. While attempting to locate an elevator that would deposit me somewhere within a mile radius of the Pacific Dining Room, I reflected on just what a potent symbol those cliffs represented – something emotional, something indefinable, something uniquely British that went along with Big Ben, red telephone boxes, and the Queen.

At my designated table in the Pacific Dining Room, I sat with an eclectic group of people who, surprisingly, were not migrants and were actually paying for their passage to Australia.

Ena, a cheerful and spirited Dutch lady much older than the rest of us, was returning to Australia after an extended holiday visiting relatives in the Netherlands. She had spent the war years in a Japanese POW camp in the Dutch East Indies.

"Young man, you are very young to be traveling on your own. What are you going to do in Australia?" She asked me.

Until then, I had been content to keep quiet and listen to the banter around the table, particularly from Winston, a paunchy but handsome Cockney in his late twenties. Winston was a Formula 1 race car mechanic; with his good-looking, curly-haired cousin, Terry, he was escaping the English winter to follow the motor-racing circuit in New Zealand. I felt a little intimidated by them; they were older than me and very self-assured.

"Um… well… I am…" I felt my face getting warmer and redder. I always dreaded talking to groups of people. It went directly to my complex about my jaw that, at times, paralyzed me with anxiety.

"Come on, mate. We ain't got all day… Here, 'ave one of these to 'elp yer relax."

Winston handed me a cigar. I had never smoked. I tried it once in the bushes at the far end of the playing field at *St. John's* with Richard Hiscock. After a few drags I immediately vomited all over him. That had been the end of my smoking days.

"I'm sorry, but I don't smoke," I said.

Winston looked at me as though I was from another planet but I was sure of my convictions.

"Very wise. Very sensible," he said, "I've read some 'orrible things lately about what smoking can do to yer."

"Then why don't you give it up?" whispered Terry.

Winston inhaled deeply on his cigar, then blew out a perfect smoke ring that billowed across the table.

"Coz I gave up reading instead!"

Ena had taken a swig from her glass of wine but before she had time to swallow, she got the joke and a wave of laughter spread upward from her belly, bursting from her face and sending rivulets of red wine running down her chin. It made me laugh and I began to feel a little easier within myself.

"I've wanted to go to Australia since I was very young." I said.

Ena dabbed at the wine on her chin. "You still very young. Too young." She sounded a bit like my mother.

"At first I'm going to stay with family friends in Canberra and…" I hesitated, suddenly realizing that I didn't know what I was going to do after Canberra.

Planning, Holman, planning is everything. Mr. Tittensor's words bounced around in my head while around the table, other heads waited for a response.

"Let's get to the Sunday joint here, young John." Winston looked at his watch. "Terry and me got a party to get to."

I forked the food around my plate. "I think I'm going to work my way around Australia in the…" I noticed a smear of red wine on the side of Ena's chin, "in the wine…er… wineries and… vineyards."

Ena smiled and raised her glass. "I think that's a wild idea, John, but a fine idea too!"

Actually it was not such a wild idea. The seed had been planted soon after I left school by a tall, bald wine merchant in the market town of Horsham. On my first day at work in his store, Gary Grove called me to his desk. Conspicuously dressed in a grey pin-striped suit, white shirt, acceptable tie and bowler hat, Grove had loftier ambitions, and Horsham was a mere stepping stone in his career path.

"Expect a 'good morning' when you arrive, a 'good night' when you leave. There are to be no exceptions to this rule. Understand?"

Arnold Bradstock, one of my co-workers, a Roger Daltry lookalike, pulled me aside later and explained. "That's not a courtesy thing. It's to let him know that you've fronted up for work on time and you haven't skived off early!"

If an employee did arrive late, Grove would berate him in front of the other staff, then give him some shady job to do, such as cleaning his private car or steaming the labels off cheaper wines and replacing them with labels from a more expensive brand.

On Christmas Eve of 1968, Arnold and I had downed two bottles of Château Neuf de Pape in the back storeroom. We got a case of the giggles and could not stop. Business was brisk and we battled to keep the shelves replenished and ourselves under control. The Piesporter Michelsburg ended up where the Sauvignon Blanc should have gone, and the Moselle took shelves reserved for the Bordeaux. A long line of customers wound out of the shop and down the street, which fortunately diverted Mr. Grove's attention away from us. We disappeared to the store-room, supped on the bottle, rushed back and restocked the shelves in the shop. The moment of truth came at 6:00pm when we had to say goodnight to the man. He sat ramrod straight at his desk by the door drumming his fingertips... waiting.

How were Arnold and I to get past him without looking like complete idiots? I could barely walk straight. I took a deep breath.

"Merry Chrissshmash, Mr… Gg … g …rove. In a hurry… missh my bussh."

I hustled out the door and did not look back.

Arnold walked the gauntlet next, like a man who had just inhaled a lungful of laughing gas – the effect of which reached its peak as he passed Grove's desk. Grove fired him on the spot.

Joining me at the bus stop Arnold waved his arms in the air and cried, "Free at last… Free at last… Lord Almighty… Free at last."

Why I did not get fired is still a mystery, but I quit the job soon after. The princely sum of seven pounds a week did not tempt me to stay. However, Grove must have gazed into a crystal ball, or maybe I had mentioned my interest in Australia, because totally out of character, he gave me addresses of some vintners he had worked for in Australia who could perhaps offer me employment should I ever stray Down Under. This information proved a key factor in the months ahead.

But back in the present, *Australis* headed south through the Bay of Biscay, the wind freshened, the sea whipped up, seasickness ran rampant for a couple of days and the smell of stale vomit permeated every nook and cranny. I felt acutely homesick but I had to believe that things would get better.

CANARY MELLOW

The sounds of the ship docking woke the cabin early. The lights of Las Palmas, the principal city of Gran Canaria, winked at us through the porthole. Despite its name, Gran Canaria is the third largest of the Canary Islands.

I struggled down the gangplank, against the tide of Spanish peddlers attempting to board to sell armloads of watches and jewelry. The warm sun on my back transformed my melancholy longing for home into an almost devil-may-care bravado: *OK, you idiot… the sun's shining, the world is your oyster, make the bloody most of it! The sooner you get to Australia, the sooner you can come home again.*

I shaded my eyes against the glare. People were lining up along the quayside to board tour buses replete with uniformed drivers, tinted windows and air-conditioning. One bus stood in sharp contrast to all the fancy buses, appearing rather lonely and forlorn, like a weathered version of the orange-colored American school buses I had seen in films. A man stood by the bus door; he was holding a flimsy piece of cardboard ripped from a box, and lettered with a blue marker: *Volcano Tower.* The man's black hair was tied back in a matador style pigtail, his handsome weathered face marred by a pair of lips that Mick Jagger would have been proud of; dangling from his lower lip was a non-filtered cigarette. The Camel packet protruded from the breast pocket of his grimy white jacket.

"You want to go tower of volcano," he said to me.

I had no idea what he was talking about. "Er… yes."

The man displayed a wide rubbery smile and miraculously, his cigarette stayed in place as though stuck to his lips by superglue.

I clambered aboard the bus. The only other passenger was an elderly lady in a white trouser suit, a bandana holding her white hair in place. She sat on the front seat adjacent to the driver.

"Good morning, young man!" She had an upper-class English accent.

"Good morning," I responded.

"A lovely day for a bus ride." She offered her hand and I shook it. "My name is Lillian Ferigno. I come from Haywards Heath. I am 77 years old. My husband's dead. Don't believe in beating about the bush… like to let people know who I am, set them at ease." She tapped the seat with the flat of her hand in invitation.

"My family lives just down the A272 from Haywards Heath!" I replied.

"We have Sussex in common then, young man, although I'm not there much. I spend my days… the days I have left to me… sailing around the world on liners. It's what I love the most."

I sat down, feeling comfortable with her.

"Now, Manolito, I'd say it's time to go. Wouldn't you?" She said to the driver.

"Si Senora!"

Ms. Ferigno and I were still the only passengers.

"Manolito's a good man. He has a nice family," she told me.

"You know him?"

"Oh yes."

The bus roared away from the docks and passed through a pretty square filled with statues of dogs.

"La Canarias…" said Manolito in terse explanation, his cigarette still dangling.

"He means dogs," Lillian elucidated. "These islands are named for the wild dogs that roamed here when the Romans landed. Dog in Latin is canis, so they called the islands *Canaria Insula*, the island of dogs!"

I'd been expecting to see flocks of canaries. Did Mr. Tittensor ever tell me that it was named for a bunch of dogs in geography class? If he did, I probably didn't hear him because my head was always filled with thoughts of Australia.

"We need stop… petrol… Lillian."

Manolito pulled over at a little service station, its white walls draped by vibrant magenta bougainvillea.

"Alright, Manolito." Lillian opened the leather handbag resting on her lap, pulled out a fistful of pesetas and handed them to Manolito. It seemed a little odd to me. Then she handed me a couple of notes too. "I'm dying of thirst… do you mind getting me a drink from the café over there? Get something for yourself."

She pointed to a dirty white building which had a Coke machine in front amid a jumble of plastic chairs and tables. A few sorry-looking, geranium-filled pots demarked the service station forecourt from the restaurant area. I pushed the chairs aside to get to the empty café while Manolito pumped the petrol. I bought a bottle of mineral water for Lillian and a Coca-Cola for myself, patted the head of a Heinz 57 dog snoozing in the doorway, then returned to the bus. Manolito was still refueling, his head bent over the nozzle of the pump, the cigarette hovering inches from the stream of petrol flowing into the tank. I assumed he knew the consequences of immolation by gas explosion, so I got back on the bus without a word.

Manolito boarded a few minutes later and announced, "We go Angostura now!"

"He means the Angostura Valley," Lillian explained. "That's where they grow the bitters that I put in my gin and tonic every night! Do you like a G and T young man?"

Gazing out the window at fields of rich black soil, I replied, "No, but my mother does."

Just the mentioning of "my mother" invoked a pang of homesickness, quickly replaced by a larger pang of… terror! Although, Manolito had reached the foot of the volcano, its terraced slopes covered with banana plantations and other tropical vegetation, I hardly noticed because he was driving like a maniac up the narrow roller-coaster road Caldera de Bandana. Ignoring niceties such as slowing at corners, he just honked the horn; if another vehicle were coming the other way, tough luck, the steep drops were unbroken by guardrails.

"Don't worry young man," Lillian said, "he does this every day."

Yes… but I didn't want this to be the one day that his luck finally ran out.

In an attempt to divert my thoughts from the bus nose-diving over a 10,000-foot cliff, and the low odds of survival, I conjured a vision of Blanche Kelleher. Blanche often spent her holidays in the Canaries. If Lillian Ferigno had been Blanche Kelleher – and had Blanche been willing, I would have happily spent the rest of my days cruising around the world on luxury liners as a kept man in a state of perpetual bliss. Blanche had an angelic face with long chestnut hair that stretched down past her compact bottom. She had the best pair of legs I have ever seen, which she showed off to maximum effect by wearing the shortest mini-skirts on earth; the word sexy could have been coined with her in mind. Blanche's son Patrick went to school with my brother Nick and me. Blanche came into our lives when she offered to share the driving duties with my mother, which made the usually boring journey to school… well, definitely not boring. When we'd pull up in front of the assembly hall at *St. John's College*, boarders would lean out of windows, poke heads around doors, and leer from the rooftops – all to better view Blanche in her mini-skirt. Blanche obliged them by sliding out of the car to open the back door for us; waiting for us to alight she would stretch casually, knowing full well the reaction she would provoke. The boarders would wolf-whistle and cheer as her mini-skirt rose up her thighs to unimaginable heights causing panic among the school hierarchy who fully expected a mass riot to ensue. Nick and I would saunter into school, half-embarrassed and half-amused because we were the envy of all. Although she was probably old enough to be my mother, I must confess an unrequited lust for Blanche.

On the bus, the flashbacks of Blanche had caused a *Mandingo* situation in my shorts, so I barely noticed when the bus reached the summit of the volcano. I was bent double, fiddling with my underpants with one hand while pretending to tie my shoe laces with the other – not an easy feat. I waited in that awkward position for Ms. Ferigno to exit the bus, then I exited swiftly and leaned casually against a wooden fence at the edge of a deep crater, feigning interest in a little white-stucco farmhouse at the bottom, while I prayed for some order down below.

"His real westward journey began from here, you know?" Lillian was saying.

"Who… who…whose did?"

"Christopher Columbus. It was near the Gran Canaria that the rudder of his caravel Pinta became loose and fell off."

"Oh! That's interesting," I said, secretly hoping my rudder would soon become loose.

"Yes. It was said that two of the crew, who were really the owners of the vessel, broke the rudder on purpose because they were frightened at the idea of the perilous voyage that lay ahead and hoped, by damaging their vessel that they would be left behind."

"I can understand that." I fidgeted and pressed up against the fence. "A few days ago I would have gladly broken the rudder on my vessel… I mean our vessel… *Australis*." I nonchalantly smoothed back a cowlick that always seemed to droop over my forehead when I got nervous.

Ignoring my inanity, Lillian continued, "It didn't happen, of course. Columbus sailed on to the island of Gomera, where he had the rudder repaired, and as the last of the Canary Islands faded out of sight, the sailors burst into tears, saying that they were sailing off upon the awful sea of darkness and would never see land again."

That was a feeling I would appreciate later on my voyage, but at the moment I gazed over the crater toward long sandy beaches where winter tourists would lay in the sun, and daydreamed of Blanche in a bikini.

After returning us safely to the dockside, Manolito kissed Lillian on both cheeks. Tears filled his eyes as she handed him another fat wad of pesetas. I never asked her what this was all about, but with the benefit of wisdom and hindsight, I am sure Lillian had a host of Manolitos scattered around the cruise ports of the world. Perhaps it was her way of giving back.

She offered me her hand again and I shook it.

"It has been a pleasure travelling with you, young man."

"Well…thank you… likewise."

"Just be true to yourself, John. Always be yourself and don't ever take yourself – or the world – too seriously." She whirled away and joined the throng climbing the gangway.

Pondering her words, words I have never forgotten, I explored the large market that had sprung up alongside the ship. Anything from fake Rolex watches to contraband whiskey was on sale, sold by hustlers with a mix of nationalities, including Chinese, Indian, African and Cuban. I bought a camera for about ten English pounds, then boarded the ship.

I stood on the foredeck and snapped away at the crumbling Spanish colonial buildings and waterfront fortresses before the night sky enveloped the ship as it sailed off *upon the awful sea of darkness.*

ATLANTIC ANTICS

Two of my cabin mates, Chris and Ian Francis were about my age, though that's where our similarities end, both were physically fit and champion swimmers in their native Grimsby. Their father, Hugh, hoped the boys would become even better swimmers in Australia. I think they were surprised to find someone as young as me traveling on my own, so they enrolled me as an honorary member of the family and included me in their activities. I joined them after dinner most nights; we usually took in a movie then went to the ballroom where we danced to *Jo and the Splendors*, an Afro-haired Greek combo in loud flowered shirts open to the waist (revealing hairy chests with the regulation gold chain dangling à la Engelbert Humperdinck).

The oldest sister, Cheryl Francis, must have thought my dancing in need of improvement; nearing the equator, and in a moment of weakness, I agreed to partner her at a dancing class. Dancing lessons were previously something I had managed to avoid, much to my mother's chagrin, but if a girl had asked me to jump off a 100-foot tower into a vat of boiling chocolate filled with piranhas, I probably would have obliged. Cheryl wanted to attempt Highland dancing but I convinced her it was a bad idea, due to my lifelong aversion to the kilt. When I was a child my parents had gone on a holiday to Scotland and brought back for Nick and me what looked like a dress that our sister might have worn, had we had a sister; my mother called the strange garment a kilt.

"It's a present for being such good boys while we were away," she said.

We were soon wishing we had been bad boys while they were away because being forced to wear the kilts at family occasions was just too much to bear.

Cheryl and I arrived for our first lesson, but she had neglected to tell me it was for Greek dancing! The class was conducted by a gentleman in the full regalia of an Evzone, a Greek National Guardsman. I stood there like a stunned wombat as he explained to us the significance of the dress in Greek history, that there are over 300 folds in a particular part of the outfit representing the 300-plus years that Turkey occupied Greece. The particular part of the outfit he described looked like a cross between a mini-skirt and a tutu, and it made my kilt phobia pale in comparison.

Observing my expression, Cheryl laughed, "Don't worry, you don't have to wear one of those!"

However, I did have to attempt the dance steps. Given that I possessed two left feet, this did not augur well: Zorba's Dance required a lot of crossing of legs while moving in a lateral direction across the floor, at the same time waving a handkerchief limply in one hand.

"In Greece," our pseudo-evzone explained, "dancing is regarded as the highest form of art. Every dance has a story to tell. Socrates said that every educated man should know how to dance gracefully to keep the body strong and supple and ready for duty on the battlefield."

What Socrates would have made of me, I hate to think. I had one memorable moment when I should have crossed right-over-left but crossed left-over-right instead, just as Cheryl was crossing right-over-left. Our feet collided and we both went down, causing a mass pile-up of dancers like cars on a foggy motorway.

Fortunately the extreme heat curtailed my woeful attempts at Zorba's Dance. The barometer rose and it got so hot that the ship developed a serious air-conditioning problem, so all physical activity was put on hold until it was fixed. For days, everyone in our dining room sat around fanning themselves with the menus, sweat pouring off faces, while waiters emerged from the kitchen looking as if from Dante's inferno, staggering around, carrying trays heaped with steaming food, which made the dining room even hotter.

At the equator, our sister ship *RHMS Patris* passed us on the port side, heading north, no more than a hundred yards away, full of Aussies bound for swinging London. The passengers cheered and set off balloons, creating a carnival-like atmosphere. I fantasized that someone would appear on the foredeck of the Patris with a large megaphone and say… *anyone changing their minds and deciding to return to England – all aboard now please!* It didn't happen and although nice to see another ship, it was a poignant reminder that it would be a long time before I would head homeward again.

The days onboard attained a pleasant rhythm; the sun shone amid a cloudless sky that reflected the azure blue of a calm sea, broken only by the occasional white crest of an idle wave. Lazy days passed watching flying fish skim across the bow of the ship and porpoises dip and dive through the wake. When the sun became too hot to bear, the Lido pool provided relief; though the saltwater stung the eyes and the sunburn, it was cool.

The evenings also were gaining a certain rhythm. After dinner I joined up with the Francis family at the ballroom, where the entertainment was corny but fun. Jeff Hudson, the entertainment director, recruited some of the passengers to sing, joke and dance their way through productions with names like 'Atlantic Antics', 'Neptune Naughties' and 'Cape Town Capers.' After the performances, Jo and the Splendors played and the rest of us hit the floor. If we were sober, the evening ended on deck, gazing at the night sky; you could see every star. The moon's reflection shone on the water like phosphorous. I had never experienced nights so warm and clear. If we were drunk, we stumbled back to our cabins to sleep till late morning. A maid brought cups of tea to our cabin at 7:30 am, but never woke us so it was stone-cold by the time we stirred. We could hardly complain when all this was courtesy of the Australian Government! I began to feel more comfortable with my situation, probably because my mother had been replaced by the maid, a Chinese laundryman, and the Pacific Dining Room!

Late one evening – or it could have been early one morning – I sat alone at a table on the edge of the dance floor. I had trod on Cheryl's foot once too often so she'd limped off to bed taking the rest of the family with her. I had drunk more than my limit of ale and was watching couples glide around the floor when I heard, "John… John… over here."

I looked around and saw Lillian Ferigno waving, beckoning me over to her table. She was sitting with a young woman with glasses who looked a little bored.

"John, I'd like you to meet Nina… Nina Van Hall. She's from Amsterdam and, like you, travelling on her own to Sydney."

Nina bowed her head but said nothing.

Lillian winked at me and nodded in the direction of the dance floor. She stifled a yawn and said, "I think it's time for my bed!"

"Would you like to dance?" I asked Nina.

She nodded, but again said nothing.

Jo and his Splendors, gold chains flying over their hairy chests, were doing their version of the Funky Chicken. While I pranced about like a constipated Rhode Island Red, with arms flapping and legs scratching, Nina's expression changed from bored to decidedly unamused. Her horn-rimmed glasses and stern deportment seemed like an impenetrable shield, which in a perverse sort of way, made her seem more attractive. I imagined that behind that exterior lived a real person struggling to get out, a bit like me.

The next day Nina lay poolside, alone in a bikini. How was I to get her attention? Immediately I saw my opportunity: the springboard.

Just before I left England I took diving lessons, not because of any desire to learn to dive but because a friend of my parents was learning to swim and I agreed to drive him to the pool in order to get some weekend use of my mother's car. To avoid wasting time, I enrolled in the diving classes at the other end of the pool. The instructor, a sinewy man in his seventies, could do all sorts of twists and turns, forward and backward somersaults, and triple-toe-loops. I was about a quarter of his age and uncoordinated, so while most of the boys graduated to the high board rapidly, I took much longer. In fact it took six weeks for me to get from diving off the side of the pool to the high board. It was the last lesson, so he must have felt sorry for me. While all the other examples of strapping British athleticism were doing twists and loops with high degrees of difficulty, all I wanted to achieve was a head-first dive with no degree of difficulty. From the top of that board it looked a long way down. A lot could go wrong in the split-second between leaving the board and hitting the water. A lot did go wrong. My take-off was pretty good but whatever possessed me to attempt a forward somersault, I don't know. I got my head tucked under, but as I rotated I was suddenly looking up at the rafters of the pool complex. In the half second I had to panic, I panicked and hit the water in a horizontal position. I remember the point of entry being somewhere close to my belly button. I remember it because it felt like being hit below the belt by Joe Frazier. I would have sucked in air or cried for help but my mouth was full of water.

So having failed with the funky chicken I saw the opportunity to attract Nina with my diving prowess. Here I made a severe miscalculation. I should have left well enough alone. After a couple of loud, well-timed coughs to get her attention, I hopped onto the springboard, did a couple of stretches, nonchalantly skipped along to the end, then jumped up and down letting the board spring me upwards. Greg

Louganis would have got it right but not me. After landing feet first back on the board I toppled forward and fell into the pool.

Spitting out streams of water, I caught Nina's eye. She was laughing.

A loud voice with a German accent emanated from somewhere near my left ear:

"Hey, you. It is verboten to dive. Please to get out of the pool."

I rubbed the water out of my eyes to see the pristine-white uniform of Lothar, the bullet-headed Master-of-Arms. He was pointing toward a large red sign that read *Diving Forbidden.*

"Can you not read?"

He was not very nice about it but I suppose he did say please. He explained to me that it was verboten because if the ship rolled suddenly so did the water in the pool. A dive could prove fatal if the $H2O$ you were diving headlong into suddenly became concrete. Before I could ask why have a diving board in the first place, a large cloud passed overhead and landed in the middle of the pool.

"The cavalry's arrived, John boy," Winston said as he surfaced.

The Master-of-Arm's hair would have stood on end, had he any. His face turned pink and he bellowed, "Diving is verboten... verboten!"

Then Terry flew in, landing feet first, sending up a stream of water, which elicited a stream of epithets from Lothar.

Winston and Terry had a history with the Master-of-Arms. They loathed Lothar because he came to their cabin every night to break up their noisy parties, so this was payback time. No sooner had they hit the water than they were out and diving in again, and encouraging others to do the same. Soon the pool was a frenzy of flying bodies and white water. The Master-of-Arms ran around the edge ranting like a man possessed.

Even with the pool, keeping fit was difficult. Getting fat was not. Three regular meals a day, plus snacks and beer, caused my girth to expand. My body passed through the doldrums, as did the ship, a region renowned for its whimsical weather which invariably frustrated sailors with unpredictable or absent winds. In the *Rhyme of the Ancient Mariner*, Samuel Coleridge described this equatorial realm as "hell"; and Sir Francis Chichester concurred, saying the "Calms were the very devil." Donald Crowhurst, a competitor in the first solo round-the-world yacht race in 1968, never left the Doldrums. Fearing that his ill-designed craft would break up and sink in the Southern Ocean, he sailed around and around in mid-Atlantic, sending false positions back to the race organizers. From his logs it has been ascertained that he had intended to insert his boat back into the fleet after they rounded Cape Horn and were heading north for home, but eventually doubts crept in about the feasibility of such a plan and he went mad. His boat was found near the coast of Brazil – minus Donald Crowhurst, who had jumped overboard and paid the ultimate price. Robin Knox-Johnston – whose splendid book, *A World of my Own*, my mother had given me as a gift prior to my departure – was the only one of a field of nine to complete the race. He gave his £5,000 prize to Crowhurst's widow.

Leaving the Doldrums and somber thoughts of Donald Crowhurst behind, I took the fitness plunge and joined 'Jeff's Jog Trotter', described in the shipboard magazine Seascape: *Follow Jeff around the sun-deck at an easy pace, no overtaking. Drop out when you wish and pick up the next time round. Girls and boys from 8 to 80 are welcome.*

Most of the runners were in actual fact from 68 to 80. One man, almost bent double with a calcified spine and not a day under 90, took off like a human cannonball. Determined to keep up with him, I flashed through eight laps before I got within shouting distance. I remember thinking, *I can't let this old geezer beat me*, but that's all I remember thinking because I hit the "wall" and collapsed like a pathetic sack of potatoes on the deck. The world was spinning. I sat there trying to make sense of things. The old boy dashed past me twice as I stumbled along to the bar. Topping up my dehydrated body with beer, I almost went mad trying to count the number of times he flashed by the window. A man can take only so much humiliation.

CAPE TOWN CAPERS

It was December 12, 1969 when I staggered up on deck before breakfast. A faint coastline flickered through the mist, a welcome sight after eight days without seeing land. The sun burned away the mist, the ship sailed into Table Bay, where dead ahead, nestled under Table Mountain stood Cape Town. I snapped excitedly with my new camera and couldn't wait to get ashore.

While *SS Australis* began its day of re-victualing, refueling and refreshing, Tom Heapy and I approached a cheery dockside café, decorated with colorful potted plants and hanging baskets. A sign on the door displayed *Net Blankes.* Oblivious, I went inside and bought half a dozen scenic postcards and a large black coffee to help me recover from an epic party in Winston's cabin. Tom hung back; when I came out he had vanished.

"Psssst... pssst..." His head popped out from behind the rear wall of the café, followed by a beckoning finger. "Come here."

He pointed toward a gray, dirty outdoor seating area next to the toilets, from which emanated a distinct odor of stale urine and decayed food. Another sign hung on the wall: *Net Swart.*

"It means blacks only!" Tom whispered.

"What?"

"It's a segregated country, lad." Tom, normally mild-mannered and self-effacing, kicked the wood-sided building. "It's a bloody disgrace."

A skinny runt of a man with a large bald patch, fringed by wispy hair emerged from the back door and said, "You got a problem, rooinek?"

"IT'S A BLOODY DISGRACE!" Tom shook his fist in the man's face.

The two of them stared eyeball-to-eyeball and what was left of the hair on the back of the café owner's head stood up like the comb of a fighting cockerel. He pointed toward the *Australis*.

"Just get back on the ship, English. Go back to where you fuckin' came from."

Tom, not normally at a loss for words, was at a loss for words. His eyes fixed on a distant crag on the side of Table Mountain. Perhaps he had been vouchsafed a revelation that no matter what a 65-year-old ex-postman from Yorkshire might think, say or do, it would have absolutely no effect on the beliefs of a bigoted café owner in Cape Town. It was more likely, however, that he just did not want a fight because he dashed off to join the throng of people lining up to get on tourist buses parked dockside.

My hangover made my head feel as though it were being squeezed in a vice. I sipped my coffee and stared blankly at the café owner, who stared back at me, but not so blankly. He was still in attack mode.

"What's your problem, boy?"

I shrugged, then headed toward the buses, but Tom was gone. I hopped aboard the first one, only to discover it was the over-eighties gadabout tour and my friend the geriatric human cannonball was sitting next to the driver.

Oh well. Sit back and relax, try and enjoy the ride. If things got rough, I could always daydream about Blanche Kelleher again.

From my smoked-glass window, the center of Cape Town appeared clean and bright with large elegant public buildings and wide spacious streets. City workers were putting up Christmas lights, something that seemed vaguely ludicrous in the middle of summer and totally ludicrous in terms of apartheid. *Would Jesus Christ have embraced this forced separation of races? I don't think so.*

Although I had few positive thoughts about my school, *St. John's College*, it was multi-racial. Having to deal with psychos like Dashwood and his ilk, I learned early on that the content of your character had nothing to do with the color of your skin. Here in Cape Town though, it was literally spelled out in black and white... *net blankes* and *net swartes*.

The bus headed south to Cape Point, the spot where the cold Atlantic Ocean meets the warmer Indian Ocean, the southern-most extremity of the African continent. The Cape of Good Hope lies a little farther to the northwest; to the northeast lies False Bay. In the days before the Suez Canal, boats would cruise down the east coast of Africa carrying goods from northern Africa. When they reached False Bay, thinking they had gone around the Cape of Good Hope, headed north and shortly afterwards found themselves stuck with the wind blowing them onto shore. As a result the bay is littered with shipwrecks, and hence the name False Bay.

I felt a bit of a wreck myself. At Winston's *Africa Ahoy* party I had downed three or four of his "mystery" cocktails, which infused me with enough courage to stare lustfully at Nina, lounging seductively on one of the bunks, her horn-rimmed specs and very short sleeveless jersey dress almost more than a man could stand. Winston stuck a cigar in my mouth, thereby creating an added edge to my alcohol-induced cool persona. He lit the phallic-shaped corona and the flames flickered atmospherically, illuminating the lower half of my face. I felt like Humphrey Bogart in *Casablanca*. I took a couple of long drags, my convictions floating out of the porthole with the smoke. Nina shook her mop of shiny hair and smiled at me. Taking it as some kind of coded signal, I swaggered manfully through the crowd toward her, preparing to confess my undying love and devotion. I continued right on past her, out of the cabin and down the corridor to the bathroom, where I spent the rest of the night with my head stuffed down the toilet, periodically emitting a plaintive cry that must have sounded like the strangulated gurgle of a choking turkey.

The long, white sandy beach at the little town of Fish Hoek looked a good spot to let the sun's rays do some restorative work until I noticed another *Net Blankes* sign hanging over the beach like a pall-bearer at a funeral. The beach was packed with families – all of the blond-haired, blue-eyed variety – either watching or participating in a surf carnival or huddled around transistor radios listening to a rugby match between Scotland and the Springboks live from Edinburgh. I thought of my father sitting by the fire watching the game on TV with the rain pouring outside and here was I, lying on this picturesque sunny beach. It wasn't just the wind-blown sand that caused my eyes to fill with tears. My feelings were a mixture of loneliness, apprehension and excitement for the unknown that lay ahead. My father had stopped in Cape Town and Durban on his way to Burma to fight the Japanese. He must have experienced similar feelings but magnified a hundred-fold because he faced the real possibility he might not return home alive.

The bus trundled round the backside of Table Mountain through Stellenbosch, the oldest wine-growing region in South Africa. I knew a bit about the region because that erstwhile boss of mine, Gary Grove, had worked here as a young man. It stretched my young imagination to picture the pinstriped, bowler-hatted figure of Gary Grove toiling in the wine fields of Stellenbosch. The concept of the "wine tour" had not yet been established in South Africa so the bus stopped only at one winery, more so the tourists could see the beautiful Dutch Colonial architecture rather than to sample what was on offer inside.

I was relieved to return to the ship after a day that had left me edgy and uneasy. I wandered into the smoking lounge to write the postcards. Tom Heapy sat slumped over looking decidedly unhappy. I sat down opposite him.

"How was your day, Tom? Mine was pretty good… for the most part."

"You didn't see what I saw, lad."

"What did you see?"

"Crossroads?"

Thinking he was referring to the TV soap opera of that name, I replied flippantly, "Bad episode, was it?"

He rolled his eyes. "Nay lad, it's a shanty town where they hide the blacks away. I took a tour and the bus stopped at a pub." Tom tightly rolled up the newspaper on his lap. "I asked the landlord for a pint so he sends this young black lad out the back to fetch it. A few minutes later he comes back… but the poor little lad had brought a glass of coke by mistake. The bastard threw the coke in his face and kicked him out. I mean really kicked him." Tom thrashed the coffee table with the rolled up newspaper.

"What did you do?"

"What could I do? I didn't give the bugger any of my business. I told the driver, who was a Cape Colored, and he said, 'I will show you something.' He drove us to Crossroads out near the airport; he weren't supposed to, but he did. Thousands of blacks live there in the direst of conditions. They come from the country to find work and end up living in cardboard boxes. You don't see that in your bloody postcards."

He bashed the table again with the paper then handed it to me. "Read the front page."

I unfolded the almost shredded newspaper. On the front page was a photo and small article about one of our passengers, Sugar Bill Robinson, a black American boxer and sparring partner of the Australian champion, Johnny Famechon, who had recently fought at the Royal Albert Hall on the same bill as Joe Bugner and was now on his way to Australia to fight. The journalist praised Sugar Bill in the article but he had to come aboard to get his interview as apartheid laws forbade Sugar Bill from leaving the ship.

"Don't make sense do it, lad?" said Tom.

"No, it doesn't make sense, Tom."

My own problems seemed suddenly insignificant. I felt relieved to be back on board and to receive a stack of letters from friends and family at home. At dinner, I learned that the nice family who sat at the next table (the father was a cultured, well-educated man and former Fijian Ambassador to Great Britain) had not been allowed ashore either. I did not tell Tom for fear he would turn apoplectic.

Instead I went to the ballroom and danced with Nina. She was warming to me... slowly. I missed my girlfriend Delia after having read a long letter she'd sent, but instantly saw that the mysterious Nina could aid in my recovery process.

INDIAN OCEAN COMMOTION

It seemed odd that our porthole had been locked down while *Australis* was in dock, but once the good ship left Cape Town, the captain advised us that he had to steer farther south than usual to avoid a cyclone. The weather became much cooler as *Australis* sailed into the Roaring Forties, named for the boisterous prevailing westerly winds that are especially strong in the south Indian Ocean, and unlike the winds in the Northern Hemisphere are not impeded by large landmasses. I learned later that the cyclone story was just a ruse to keep the passengers happy: the *Australis* regularly took the more southerly route to make up time because the faster Suez Canal route had been closed since the Arab-Israeli war of 1967. The wind blew like the clappers from west to east, allowing the ship to use less fuel and save the Greek owner, Mr. Chandris, a bunch of money.

A day out of Cape Town, the ship rolled twenty degrees off vertical, causing me to wake up in the early hours of the morning. The Boer War suitcase slid back and forth across the cabin in time with the ship's roll. Hugh Francis switched on a light, lit up a cigarette, took a few puffs, then lifted himself onto one elbow to look around a cabin that resembled a student frat house after a wild party – magazines and books strewn across the floor; cupboard doors open and contents flung out.

"The bloody ship doesn't have stabilizers." An ex-navy man, Hugh knew about these things.

Tom Heapy who normally did not sleep well, slept like a log. Not me; no nightmares this time, I was really worried about the ship sinking.

At daybreak, Ian Francis and I went to the aft deck and were awed by huge waves whipped up by freezing winds; the crests of some were at eye level and sent the ship careening from side to side from their impact. It reminded me of footage I had seen in 1965 of Sir Francis Chichester rounding Cape Horn in his yacht *Gypsy Moth*, a tiny boat dwarfed by cathedral-like waves. I now understood why Crowhurst was so worried. I could not imagine being out here alone in a small boat.

Three days out of Cape Town, the seas grew even bigger. Few souls ventured topside and fewer still showed up for meals. Mass seasickness reappeared. Hugh told me that the best place to avoid seasickness was out in the open with the wind in your face, so I braced myself on deck and watched the giant albatrosses following astern, gliding effortlessly on currents of air, a thousand miles from the nearest land.

Eventually, the warmth of the smoking lounge beckoned. Lillian Ferigno spotted me and waved me over to her table. Rain slashed against the large picture windows, the seas heaved but the room exuded an air of coziness in the eye of the storm. There were a lot of people sitting around card tables.

"Ah… John! Can you play whist? Mrs. Smith here is looking for a partner."

The fact that Nina was also at the table kept me rooted to the spot.

"Well. Yes. We used to play at home on Sunday evenings."

The thought of Sunday evenings at home, sitting around a blazing log fire playing whist brought forth a wave of emotion that for a moment sucked the life from me. I bit down on my lower lip, a considerable feat considering how far removed it was from my upper lip.

Mrs. Smith, a spritely white-haired lady standing next to Lillian, looked me up and down (but mostly up because she was a dwarf compared to me and I reached only about 5' 9").

"OK boy. Let's show 'em what-for."

I sat down at the green felt-covered table; the air so thick with tobacco smoke that across the table Mrs. Smith resembled a ghoul emerging from a London fog. Lillian sat to my left. To my right sat Nina. Mrs. Smith shuffled the cards and offered them to Nina to cut for trumps, then she gave the cards to me. I dealt the regulation thirteen cards apiece and we were off.

The ghoul and I won the first go-round seven tricks to six. Nina and Lillian won the second round. So it was all down to the third rubber, which meant if Mrs. Smith and I won, we got some prize money and moved on to the next round.

Mrs. Smith had a gleam in her eye. She could taste blood. She dealt like a woman who meant business, a whirlwind of flying cards and flashing eyes. She leaned toward me, cupped a small hand around my ear and whispered, "Look for me sign, sonny... if I pull out me 'andkerchief and dab me lips with it, it means I want you to use your trump card if you have one... or any card that beats mine, even if it looks as though I can win it... unnerstand?"

"I think so... handkerchief ... trumps?"

"Yes. But be sure and wait for the signal."

And so it came down to the penultimate hand. We had five tricks. Nina and Lillian had six tricks. Tension was palpable. Mrs. Smith's eyes darted back and forth, her mind working overtime. Mine was not working at all.

Nina laid a ten of hearts. I didn't have any hearts. I had a king of spades and a ten of spades and spades were trumps. Mrs. Smith gave a funny little sneeze. It wasn't really a sneeze at all, more like a little *snitch*. She pulled out her handkerchief and put it to her nose and gave a dainty blow, so I laid my king of spades. Immediately I felt a sharp pain in my right ankle then another pain in my left. Mrs. Smith was kicking me under the table. Could she be Dashwood's granny? Her face drained of color. She really did look like a ghost now. She tapped her lips with a gnarled finger.

"Lips, sonny, lips," she hissed, "I told you to wait for the signal!"

"We won the trick, didn't we?" I hissed back.

"Yes… but I coulda won it with a jack of hearts."

Mrs. Smith had done the numbers and knew we couldn't win the last hand with the cards we had. She was right. Ms. Ferigno won. Mrs. Smith lost. She stormed from the Smoking Lounge and I never saw her again. I often wonder about that given what happened next.

"Oh my Gott…" Nina cried, the first words I had heard her utter since Cape Town.

She stared out the big picture window, her eyes transfixed on a massive rogue wave building a few hundred yards away. It towered above all others. It came hurtling towards us like the opening scene from the *Poseidon Adventure* … except the film hadn't been made yet.

"Hold on!" I yelled.

The card tables were not bolted down like the other furniture in the Smoking Lounge. The big wave smashed into the side of the ship, clouds of spray lashed the window, the ship keeled over and the card players slid, *en masse*, across the parquet floor, hitting the wall on the far side. Lillian's chair flipped over and she slid on her back, thumping into the logjam of people, tables and chairs that had hit the wall ahead of her. The ship lurched back the other way and the tangled pile started to slide in reverse but the ship shuddered briefly, like a dog shaking off water, righted itself, then continued its progress toward Western Australia.

Nina placed two delicate hands on my shoulder and pushed herself up. It sent a glorious frisson down my spine, the only real physical contact Nina and I ever had. We were two shy people in a noisy world. I knew why I was shy but I never figured out why Nina was. Perhaps I should have tried harder.

Lillian was trying to get to her feet amid the jumble of bodies. I offered a hand and pulled her up. She looked none the worse for wear.

"Are you alright?" I asked.

"Of course. Take more than that to shake up an old sea salt like me!"

She was lucky. All around us elderly people were groaning and moaning, some bleeding; rivulets of blood stained the floor. Crew-members appeared and ushered the injured off to the sick bay. That night, three old folks died from their injuries. The Captain, a thousand miles from land with nowhere to store the bodies, ordered a short funeral service then the corpses were dumped overboard in canvas bags. The families awaiting them in Australia were in for a big surprise.

The ship headed out of the Roaring Forties into calmer seas and a more northerly course. Shipboard life returned to normal. The night before we arrived in Fremantle, Captain Ikiadis held a farewell cocktail party. The Captain and the chief purser stood at the door while several hundred people filed into the main lounge and were announced by name. The Master-of-Arms gave me an imperious glare along with a half-hearted handshake. Winston and Terry did not turn up. The party to end all parties had already started in their cabin. They knew exactly where the bullet head was. Waiters flew about the room with large trays of watered-down cocktails. I downed six martinis and three whiskies and declared the substance barely alcoholic …alco…mo… holic content to be barely minim…eral… oh well, I was still on my feet as the band played on.

The Captain made his farewell speech in broken English, expressing his hope that we had enjoyed the trip. Wishful thinking after the last week, I thought. When the band struck up 'Now is the Hour (that we must say goodbye)' it seemed a bit premature as many of us still had another 2000 miles to go to Sydney and some were heading for New Zealand.

Hot on the heels of the farewell cocktail party the kitchen staff hosted the farewell dinner. The diners donned party hats. The meal commenced with the usual questionable soup (the same stuff often turned up as gravy), followed by lobster thermidor. The *piece de resistance* came at the end – the lights faded to black and out of the kitchen floated trays of a flaming substance. One tray descended toward our table, and from underneath it appeared our grinning waiter, who Winston had nicknamed "Hot Potater." The lights went on and the flames went out to reveal a sort of bombe Alaska which had a sugary taste with a decided hint of methylated spirits!

In the ballroom, the *Big, Big Farewell Show* was getting underway. There had been no shortage of entertainment throughout the voyage – shortage of talent, yes; entertainment, no. A few genuine comedians and singers did come forth. The boxer Sugar Bill Robinson had a gravelly voice and sang a fair rendition of "King of the Road." Leonard Weir, who had been in the original cast of *My Fair Lady* with Rex Harrison and Julie Andrews, brought the house down. The audience sang along to his version of "Knees up Mother Brown", "Don't Dilly-Dally", "Lambeth Walk" – all the old Cockney songs I knew so well from my father (who claimed to be a Cockney but to be a true Cockney you have to be born within earshot of the bells of Bow Street church in the East End of London. In actuality Dad had been born in Eastbourne on the south coast).

Streamers flew and softballs zig-zagged across the room. An old inebriate – it could have been the human cannonball, now I come to think of it – stood and gave his rendition of the "Scottish Soldier." Then he sang "Auld Lang Syne." Tears were streaming down faces, for tomorrow many would be emerging from this little cocoon we had been immersed in for weeks, and life would begin again with all its harsh realities and surprises.

TERRA AUSTRALIS

I went up on deck for some fresh air, the sea dead calm and the air noticeably warmer than it had been for nine days. Someone shouted, "Land. There's land ahead!" I proceeded with Chris and Ian Francis to the top deck above the captain's bridge, an area that had been cordoned off since Cape Town. The ship passed a small sandy island – Rottnest Island – and in another half hour we reached the pilot station, where the pilot came aboard to guide us into Fremantle. The sun-drenched coast of Western Australia was clearly visible now, a coast known in 1829 as New Holland, the year it was formally taken possession by Captain Charles Howe Fremantle for His Britannic Majesty George IV.

SS Australis plied down the long, narrow harbor and came to rest at the terminal. Thousands of cheering people lined the docks. Immigration officials came aboard to check passports and vaccination certificates.

Nine days since I last stood on dry land, my dream became a reality: I stepped off *SS Australis* onto *Terra Australis*, the Great Southern land.

The wind known as the Fremantle Doctor took the edge off the heat and blew gusts of sand as I strolled down the main street. I half expected to see John Wayne come flying out the swinging doors of one of the many saloons. I pushed through the Wild West-like doors of one pub. No cowboys; just a bar crowded with office workers on lunch break. The standard dress of the working male in Fremantle resembled the standard dress of the working male in Fish Hoek: long white socks to just below the knee, Bermuda-type shorts that stopped just above the knee, white short-sleeved shirts, some worn with a tie, some without. Watching those workers guzzling down their beers in the hour allotted to them made me realize that my party was almost over. I still had the final leg of my journey to Sydney to look forward to, and reuniting with the Eliots in Canberra but after that … work of some kind. I swiftly downed a schooner of Swan lager. *Heck… That's weeks away. No sense in worrying about it yet.*

I stepped out of the saloon onto the dusty main street. The lager was stronger than I had thought so I decided to give the dust and heat a miss and return to the air-conditioned shipping terminal. Christmas was just a week away. En route I observed locals putting up multi-colored flags instead of lights. *How bizarre!*

Three letters awaited me at the terminal, one from Delia, another from my mother and father, the third from auntie Doreen in London – a welcome event, as I felt like I had been cut off from the world for the past two weeks. Delia hinted that my brother Nick might be taking her to a dance. So much for loyalty!

Calm seas prevailed around the southwest tip of Australia and through the Great Australian Bight to Melbourne, a distance of roughly twelve hundred miles. Most of the "entertainers" had disembarked in Fremantle, so the evening entertainment was replaced by boring slide shows put on by immigration department officials about aspects of Australian life. The atmosphere felt like it had been plucked from the ship by some invisible force. Christmas decorations appeared in the dining room. I had never known it less like Christmas.

Lillian Ferigno and Nina had both departed in Fremantle to

take the train across country – Lillian to connect with another cruise ship in Sydney that would take her home to Haywards Heath, Nina to connect with a former lover in Sydney where she hoped things would resume where they left off. They had never really started off with Nina and me. Whereas I was an introverted extrovert, or at least an introvert busting to be an extrovert, Nina was an introvert through and through. She was quiet and liked it that way; I was quiet but hated it that way.

And so with another lost love gone from my life, I went along with Tom Heapy to play Bingo, about the only shipboard activity I had not yet participated in. We entered the garishly lit room filled with little old ladies who gave us sidelong glances from behind their bingo cards. Tom handed me a card and we sat down in the front row.

He whispered in my ear, "It's the Christmas Snowball tonight!"

"What does that mean?"

"Just wait and see, lad!"

A portly middle-aged man stood at the end of the room, dipping his hand into a barrel. His hair was dyed orange, his torso clad in a shiny maroon jacket with a black velvet collar. The ladies hung on his every word.

"Sunset Strip... number 77."

Tom looked at his own card and then mine. His eyes opened wide and he pointed, "Cross it out, lad...cross it out."

Orange Hair dipped his hand in the barrel again and came up with... "Legs eleven... number 11."

I crossed that one out.

"Staying alive... number 85."

I crossed that one out too.

Tom's eyes hovered about six inches from my card. He squirmed around in his seat.

"This is it lad. This is it... one more."

My hand started to shake. Orange Hair stuck his hand in the barrel and slowly drew out the last ball.

"Wait for it, ladies and gents...It's... it's... Bobbie Vee... number thirty-three."

I looked at my card.

"I've got it," I whispered.

Tom didn't hold back. "HOUSE! HOUSE!"

I glanced around, but nobody else seemed too excited that I had won £5.

"Roll it over into the snowball, lad," Tom advised, "I can feel this is your lucky night!"

I did roll it over until the snowball reached £30.

"Last number coming up in our last game of the night... and our last night of bingo... the last-chance saloon but... *we'll meet again... don't know where don't know when... but I know we'll meet again some sunny day...* now it's... snowball time! Wait for it now... wait for it!"

His hand shot into the barrel. He wiggled it about. He pulled out a ball. He held it up in front of his eyes. He squinted and turned the ball slowly in his hands.

"It's... it's the BRIGHTON LINE... number 59!"

I almost choked on my hotdog.

"I've got it! I don't believe it, but I've got it."

Tom jumped about three feet off the ground, grabbed my card and handed it to Orange Hair, who doled out the money.

Tom held tightly to my arm as he led me swiftly from the hall, away from the mutters and prolonged hisses replacing the vacuum of stunned silence.

"They weren't too happy about you winnin' lad... some of them 'ave been trying to win the big prize since ship left Southampton, then you come along and win the bloody lot first time out!"

Had I known the significance of that £30 in the struggles that lay ahead, I might have stormed the bridge and ordered Captain Ikiadis to turn the ship around and head back to England.

On the last leg its marathon journey, SS *Australis* steamed out of Port Melbourne and steered north toward Sydney.

On our last night together, Winston uncorked a bottle of bubbly. "Just a little tiddley before yuz leaves Terry and me." He poured the frothy contents into our fluted glasses and raised his. "Nice knowing yuz all. Ena, you're the Mae West."

Ena winked at him. "You not so bad yourself!"

"And John boy, hope yuz make lots of bees and honey in the land down under."

"Well. It's certainly going to be an adventure." I raised my glass to him. "Hope we can all meet again someday."

I was going to miss Winston and Terry; especially their humor.

Ena gazed at me with a motherly eye. "Take care, John. You will do fine if you just be yourself."

I had already heard this advice but it was a little hard to get my head around when I did not really know who the "yourself" was.

As usual Winston had the last word: "Yeah, and watch out for them Aussie sheilas! They'll eat yuz for dinner, mate!"

Now that was something to look forward to!

Later I joined Cheryl, Chris, and Ian to stagger from party to party until 3:30am, when we headed back to the cabin for some shuteye. A sheet of paper was pinned to the door – *DO NOT DISTURB.*

We found Hugh Francis at a party in a cabin down the hallway. I stretched out on a spare bunk and closed my eyes. Someone shouted "Land ho!" Glancing out the porthole I saw cliffs and realized we were sailing through the heads of Sydney Harbor. Some minutes later we passed Rushcutters Bay, where British Prime Minister Edward Heath was preparing his boat *Morning Cloud* and its crew for the grueling Sydney-to-Hobart yacht race, which began on December 26. (He won the race and some say the good publicity also won him the next general election.)

At that moment I would have given anything for the ship to turn around and head back to England on another four-week cruise. Instead, *Australis* docked at Woolloomoolloo, derived from an Aboriginal word 'Walla-mulla' meaning young male kangaroo. I suspected it had been many years since kangaroos had frequented these parts. Before me were the half-completed sails of the new Sydney Opera House, and behind that 'the coat-hanger' itself, the Sydney Harbor Bridge. I should have been excited but I felt hungover and mostly sad to be saying farewell to my companions of the past four weeks. I wandered into the big customs hall and met up with an immigration official who gave me the lowdown as to what would happen next.

As the *SS Australis* disgorged its passengers and reloaded for its Pacific cruise, I passed uneventfully through customs and wheeled the Boer War suitcase out into the street. It was December 22, 1969, and reality was about to bite.

PART THREE: THE ODYSSEY

There is something elusive and mysterious in this land, some soul I cannot find, some spirit I have never seen; something I can only feel.

EB Mackennal

CHRISTMAS IN CANBERRA

Sitting curbside amid the hustle and bustle of the docks with two English nurses who were to travel with me to Canberra, thoughts of my family set off a fresh wave of anxiety and homesickness, broken only when our taxi to a new world arrived and whisked us out to Kingsford-Smith airport.

The nurses and I waited in the terminal to board. Through a large observation window, as if someone had turned a heavenly switch, the bright blue sky turned black and the rain cascaded down with such intensity that day suddenly became night. Twenty minutes later it stopped, the skies cleared and we boarded our little plane (still courtesy of the Australian Government.) There was so much turbulence en route that I regurgitated both my previous night's dinner and the morning's breakfast.

At least the plane felt cool, leaving me unprepared for the blast furnace that hit me when the aircraft door opened at Canberra airport. The heat from the concrete runway crept through the rubber soles of my plimsoles and made my feet tingle. The surrounding sunburnt hills shimmered in the intense light. I shaded my eyes. I'd been ten when I last saw Noel Eliot so I pulled a photo from my breast pocket and glanced at it. Only a half-dozen people stood in the enclosed grassy area in front of the small terminal; the tall, craggy figure of Noel Eliot towered above them all.

With outstretched hand Noel said, "Welcome to Australia, John. We're glad to have you here."

I attempted to crack a smile but my dry lips cracked instead. The weight of the Boer War suitcase severely tested the suspension of Noel's Holden station wagon but fortunately we drove less than a mile before turning onto a long dirt driveway overhung with pine, wattle and eucalypts. A weathered sign displayed *Cambrey Farm*, our destination. At the end of the driveway stood a white weatherboard farmhouse.

Still with a trim, fit-looking figure Enid ran toward me, her arms spread wide. "John, it is so lovely to see you after all this time." She wrapped her arms around me in a hug. "I want to hear all about your trip. You must be hot... I will get you a nice cold lemonade. Come along inside."

Enid showed me where everything was in the house and I felt at home immediately. I had a small room of my own, a welcome change after four weeks sharing a cramped cabin with five other men. I unpacked the Boer War suitcase and Noel showed me around the 25-acre farm, where he grew a variety of fruit and kept chickens, a Jersey cow and three horses. The farm generated enough income to supplement his RAAF pension and provided the family with fresh produce. At the back of the farm, we wandered through a paddock of dry wispy grass to the muddy Molonglo River, which had been dammed to create the centerpiece of Canberra, Lake Burley Griffin.

"You know, your Uncle Johnny always wanted to come here," Noel said as we gazed through the willows toward the city of Canberra shining in the distance.

"I didn't know that."

"Yes. He talked about coming out here for a visit after the war was over..." Noel continued to stare, then turned and patted me on the back. "So we're really happy you could come, John!"

A tall girl with a mass of freckles and red hair arrived. Lindy did not look a lot different from the little girl who shinnied up that tree, except she was now a pretty young woman.

"Giddai, John. Welcome to Australia and a Merry Christmas!" She smiled and those freckles seemed to dance around her face.

"Well thank you... although it does not seem much like Christmas to me."

I had forgotten it was Chrissie, as Enid called it, but that night they had a festive cocktail party. Since Canberra was the capital city, many of the Eliots' friends were either diplomats or worked in some capacity for the government. My head started to spin after a couple of hours of chatter. I was talking with Lindy and her boyfriend David when I felt the floor move as if I were still on the deck of the ship. My eyelids began to droop. I shook my head to stay awake.

"You should go to bed," suggested Lindy. "You've had a long day!"

Lindy had been ten when I secretly pledged to come to Australia one day to marry her but now, eight years later, she had a boyfriend; I suppose I should have known, but she did not mention him in her letters. I slept fitfully that night, not because I dreamt about the loss of my one true love to another, but because I dreamt a giant spider was crawling up the wall above my head. I sat bolt upright and switched on the light. A giant spider *was* crawling up the wall above my head.

It crept onto the ceiling and disappeared through an air vent. I lay awake all night anticipating its return.

Over breakfast I told the Eliots about the visitation. Enid laughed as she poured corn flakes into a bowl.

"Yes," she said, "His name is Fred. He's a tarantula and quite harmless, really. He helps to keep the mossies at bay."

I must have looked puzzled.

"Mosquitoes, dear!"

She sprinkled fresh homegrown strawberries and passion fruit on the corn flakes. This was a revelation. Never had we mixed fresh fruit and cereal in England. It tasted rather good and I followed it with eggs from their hens and whole meal toast spread with butter churned from the milk of their Jersey cow.

Enid and Lindy invited me to go Christmas shopping at the Civic Centre. I wandered about marveling at the modern, enclosed, air-conditioned shopping complex with its walls of glass and different levels connected by escalators. It would be many years before shopping centers like this appeared in English towns.

I climbed to the top of City Hill, where I stood by the flagpole to take in the view of Lake Burley Griffin. I found it difficult to comprehend that this dry barren country would be my home for at least the next two years. It seemed unreal after four weeks at sea where nothing had been permanent. Though, I had long tried to imagine what Noel and Enid's home might be like, my imaginings had all been of the *Australian Womens Weekly* variety: sweeping plains, wide rivers, eucalyptus trees and sheep. These fantasies did not include the emotions of a stranger in a strange new land – a longing for family and familiar friends. Contemplating the city below me I thought to myself... *What the hell are you doing here? You know if you don't overcome this homesickness, this emptiness, you are going to have a miserable time and the next few years will seem like an eternity. Snap out of it!* I slapped my face a couple of times – hard – and it helped.

It also helped when I spent the afternoon with Noel delivering care packages. Christmas was an especially busy period for his charity, Legacy, which provided financial help, companionship and assistance to the dependents of servicemen who had died in Australia's wars. Crisscrossing the city, visiting those widows and orphans with their smiles and genuine gratitude for the hams and turkeys and toys we handed out, nearly convinced me that I didn't have it so bad.

I knew a bit about Canberra from my school geography projects. Both Melbourne and Sydney had vied to be the nation's political center, but neither would give an inch so the Aussies created something from nothing in the bush. Chicago architect Walter Burley Griffin won the right to design the city in an international competition sponsored by the Australian government. It did not feel like any city I had been to. For one thing there was so much open space. Even the center of town had a park-like feeling. Dotted about on wide tree-lined streets were a lot of impressive public buildings of a high architectural standard, all connected by sweeping ring roads, roundabouts and gardens. Every house seemed to be separated from every other house by acres of lawns and trees.

Noel turned the station wagon down the driveway toward the farmhouse.

"So John, what do you think of our little town?"

"The whole place is one giant park. It's all so green compared to this." I pointed to his brown stubbly fields and the hills beyond the airport.

"Yes. They use a lot of water from the lake to keep it that way. A lot of Aussies hate Canberra because they say it's too planned, but I think it's more the fact that they hate politicians… and most of them live here!"

There were not many politicians in the semi-rural suburb of Pialligo. I took a stroll along one of its thoroughfares, Beltana Road, a road that fronted *Cambrey Farm*, other poultry farms, fruit farms and nurseries. The hot dry air was laced with an aroma which reminded me of the eucalyptus vapor that my mother inhaled from a steaming bowl of water to clear her sinuses. Vicks Vapor Rub could be bought in little blue bottles at chemists in England, but in Australia, it evanesced from trees!

Further down the road this balsamic bouquet was diminished by the more pungent smell of poultry manure. Soon, thousands of flies descended from all parts of Australia to drink the gallons of sweat dripping from my body. They crawled up my nose, into my ears, eyes and mouth, and nothing I did would make them go away. I was not prepared for them or the extreme heat. What I considered lightweight clothing in England was nowhere near lightweight enough in Australia. My saturated 100% polyester tee-shirt clung to my body like another layer of skin.

Unable to outrun the flies, I jumped at the opportunity to go swimming with Lindy at Mugga Way, a ritzy street close to Parliament House where the foreign embassies and consulates are found.

"You'll like John Garran," Enid remarked as I threw my beach towel onto the rear seat of the Holden station wagon, "He's the son of Robert Garran who wrote Australia's constitution. A suburb in Canberra is named after him, you know."

No I didn't know. I didn't even know that Australia had a constitution. Obviously I had a lot to learn.

A tall sixty-something gentleman with presence, Mr. Garran chatted with us poolside at his elegant two-story whitewashed mansion with a panoramic view of the city. Hordes of children, some barely of walking age dived in and out of the pool in perpetual motion until a beautiful woman in her late forties, but looking much younger, appeared with a white bathrobe wrapped loosely around her tanned body. She gave Mr. Garran an affectionate hug, and then poured mugs of ice-cold ginger beer from a glass pitcher for the children.

Lindy whispered in my ear, "That's Mrs. Garran!"

Mrs. Garran stretched out her lissome frame on a lounge chair beside us and asked if there was anything we wanted. Instantly, I wanted Mrs. Garran. Like Blanche Kelleher, she possessed the seductive power of an older woman but there was something more: Mrs. Garran oozed class and intelligence, a very potent combination against an 18-year-old boy who oozed nothing except acne. I watched her laugh as Mr. Garran playfully tossed one of the freckle-faced tots into the deep end. I have never been one given to envy, but I was envious of him. Not just because he had a gorgeous wife, although that would be reason enough to be envious, but because of the kids. They were so at home in the water. I was twelve before I learned to swim. In Australia it seemed they swam from birth.

Mrs. Garran rolled over onto her side and the robe slipped off her shoulder, exposing a suntan so uniform it looked like she had been dipped in caramel. She smiled at Lindy and her perfect teeth sparkled in the sunlight.

"He's writing a book you know?"

"No. I didn't know," Lindy responded.

"Tentatively it's to be called *Merinos, Myths and Macarthurs*. The history of the Merino sheep in Australia." She tossed back her auburn hair, then looked at me with the same sparkling smile and laser-like blue eyes, "Mr. Garran is an authority on sheep, John."

"Golly…" I said, fiddling with my towel, arranging it baggily around my lower body like a poor man's *Gunga Din*, in order to disguise another potentially embarrassing moment. "I've always been interested in sheep," I lied.

"Yes, he probably knows more about the Merino sheep and their history than any other man in Australia."

"My great uncle Frank back in Sussex is an expert on the Southdown breed," I said, trying to impress her, but that was actually true.

"Oh really…" she said.

One of the tots began to cry. When she turned onto her other side to attend to him, her robe slipped, revealing more of her beautifully proportioned body. I rolled onto my stomach, stuffed my fingers in my mouth and bit down hard, thereby restricting the emission of an involuntary vulpine howl.

"Gosh, it's hot! Think I'll have another dip."

With the towel firmly wrapped around my midriff, I strolled casually toward the pool and plopped into the deep end, where I remained immersed in cold water until Lindy told me it was time for us to leave.

On the way home she informed me that Mr. Garran owned two sheep stations, one bordering Canberra, the other a few miles out of town. In retrospect, I should have tapped him for a job on one of those sheep stations but I was just beginning to enjoy myself, so any stray thoughts of work that filtered into my consciousness were quickly pushed out again. Besides, the obvious distraction of Mrs. Garran would have been more than a man could stand.

My first Christmas Day away from home was blazing hot

from the get-go and featured a whirlwind of parties and social activities. The family gathered at dawn around a Christmas tree. Where they found such a thing in the heat of mid-summer in Australia, I had no idea, but a pile of neatly wrapped presents was stacked underneath it. Lindy handed me a gift; I unwrapped it and was pleasantly surprised to find two tee-shirts and a pair of Stubbies (short shorts), all in 100% lightweight cotton.

"We were a bit worried about your wardrobe!" Lindy commented. So was I. If I'd migrated to Sydney, Nova Scotia, instead of Sydney, New South Wales, my wardrobe would have been perfectly suited to combat the chill winds blowing off Hudson's Bay, but here in your actual sunburnt country, it was a problem.

Lindy and I delivered presents to the home of her best friend, Elisabeth Mackay, whose family owned a neighboring fruit farm.

Elisabeth was a strikingly attractive blonde with all the curves in the right places and fit-looking, in an outdoorsy Australian way. If ever I believed in love at first sight, it was now. Too awestruck to say anything sensible, I said nothing. She and Lindy discussed mutual friends and school and I was out of it. So I started a conversation with her grandmother who was eager to impart her knowledge of the dangers to fruit farming posed by an infestation of the Mediterranean fruit fly in South Australia. By the time I was fully briefed, Lindy was ready to go.

"Nice meeting you, John." Elisabeth extended her hand as I stood to leave. The gesture surprised me. Girls I had known in England did not shake hands.

"You'll have to meet Charlie sometime," Elisabeth suggested.

"Charlie?"

"My horse. Lindy says you're quite a horseman."

I blushed slightly and rubbed the side of my jaw as if the action would somehow draw their attention away from it. I felt embarrassed that I was embarrassed.

Our next port-of-call – a garden party under the midday sun at a diplomat's home in the suburb of Red Hill, where we hobnobbed with the rich and famous: the US air attaché, the Prime Minister's press secretary, the director of De Havilland aircraft and the head of the Department of the Interior. The political correspondent of the *Sydney Morning Herald* advised me on what I should see while in Australia, but all I really wanted to see was Elisabeth Mackay.

Returning to *Cambrey Farm*, I was ready for bed, but Enid started to prepare Christmas dinner. The evenings allegedly being cooler, it made sense to eat then, although the temperature remained about 99 degrees Fahrenheit in the shade. The guests, Norman and Marjorie, arrived. Norman had been Noel's commanding officer after the war and was now the current commander of Amberley Air Force Base in Queensland, where they were readying to take charge of the new F-111 fighter jets that Australia had purchased from the United States. One had inconveniently crashed that week, causing a political furor and a major headache for Norman, although he did not appear to be unduly worried at F-111s falling out of the sky, as he tucked into a sensible Christmas dinner – cold cuts of turkey and ham with a variety of salads and condiments.

The talk turned to Australian politics. Norman spoke of the perilous situation in Vietnam, in which Australia was heavily involved, and referred to Prime Minister John Gorton as a contemporary of theirs. Much gossip drifted around the table over Gorton's appointment of an attractive 22-year-old, Ainslie Gotto, as his principal private secretary. Gorton loved both drink and the company of young women, but they felt Ainslie wielded too much influence over her boss who had taken over as Prime Minister in January 1968 following the mysterious disappearance of Harold Holt while swimming in heavy seas at Cheviot Beach, Victoria. There were many conspiracy theories and one held that the CIA had Holt assassinated because he was about to withdraw Australian troops from Vietnam. This theory was supported when Gorton increased the war effort, but it remains a mystery to this day, as Harold Holt's body has never been found.

Lindy and David invited me to a party in Woden, a brand-new suburb created from virgin bush that abounded with kangaroos and opossums trying to find their way home amid the cardboard cutout houses. That the gorgeous Elisabeth Mackay was my date made the party more interesting than it should have been. We talked about horses on the way home, tightly squeezed in the back of Lindy's Fiat Bambino, a very small car indeed – a car that made my mother's Mini-Cooper look positively roomy. Suddenly Australia was fun.

This feeling was enhanced the next day when we visited a drive-in movie theatre. Though ideally suited to Australia's meteorology, this idea imported from the USA was not suited to its entomology. Huge moths and other creepy crawlies came from the four corners of the outback attracted by the bright lights of the big screen; their size magnified by the beam of the projector, sometimes obscured the screen completely. Squeezed next to me in the back of the Fiat, Elisabeth made it clear that one did not really go to a drive-in to watch a movie anyway; it was just a convenient place to park. I really was beginning to like Australia.

On the dawn of a new decade, the four of us motored a hundred miles to Canberra's closest beach, Bateman's Bay on the New South Wales coast, where the temperature was decidedly cooler than the hinterland, but still warmer than Brighton on the best of summer days. Sitting on the coarse golden sand of the beach, I struggled to pull on my swimming trunks under a beach towel.

"You can't do that!" Lindy said.

"What can't I do?"

"Change on the beach!"

"Why?"

"Because," said David, "It's against the law." He pointed to a brick building at the edge of the strip of sand. "There's changing rooms up there. You can get arrested for exposing yourself like that."

Even in 1970, Australia outwardly reflected an image of a morally puritanical country. Most beach communities provided changing rooms, but I still preferred the English method of struggling under a towel.

Lindy suggested I try body surfing.

"Look," she said, "You just dive in front of the wave and let it take you in."

"What! Without a board?" I responded.

"Watch."

She ran down the sand and dived in front of a head-high roller, then shot toward the beach, arms pressed to her sides, like a torpedo just launched from a submarine.

Jumping to her feet with water cascading down her trim, fit body she said, "See. It's easy."

Taking my cue from a towering wave that came thundering toward me, I dived in front of it. Somehow it knew I was an amateur at this game because it picked me up and dumped me headlong into the sandy bottom. I felt like a rag caught in an endless spin cycle of a giant washing machine. I struggled to the surface, gasping for air, not knowing which way was up, when another wave hit me and deposited me halfway up the beach.

Lindy and Elisabeth peered down at me while I lay there belching sand and seawater.

"You've got to be able to tell the dumpers from the rollers, mate!" Lindy said.

I had much to learn about the powerful Australian surf. But, never in my wildest dreams could I have imagined that one day, a child of mine would become a talented surfer riding the swells along the central California coast.

On the highway back to Canberra, our little Fiat ran ahead of a powerful storm that blew in from the Tasman Sea and curtailed our day at the beach.

Elisabeth shielded her eyes and looked toward the horizon where clouds of red dust blotted out the sky.

"I'm worried about Charlie, my horse. He gets freaked out in the wind."

Back in Pialligo, we exchanged the Fiat for Elisabeth's Ford pickup, then motored along a dusty track on the eastern edge of Fairbarn RAAF base while brightly colored budgerigars flew ahead of us.

Her horse, a small chestnut gelding, was galloping around in a dirt corral and occasionally bucking. Upon seeing Elisabeth, Charlie seemed to calm down and trotted over to the fence. Elisabeth pulled a sugar cube from her pocket and offered it to him on her open palm. He took the sugar and gave Elisabeth a fond nuzzle. She rubbed his neck and said, "Let's go up to the homestead. I'd like you to meet Mrs. Tinker."

A wind pump stood near a rather dilapidated farmhouse encircled by a shaky wooden verandah. A stocky woman opened the front door. She was dressed in a floral patterned dress, her hair tied back in a bun; she looked every inch the tough, no-nonsense farmer's wife.

"Hello Darl." She gave Elisabeth a hug, then looked at me and winked, "Who's your boyfriend?"

"Edna, this is John. He's staying with the Eliots. Just arrived from England."

"Come on in, love. I'll make youse a cuppa – or something stronger, if youse like."

"No, tea will be fine," Elisabeth assured her.

Edna grinned, revealing a missing front tooth.

"A pommie, aye? Well, youse're welcome here, luvvie."

"Thank you."

Edna led us along a dark corridor to the back verandah, where she offered seats on a swinging lounge overlooking the air base. I shielded my eyes from the glare. An RAAF Hercules rumbled up the runway; a big heavy transport plane, it rattled the corrugated iron roof of the farmhouse.

"Heading for Vietnam," Elisabeth informed me as Edna went into the kitchen

"By the way," I asked, "Where does the word Pommie, come from exactly?"

She smiled and said, "I heard it's in reference to the red

cheeks of you English immigrants, looking like pomegranates."

"At school they said it goes back to the convict days when they had P.O.M.E, Prisoner of Mother England embroidered on their shirts…" I replied.

"I'll take care of you, you bastard!"

Elisabeth and I both turned toward the back door. Edna came running out with her arm extended, holding the tail of a writhing four-foot brown snake. She swung it around and around and smashed its head against a tree… once… twice… until it was dead, then she nonchalantly flung it into some bushes, rubbed her palms together and returned to the verandah.

"Now where was I, darl? Ah yes, tea."

My mouth hung open. Elisabeth grinned.

Edna returned with a tray of tea and cookies, "Here for a while are you Pom?"

"A couple of years, I hope."

She placed the tray on a small sun-bleached patio table, then plopped herself down to pour from a stainless steel teapot.

"Ten quid tourist, aye?"

"What?"

She handed me a mug of the muddy brew. "Here today, gone tomorrow – all at our expense."

I was a bit taken aback. "I didn't think of it that way."

"Course not, love, but I wouldn't tell too many folks. You'll do all right if you fit in with our strange ways. We can whinge and criticize ourselves but we don't like anyone coming from outside and running us down… especially pommies!" She smiled another toothless grin.

"I've nothing to complain about so far, but I'll take your advice."

"You do that, love. You do that. Now have a bickie before you go."

"Thank you."

"He's very polite, isn't he?" She winked and pushed a plate toward us laden with Arnotts Tim Tams and Lamingtons.

Noel rousted me out of bed the next day at 6:00 am, the earliest I had been up in well over a month.

"Rise and shine. It's time to vaccinate the chooks!"

Still groggy, David and I ran around the henhouse ensnaring Noel's panicky Australorps, then holding them securely while he pulled open a wing and gave each one a jab with a syringe. The hens apparently knew what was coming and did their best to escape our clutches. Getting down to the last two or three stubborn ones, I dived this way and that in the dust and poultry manure while they screeched and squawked around the henhouse.

I finally got one blighter in hand and blushed somewhat when I saw Elisabeth hands on hips, standing in the doorway dressed in cowboy boots, Levis and a plaid shirt that hugged her curves.

"I thought you might like to go riding but if you're too busy?"

"No, he's earned his keep for today," Noel said, jabbing a wing with the syringe.

I released the bird and it scuttled off to join its mates huddled in the corner.

I was glad of Elisabeth's company. With the coming of the New Year, Lindy had started a job that would keep her busy until she began University at the end of the summer.

I sat on the top rail of a corral watching Elisabeth gently holding the end of a lunge rein, cantering rider-less Charlie in a big circle. The corral shook and I had to hang on for fear of toppling off it.

"Giddai Pom!"

Mrs. Tinker was leaning against the fence.

"Good Morning, Mrs Tinker."

"He's a Waler, you know?" she remarked, nodding toward Charlie.

"A Waler?"

"Yes. A breed named for the state of New South Wales. Charlie's a smidgen over fourteen hands, so a bit small – the ideal height's about sixteen hands."

I looked at the horse's small, neat head and flaring nostrils.

"He reminds me of Sunny Jim, a little horse that my brother Nick and I used to ride," I told her.

Mrs. Tinker climbed to the top of the fence and swung one leg over so that she straddled it like a horse.

"I think cheerful Charlie's got a bit of Arab in him, but don't tell Lissie or she'll be liable to go right off yer."

I laughed because Grampy was not too keen on the Arab breed either; in his opinion, they were not sturdy enough to withstand the rigors of a day's hunting in the mud, cold and damp of an English winter.

When Elisabeth finished her session with the lunge rein, she beckoned me over. She held Charlie's head while I placed my left foot in the stirrup, swung my right leg over and sat down gently on the stock saddle. After adjusting the length of the stirrups, I sat upright in English fashion, ensuring my heels, hips and shoulders were in alignment.

"Did you ever see the film *Forty Thousand Horsemen* with Chips Rafferty?" Edna shouted as I squeezed Charlie's ribs gently with my heels and walked him through the gate.

"No."

"Well, it's an Aussie movie made God-knows-when… but it's all about the Australian Light Horse regiment in Palestine during the First World War. It's where the Waler earned its stripes. It became famous for its endurance and soundness in crossing the deserts and charging obstacles like sandbag walls and trenches."

The little horse had a lot of stored-up energy, and felt a bit like a spring ready to uncoil. I jog-trotted him down a farm track while Elisabeth followed in the pickup. We passed through an open gate and I let Charlie have his head a little. He cantered across a vast paddock, stirring up the dust until reaching a crack in the ground, a dry gully created by centuries of storm runoff. Easing up, we ducked down the gully and cantered up the other side, passing through another gate into a pine forest and out into an area of eerie black stumps – eucalyptus trees blackened by a recent fire. Amid the burnt-out landscape there were giant mounds – the nests of the fire ant, half an inch in length with an unpleasant bite. The flies were becoming a problem too, arriving posthaste to drive Charlie and me nuts as they invaded every crevice in our bodies; unlike English flies these too had a nasty bite. I spotted Elisabeth up ahead getting out of the pickup armed with a can of fly spray. She came over and drenched Charlie and me in the foul-smelling stuff.

"Hit 'em high, hit 'em low, hit 'em with the old Pea-Beu!" she sang.

The old Pea-Beu worked for about thirty seconds and then the strongest and fittest were back. I might have seen Darwin's theory of natural selection right before my very eyes if my eyes hadn't been filled with flies.

"You're a decent rider," Elisabeth commented. "You should see about getting work on a sheep or cattle station as a Jackeroo."

"A what?"

"A Jackeroo!" She walked alongside me holding onto the stirrup leather, spraying any errant horse fly that dared to rest on Charlie's rump. "It's our version of the cowboy."

"A cowboy? That sounds exciting."

As children, my brothers and I had loved playing cowboys and Indians, riding bareback over Grampy's big field, pretending we were characters out of Wagon Train or Rawhide. I always fancied myself as a Rowdy Yates or a Gil Favor, but in reality I was probably closer to Wishbone, the cook who drove the chuck wagon!

"Hmmm… a Jackeroo. How would I find a job like that?"

Elisabeth moved ahead of the horse and swung open a metal gate.

Charlie trotted through it onto a dirt road, his withers covered in white frothy sweat, more from the baking sun than the workout I had given him.

"Just follow me and walk him slowly back to the corral, let him cool off a bit."

Elisabeth got into the pickup, closed the door and stuck her head through the window.

"You would need to apply through a stock and station agent. All the big ones – like Elder, Smith, Goldsborough and Mort – have their headquarters in Sydney. They manage properties all over the Northern Territory and Queensland."

Back at the farmhouse Mrs. Tinker was ready with a cuppa. I never met Mr. Tinker but Mrs. was the salt of the earth. I met a lot of people during the time I spent in Canberra but I liked the farmers and bush characters the best.

"I see you've learned the great Australian salute." Mrs. Tinker remarked as we sat on the verandah watching more transport planes take off from the air force base.

"Uh?"

She mocked me swishing the flies away from my face.

There were no flies in the air-conditioned Officers Mess at Fairbarn, the RAAF base. Noel had offered to show me around the same base I had been looking at from Mrs. Tinker's verandah just an hour earlier. Sitting with a schooner of beer while staring through large panoramic windows at sterile concrete runways, I asked Noel what he remembered of my namesake uncle.

"Johnny was about your age when he enlisted and became our rear-gunner or 'Tail-end Charlie' as we liked to call him. He had a small build, always cheerful with a half-smile on his face and a soft, almost singing Sussex accent. We became close friends," Noel told me.

"Did you ever come down to Bowshots farm?"

"Yes. He invited me down if we had a day off, which was not often. Your grandfather always made sure we had mounts so we would go out with the local hunt. I think he expected me to come a cropper over the jumps but I'd grown up on a sheep station in Western Australia so I knew how to ride well enough. I think I impressed him with my equestrian skills!"

"That took some doing!" Grampy was not easily impressed. Just the thought of him made me smile.

"Johnny had a wonderful way with horses," Noel continued. "He would have made a great steeplechase jockey.

Your grandfather had high hopes for him."

I watched a helicopter touch down at the far side of the airport.

Noel seemed to welcome the distraction, and said, "For security reasons all VIP flights come in and out through Fairbarn. We train helicopter pilots here to serve in Vietnam."

But I wanted to divert his attention back to another war. "I know the story of how you were attacked returning from the bombing raid, but when did you know that Uncle Johnny had been killed?"

Noel leaned back in the leather mess room chair and put his fingers together, almost as if in prayer. He touched his lips with his fingertips, then let out a long slow breath.

"Much later, when I was hiding in the Forest of Freteval I learned that four of the crew died in the aircraft, and Johnny was killed in his turret. Why the others did not get out, I don't know."

I was stunned, thinking about the vulnerability of a nineteen year-old boy, a few months older than me, alone in a dark turret at the tail end of a Stirling Bomber eleven thousand feet above France, feeling exposed, frightened and cold, only seconds from a terrible death.

"You said he wanted to come to Australia?" I asked.

"Yes. He liked the idea of the wide-open spaces and the freedom. He was such a fine horseman; he would have fit in really well. He could have been..." Noel looked away for a moment as another big Sikorsky touched down on the runway.

"A Jackeroo?" I filled in the blanks but it was as if someone else had fed me the words.

Noel turned his head and half smiled. "Yes, a Jackeroo..."

I cannot say that this was an epiphanal moment – but for the first time on this journey – and not for the last – I had a feeling I was not travelling alone.

Noel interrupted my reverie. "Finish your beer; I have some work to do. I'm still in the RAAF reserve, you know. I have to do three months service here every year. While I'm on duty I record flight plans for all aircraft leaving the base, including those VIP flights."

My own flight from Canberra was imminent. Behind a bank partition of rich Australian hardwood, a blond-haired, clean-cut young man smiled.

"Can I help you, mate?"

I handed him my green pass book. "Yes. I'd like to withdraw $20 please."

He passed four crisp colorful $5 notes across the counter and wrote in my new balance. I was shocked at what I saw. I had less than $200 left! When I left England I had the equivalent of $400. Now it was time to push the panic button, a decision had to be made about a job – fast! As usual I had no real plan, just a new buzz word in my vocabulary: Jackeroo. The word fueled a fresh objective: to work on my suntan while rounding up cattle or sheep somewhere in the Outback.

A few days later I loaded the Boer War suitcase into the luggage compartment of a Pioneer bus at Canberra Civic Centre, and headed for the big city in search of a job as a cowboy. Mr. Tittensor would not have been amused.

I left my surrogate Australian family with a feeling of sadness. Trundling along on that bus toward Sydney, through dry parched hills and gum tree forests, I felt lonelier than I had for some time. I already missed the Eliots – and I missed Elisabeth. As it turned out, I would see her on just one more occasion, and under very different circumstances. My time was soon devoted to survival, however, so romance had little room to flourish.

SOJOURN IN SYDNEY

Gazing through the window of the crowded bus, my first impressions of Sydney were of a vast sprawling metropolis; its western suburbs not particularly attractive with tracts of uniform red-roofed homes fronted by neat little strips of lawn and flower borders.

A yellow taxi deposited me in front of a modest semi-detached cottage at the end of a short cul-de-sac. A tall, handsome, suntanned man, dressed in white tennis shirt, shorts and sandals was mowing a narrow strip of lawn. The mowing man, who I estimated to be in his late thirties, resembled pictures I had seen of a young Frank Sinatra. I felt nervous when I lumbered up to the front door with the Boer War suitcase.

"Giddai. I'm yer cousin John," he said, not sounding at all like Frank Sinatra. "Welcome to Bondi. We've been looking forward to you coming… Mum, Mum, John's here!" he shouted. "Here I'll take that for you."

He tried to lift the suitcase and almost had a coronary on the spot. "Jesus Christ. What you got in there – lead?"

I started to explain the trunk's history vis-à-vis my grandfather and the Boer War when a small woman with a world-weary, weather-beaten face and stooped posture shuffled through the door and the thought crossed my mind: *How could a woman this tiny produce a son as big as John?*

"Great aunt Mary?"

Tears filled her eyes as she greeted me with a hug. "I'm so pleased you're 'ere, son."

My eyes welled up too. "So am I."

I followed them into the house. She showed me a small bedroom and pointed to a bed near the window.

"This is your bed, John. Afraid you will have to share with your cousin, but he don't mind if you don't."

"No. No. I'm just happy to be here."

Cousin John dropped the Boer War suitcase inside the door. I wondered if Mary recognized it as once having belonged to her lover, my paternal grandfather, Samuel Holman, a man I never knew. He had died soon after I was born.

Great aunt Mary ushered me into an armchair in the living room, then proceeded to make a pot of tea. I watched her pour the tea from a fine bone china teapot into a fine bone china cup, much like my mother would be doing at this time of day back in England.

"So why did you come to Australia?" I inquired.

Her eyes flickered a moment. "Well, I met my husband, Frank Davis, at the hospital I worked at in London towards the end of the First War. He was a patient, and had terrible lung problems from the mustard gas, you know?"

I didn't know, and felt terrible that I knew nothing of her life.

"He were also crippled up because of the toes he lost from frostbite in them cold, rat-infested trenches. The doctors told him he needed to move to a warmer climate if he wanted to live." She handed me the cup and sat down in an armchair that practically swallowed her up. "Frank took sick on the ship coming out. When we arrived he was admitted to a military hospital. He spent a year in that place."

"So what did you do?" I asked.

"Well. We didn't have much money. No friends. No family." She glanced away for a second, then turned back. She had bright, alert hazel eyes. "I didn't know if Frank would survive, but I had to find work, you see. It was hard at first but I found a job as a live-in housekeeper to a wealthy family. They were good to me and eventually I was able to afford to move out and rent a house in Bondi... not far from here."

"It must have been a lot different then," I replied. I had seen street after street in this most famous of Sydney suburbs, lined with densely packed red or blond brick houses and multi-story brick apartment blocks.

"Too right. It were just sand hills in them days. Have a piece of this?" She cut a large slice of homemade fruitcake and handed it to me on a dainty china plate with roses round the edge. "During the Depression, Frank and me ran a chicken farm in the bush up near Newcastle, about a hundred miles north of Sydney. Frank always wanted to be a farmer, but I didn't. Trouble was Frank took poorly again, so I had to run the place on my own."

Mary's lower lip began to quiver. She stared out through the window at a dark spot on the white wall of the house next door, a house that looked exactly like the one we were sitting in.

"Gosh, that must have been hard?" I eyed another piece of cake. I hadn't eaten breakfast and it was now late afternoon.

"Go on, help yourself. John won't eat it!"

I cut into the scrumptious cake and waited for her to continue, but she apparently felt she had said enough for now. She collected the dishes, piled them into a plastic bowl sitting in a stainless steel sink, turned on the tap, squirted in dishwashing liquid and began to wash the dishes with a long-handled sponge.

"Have you ever seen one of these before, mate." John waved a dishcloth above his head then tossed it my way. Embarrassed, I caught it, rose from my comfortable position and started to dry the dishes.

"So what do you want to do while you're here, son?" Mary asked.

"My main priority is to get a job – hopefully, as a Jackeroo on a cattle station to earn enough money to do some travelling." The densely packed suburb seemed a long way from an outback cattle station.

"You're welcome here, son, as long as you want to stay."

I thanked her, and then asked her how I could get to *the* beach. John obliged by taking me down to the world-famous Bondi Beach, about a mile from their back door. He admitted to me he hardly ever went there and I admitted to him I found it disappointing. The white sandy crescent of a beach would have seemed pleasant if I could have seen it, but it was covered from end to end with nearly naked sun worshippers, and the surrounds appeared shabby and run down – somewhat like Brighton transposed 12,000 miles to the south. Located in the crowded Eastern suburbs and in close proximity to the City of Sydney, Bondi had gained its reputation as Australia's most popular beach not because of its beauty but by dint of the sheer numbers using it.

I adapted quickly to the rhythms of the city but I missed the bush life. Pialligo and Elisabeth seemed a million miles away now.

One hot sultry day, I took the train over the Harbor Bridge to the leafy north shore suburb of Lindfield, named for the village in Sussex, just a few miles from my own family home. I consulted my Gregory's Street Guide before walking a mile through the up-market residential suburb with its solid brick-and-tile homes sporting stained-glass windows and wrought iron verandas, amid lush subtropical gardens with tall trees from which green and chartreuse Lorikeets squawked and flocks of Sulphur-crested Cockatoos swooped.

This southern hemisphere version of Hampstead ended abruptly at a set of solid double iron gates that opened onto rows of ugly corrugated iron Nissen Huts. The Bradfield Park Migrant Hostel reminded me of a factory chicken farm I once worked at during my school holidays. The only clucking hens here, however, were young mothers hanging out laundry on long washing lines, while their bored-looking husbands sat idly in doorways and their children kicked footballs along the dusty walkways. I passed a long line of people queuing to get into a roofless cinderblock construction. Clouds of rising steam billowed from its open showers, creating mini-cloud formations that evaporated in the hot dry air.

A couple of huts past the shower block, I found hut 318, where I saw a familiar face smoking a cigarette and reading a newspaper on the front step; the hut was otherwise identical to all the other huts.

"Hello, Hugh!"

"My God, Johnny boy! It's good to see you."

He stubbed out his cigarette on the asphalt walkway, then invited me inside a hut barely bigger than the cabin we had shared aboard *Australis*.

Julie, Cheryl, Chris, and Ian sprung out to greet me from whatever privacy existed in two small rooms that appeared devoid of any washing, toilet or kitchen facilities and furnished with only bunk beds and some ugly wooden furniture.

I must have looked as shocked as I felt.

"If you want a pee, you'll have to wait in line down the way!" Susan said with a smile as she gave me a hug.

"Welcome to Butlins, John!" said Ian.

"Yeah..." interjected Hugh, "Butlins without the laughs!"

"And if you want to eat, you'll also have to stand in line for the canteen!" Cheryl exclaimed.

"What about dancing lessons?" I asked with a straight face.

Cheryl laughed at the reminder of our Greek terpsichorean tangles.

"Well, at least we don't have to worry about the canteen today," Susan said, patting a hamper sitting by the door.

Ian grabbed one of its handles and I grabbed the other. Chris hoisted a large cooler onto his shoulder. We marched single-file through the hostel gates and down a dirt track into a wooded valley, through which flowed the muddy Lane Cove River. Susan spread a blanket in a meadow by its banks.

"We come here most days, John," she said, opening a Tupperware container bursting with deviled-egg and cucumber sandwiches.

Hugh opened his arms expansively to embrace the other migrant families dotted around the meadow.

"This is our escape from that horrible place. Helps keep us all sane."

"But we're moving out to Manly next week," Susan said as she passed the container around. "Hugh has found a good job at a medical laboratory and we have a nice house that we are going to rent near the beach."

"It was always our objective to get out as soon as possible," Hugh said as he uncorked a bottle of Lindemans Riesling and poured liberally into clear plastic cups. "There's no stopping us now."

Cheryl handed out the vino then lay stomach-down on the blanket, letting the sun do its work; her English pallor – all but gone. I eyed a stack of Mars bars sitting temptingly in the bottom of the cooler. Hugh tossed me one, then lightly flicked a towel at Cheryl's behind.

"Come on, let's get wet."

He ran to the bank, leapt onto a rope swing dangling from the branch of a tall eucalyptus and swung out over the river, dropping with a splash into the murky water. The rest of us followed suit, assiduously leaving enough of an interval so that nobody landed on the preceding jumper's noggin. Chris and Ian raced each other to the far bank and back again. I knew I couldn't match their swimming prowess, so I wore out the rope swing instead.

Late in the day, as Hugh emerged from the depths of the river for the umpteenth time, his lighthearted manner turned grave. He pointed up the hill toward the hostel.

"Some of the folks up there are finding it really difficult to move out. There's a housing shortage in Sydney, you see, which they weren't told about by the immigration people. The hostel was never meant to house families; it was built in World War II as an embarkation depot for the RAAF. We're OK because we sold our house back in Grimsby so money's not a problem for us, but a lot of them don't have any money. Some have been stuck up there for months – even years, in certain cases. Of course, I don't know how hard they've been looking for work but living in those huts is probably a lot worse than the council houses they left behind in Britain."

I was aghast. "So what happens to them?"

"They just give up and go home."

Not Hugh Francis. A total optimist, he and his family were well aware of the opportunities that Australia offered them.

I was naively unaware of the opportunities Australia offered me. I just felt lost and homesick for my own family. After our picnic, I walked away from that peaceful valley, leaving them lazing on the banks of the Lane Cove River, enjoying their freedom away from the confines of Bradfield Park, a grim place that provided a wholly different kind of entry into Australia than the one I had experienced. I never saw the Francis family again, but I have never forgotten them or their kindness toward a young stranger.

As the mercury rose in that hot summer, my bank balance continued to fall – as did my capacity to think logically. My reasons for coming to Sydney had somehow just vanished from my mind in the comfortable environment that great aunt Mary provided; I managed to convince myself that my sole purpose in Australia was to have a good time and that's all there was to it.

I happily drifted along with cousin John and his friend Sue Jilek on a tour of Ku-rin-gai Chase National Park, a wonderful wild place just north of Sydney that declared itself the home of *Skippy, the Bush Kangaroo* and looked a lot like Lane Cove National Park on a grander scale.

The darkening clouds unleashed their fury and the rain came down in sheets, so I ran for the shelter of an overhanging roof at a visitors' center. I use the term "shelter" loosely because simultaneously with a loud clap of thunder, a blinding flash of lightning struck the awning above my head and sent bits of burnt wooden tile cascading around me. I was scared shitless. Taking it as a wake-up-call, the next day I trudged around the busy streets of Sydney, hunting for a job – as a cowboy! (That, alone, illustrates how delusional I had become.)

After knocking on the door of every stock-and-station agent on Pitt Street from Dalgety to Elders, I quickly ascertained that they needed young Englishmen seeking the outback experience like Eskimos needed snow. It was apparent that I did not have much to offer anybody: no skills, a questionable education and little experience in anything worthwhile ... but, hey, this was a blue-collar country, the land of the working man, so something would turn up.

In great aunt Mary's postage-stamp sized back garden, the sweet scent from a frangipani tree almost made me giddy as I perused my address book from the comfort of a deckchair. I rediscovered the contacts given to me by my former boss, Gary Grove, and rang several wine growers, but these leads proved fruitless until I reached Len Evans; I did not know at the time that he was a major figure in the Australian wine industry. He provided me the telephone number of McWilliams Wines in Pyrmont and said to mention his name. Somehow, I left the McWilliams assistant manager with the impression that I was related to their shipping agents in Bristol, but I did not attempt to put him straight because he sounded quite enthusiastic.

"She'll be right, mate. I'll speak to the chief. See if we can find you something."

A couple of days later, the phone rang. "It's for you, son. Sounds important."

The grape harvest (or vintage) was about to begin at their winery near Griffith in the Riverina district of southwestern New South Wales, and they needed seasonal workers.

I was in.

Although Mary loved having me around the house, she was ill, the fallout from a hard life. She had not spoken to me about the affair with my grandfather. I could only imagine the torments she must have endured, knowing their affair had led to the breakup of the family. Had they been in love? How long had the affair lasted or had it been just a one-night stand? In this day and age having a liaison with your sister's husband might not have such long-term repercussions, but back then it constituted a major scandal. Mary had a perky, Cockney-like sense of humor but an air of sadness hung about her.

The day prior to my departure for Griffith, another hot sultry day in a summer of hot sultry days, I staked out my three-by-six rectangle of sand on Bondi Beach, along with 25,000-or-so others. At the foot of the steps to the beach stood an "oil station," where for twenty-five cents a leathery man sprayed you from head to toe in baby oil, guaranteed to make you fry like a Kentucky chicken. The idea that lying in the sun could be dangerous to your health was decades away; in retrospect, I wonder how many people contracted melanoma thanks to him.

Among the masses on the beach were hundreds of fit, edgy-looking young men conspicuous because of their accents and "short back and side" haircuts at a time when most young Australian males were sporting long hair. These were American servicemen on "R & R" from Vietnam. Sydney rated highly as a destination due to the hospitality of the locals and the fact that those locals spoke a form of the same language. Some soldiers found Australian girls to their liking and returned to settle in Australia after the war. Some made their way to the red light district of Kings Cross, where a more instant form of gratification was on offer – although Hooker House in downtown Sydney was not a brothel, as many discovered to their displeasure, but rather the headquarters of one of Australia's largest real estate companies, L.J. Hooker. Others went AWOL and did not go back to Vietnam at all, considering any punishment better than that, but most of them reluctantly returned to a decidedly dodgy future.

I attempted to body surf, but tired of feeling like an out-of-control missile mowing down great swathes of humanity in a vast watery bowling alley, I weaved my way back to my towel, trying to avoid the not-so-unpleasant experience of stepping on the derrieres of wall-to-wall bikini-clad women.

The loud wail of a siren woke the crowd around me, like Jesus waking Lazarus from the dead, and the word "shark" reverberated up and down the beach. I shielded my eyes against the glare. All the people in the water were rapidly trying to get out of the water. Beyond the threshing mass, two young boys on surfboards paddled feverishly toward shore while behind them, scything menacingly through the foam, was a grey fin.

I walked to the water's edge to get a better view of a wooden dory manned by six fit-looking lifeguards wearing nothing but skimpy Speedos and skull caps, trying to put themselves between the surfers and the shark. The shark kept coming toward the beach.

"It's a Grey Nurse," someone cried.

"Bloody menace they are…so much for the bloody nets," said another.

Whatever shark it was, it was big – I estimated at least ten feet from nose to tail. A lifeguard stood up in the boat and took a whack at the shark's fin with an oar. The Grey Nurse thrashed its tail, opened its massive jaws and tried to take a bite out of the oar.

The two young surfers stumbled out of the water and collapsed on the sand next to me, gasping for air. The shark cruised away from the dory, parallel with the beach, and put on a show for the thousands watching from the shore. The dory shadowed at a distance. Soon the big fish appeared bored with the whole thing, swam back out to sea and disappeared. After a while, another siren went off. I shook my head in puzzlement.

A bather next to me said "All clear, mate."

With that he and many others went back into the water as if this had been just a minor irritant.

I returned to my towel but the cupboard was bare. Along with my stolen clothes was the bus fare to great aunt Mary's. I walked back in a miserable mood, getting angrier by the minute. A southerly buster blew in, drenching me and my only decent pair of sneakers. When I went to bed that night, my sneakers were still wet so I left them on the porch to dry.

In the early hours of the morning, a scuffling noise outside the bedroom window woke me. I looked outside and saw a big dog making off up the road with one of my shoes in its mouth.

I pulled on some clothes and set off in hot pursuit. After a short chase and a brief tug of war, the dog realized resistance was futile, gave up the mangled shoe and slunk away in disgrace but it seemed like a bad omen.

RAILS WEST

The Boer War suitcase and I waited for a taxi in front of great aunt Mary's. I had spent the previous evening doing complex mathematical equations approximating mass, weight and density and given that I could barely lift the thing empty, I saw no alternative but to travel light. Great aunt Mary stood in the doorway next to John, dabbing her eyes. She thought of me as a schoolboy and confessed unease at my plans to head off into the "wilderness."

I admit that I felt more than a little uneasy myself. For the first time I was truly on my own.

The taxi driver deposited me at Central Railway Station. Unhappy World War I troops had caused a riot at Central Station in 1916; I was not feeling all that happy in 1970. I stared at a small bullet hole in the marble at the entrance to platform one, the only visible remnant of that riot. Virginia Woolf wrote a story which began with her staring at a mark on the living room wall, imagining it having been made by an officer's sword, then being transported off on a stream of consciousness to the evils of colonialism and the brutality of the British Empire. The mark Woolf saw was the remains of a dead moth, and the only stream of consciousness I went off on was the Western Flyer that transported me through miles and miles of suburbia, then miles and miles of dry, hilly country dotted with various species of eucalypti. The train for the first leg of the journey to Junee was comfortable. I read *The Population Bomb* by Dr. Paul Ehrlich. The apparent emptiness of the Australian bush made it hard to relate to overpopulation in the rest of the world. The slow train stopped at every little town and hamlet.

A few passengers boarded along the way but mostly the train picked up mailbags and parcels. Two girls sitting opposite invited me to participate in a game of cards, and we were soon joined by a hardened but happy-go-lucky Ocker named George, who could not sit still. A bald man, his stomach bulging from under his white singlet and overflowing the waistband of his shorts, he wandered up and down the carriage, joking and singing old World War I songs. I knew they were from that era because Grampy used to sing them.

What's the use of worrying, it never was worthwhile
So pack up your troubles in your old kit bag,
And smile, smile, smile.

"Cummalong now… youse all know this one."

He pointed one finger in the air and moved his arm up and down as though conducting an orchestra, his belly flopping in time with his finger.

It's a long way to Tipperary.
It's a long way to go.
It's a long way to Tipperary
To the sweetest girl I know.

Soon everyone in the carriage was singing along. This would never have happened on the 7:36 to Waterloo!

I switched trains at Junee onto a rickety two-carriage steam train. The two girls departed but George stayed with me for the next hundred-mile leg. The windows had to be opened to get any relief from the stifling heat, but with the air came clouds of dust.

Some fifteen years earlier, cousin John had worked in this area, at a town called Leeton.

"What's it like out there?" I had asked.

"Hot and dusty" had been his entire but fully accurate response. When we reached the town of Narrandera we were officially in the Murrumbidgee Irrigation Area (MIA), more poetically known as the Riverina. One of Australia's great engineering feats, this irrigation system brought water from the Snowy Mountains to transform flat semi-desert into the food bowl of Australia. The train chugged toward Leeton, and an endless forest of citrus trees flashed by the window. I tried to read, but George kept jabbering.

"Waddya know about Leeton, mate?"

"Not much," I replied. "I know they have a GJ Coles department store. My cousin used to work there."

"Rice, rice and more rice," George said. "It's the main crop, mate – has been since the 1920s – and it's so bloody good they send it to Japan! Waddya know about Griffith?"

"Not much."

"Well, they've bin suckin' water out of the Murrumbidgee for fifty years just so them city slickers in Sydney can get fruit and veg every day. A few years back, the curse of the outback caught up with them."

"The curse of the outback?"

"Salt! Contrary to popular opinion, growing ready-salted vegetables just don't work. To stop the salt rising they removed all the topsoil, concreted the fields and then put the soil back. Voila, no more salt could come up…"

I raised an eyebrow.

"…I know, I know, you're overcome with disbelief!"

The train shuddered to a halt. George heaved himself off the seat, swung his rucksack from the overhead rack onto his back and stepped out onto the platform.

Click go the shears, boys.
Click…Click… Click…
Wide is his blow and his hands move quick…
The ringer looks around and is beaten by a blow
And curses the old…

George's voice trailed off as he disappeared down the platform into the balmy night.

I was the only person left in the carriage as the bone-shaker chugged out of Leeton on the thirty-mile leg to Griffith. Alone with my thoughts, I felt a little frightened, as giant moths and grasshoppers swarmed through the open windows, seduced by the bright light of the carriage.

John Oxley had been the first European to explore this area in 1817. Unimpressed by what he saw, he wrote: *"The soil a light red sand parched with drought, a perfect level plain overrun with acacia scrub…there is a uniformity of barren desolation of this country which wearies one more than I am able to express. I am the first white man to see it and I think I will be undoubtedly the last."*

The little train pulled into Griffith at 10:00 pm. Fourteen hours after my departure from Sydney, I had arrived at my home for the next few months. My first thought was to find a room for the night so I dragged the Boer War suitcase out of the station and fought with it down the street. My paternal grandfather probably had servants or porters to lug it about, but I had just me.

I booked a room at the two-story, verandah-wrapped Griffith Hotel and flopped on the bed, sweat soaking through my clothes and onto the sheets. I was too exhausted even to take a shower.

THE GRAPE ESCAPE

My first day in Griffith broke even hotter. I had never been so hot in my life. The hotel manager said it was quite cool for the time of year.

I rose early and made my way out into the sunshine. Established around 1916, the town was spaciously laid out with a grid system of streets in the American style, which can be explained by the fact that an American designed it: Walter Burley Griffin (of Canberra fame), a Chicago architect from the Frank Lloyd Wright School. With his trademark tree-lined streets, roundabouts and parks, Griffin also designed the other Riverina town of Leeton.

Banna Avenue, the main street of Griffith, is the longest main street of any country town in Australia. Its length due in part to Walter Burley Griffin's idea of having shops on only one side of the street; the other side given over to parks and gardens. Indeed, down the center of Banna Avenue a wide strip was planted out to lawns, flower borders and trees; a single traffic lane passed along either side.

Griffith was named for Sir Arthur Griffith, the first New South Wales minister of Public Works. Sir Arthur read progressive literature and so perceived the basic social problem of the late nineteenth century as "the upheaval ... against the grinding tyranny of industrial monopoly." I would experience some of that grinding tyranny myself in the ensuing weeks.

I located my bank. The teller directed me to a couple of guest houses on Yambil Street, which ran parallel to Banna Avenue. Mahers Guest House looked the better of the two. It had a dozen rooms spread around a single-story faded yellow weatherboard house with a red tin roof set in a large but unspectacular garden.

Mrs. Maher, a late-middle-aged lady of Irish descent, blocked the doorway as she eyed me up and down. Short, wide, and wearing a shapeless smock-like dress; she looked formidable, even with her thinning hair in curlers, swathed in some sort of headscarf. Her prominently veined feet beat impatiently.

"So you want a room?"

Why else would I be here?

"I only rent to men."

I was OK there.

"I don't allow women on the premises."

You must be joking.

Jaw jutting, arms folded against a substantial chest, Mrs. Maher resembled Mussolini rallying the faithful. She unfolded her arms and wagged a finger at me.

"If I catch you with a woman in your room it will mean your immediate ejection from my establishment, understand? There can be no parties, no noisy or riotous behavior, and no alcohol. First and last months are due in advance."

As I started to walk away, I sensed her eyes burning into the back of my head.

"The rent is $10 a week... with breakfast."

I stopped halfway down the path and began to ponder: *Look, you don't have much money. The Griffith Hotel is not exactly a five-star joint and it's $48 a week!*

The hinges squeaked on the garden gate and through it walked a bearded, long-haired young man who looked like Jesus Christ in Levis.

"Name's Ivan... Ivan the Wonderful."

When I just stared, like a stunned mullet, he said, "Things can't be that bad, can they?" His Australian twang had a slight trace of Eastern European.

"Well. They could be better," I replied.

Ivan looked past me at Mrs. Maher standing rigidly in the doorway.

"The old girl's not so bad. Bark's worse than her bite."

"Hmmm…" I rubbed the side of my jaw.

"You won't find cheaper rent in Griffith," said Ivan, "and she makes a killer breakfast!"

OK. Maybe I can put up with her for a few weeks until I get on my feet.

I took a deep breath. "Alright, I'll take the room."

I had no time to negotiate which room as I needed to locate my new place of employment.

But before that, I had to settle my hotel bill and move the Boer War suitcase from point A to point B. My finances were so low I could not afford to waste money on a taxi so I dragged the suitcase down the street, stopping every few yards to sit on it and catch my breath. By the time I reached Mrs. Maher's my hands were raw, my clothes were soaked through with sweat and I felt physically sick. To make matters worse my room was not ready.

Seeing my plight, the hard core Mrs. Maher softened a little and poured me a glass of homemade pink lemonade. I flopped down on her patchy dry lawn in the shade of a mangy bottle brush. It took me an hour to rehydrate sufficiently to set off for McWilliams Winery.

"There's no buses going that way. There's nothing much out there," Mrs. Maher informed me. "You might be able to hitch a ride. People are usually good about stopping around here."

She was right. A lady with two infants picked me up immediately but she travelled only about a hundred yards in my direction, so I walked for a mile or two on a red dirt road through vast lemon and orange orchards until an old Italian man, driving a Ford F100 pickup, took pity on me and drove out of his way.

Hanwood had tall aluminum silos, looking like booster rockets from Apollo 11, dominating its skyline. Behind the silos, a large two story building, open on all sides, housed the winery; surrounding the winery, thousands of acres of vines stretched to the horizon.

"Plant a six-inch nail in this soil, water it, and in a year you will have a crowbar," JJ McWilliams famously said after planting forty thousand grape cuttings here in 1913, which gave a boost to the wine-making industry that had been started by Italian migrants attracted by the similarity of climate and landscape to that of their home country.

The old man deposited me next to the office where I met Mr. Glenn McWilliams, the winery manager and grandson of JJ. Mr. McWilliams did not look like a member of one of the most prestigious winemaking families in Australia. Of course, I did not know how a vintner should look, but he looked somewhat studious; grey-haired with oval glasses and grey short-sleeved shirt, grey shorts, white socks that reached just below the knee, and brown elastic-sided work boots. Immediately I sussed that this was a man who was a "hands-on" manager, someone not afraid to get dirty.

He stuck out a wine-stained hand and said, "Glad you could make it out here, John. How's the family?"

I fumbled for words. "Oh! Yes. Very well, thanks… at least the last time I saw them, but I…"

I was about to come clean and tell him the truth when he said, "It's the least we could do having you out here after all they've done for us. We do a fair trade in the UK now, you know."

"Yes. So I've heard but…"

A stocky man in his late fifties appeared in the doorway; he was dressed in slouch hat, blue singlet, shorts and work boots.

Mr. McWilliams said, "Albert, here, is our foreman. He'll show you around. You can start tomorrow. $49 a week OK?"

"Yes… fine." It actually sounded very fine, as I calculated my last salary at Southwater Brickworks had been about half that amount.

Albert gave me a lift back to town in the firm's minibus along with the rest of the workers. On the way, the skies darkened, lightning flashed, thunder roared and clouds of red dust blotted out the sky over Griffith. Then the rain started to pelt down. It never seemed to rain without it being a thunderstorm. I had yet to see a steady drizzle as in England. In Australia, rain arrived with great gusto, poured hard for fifteen to twenty minutes then died away quickly.

It died away quickly before the minibus pulled up next to the footbridge spanning the main irrigation canal that ran through the center of town. Crossing over the bridge, I followed a slushy dirt footpath to Yambil Street and looked forward to hibernating in my new room for a while… at least until I saw my new room. It was plainly too small to swing a cat in – about six feet wide by eight feet long – with a door midway and a window at the end with louvered slats. I literally could not shut the door with the Boer War suitcase in there.

I lay down, exhausted and read for a while; the happy-go-lucky feeling that prevailed in Canberra and Sydney had vanished, replaced by uncertainty and loneliness. I drifted off to sleep, and woke in the early hours dripping buckets of sweat. I opened the slatted window and a multitude of unknown bugs and mosquitoes swarmed in. Faced with a dilemma, I chose the sauna. Those mosquitoes that remained after I shut the window feasted on me.

The alarm sounded at six o'clock as work began at 7:30. I availed myself of the outdoor showers, then set off up the street, down the footpath and over the canal footbridge to wait under the shade of a gum tree for the minibus. A kookaburra kept me company and apparently found me very amusing. The bus, driven by Albert, was packed with workers.

The first few days were spent testing dozens of oak barrels for leaks. Albert's youngest son, a nice lad named Phillip, showed me how to place the barrel on a turntable, fill the barrel with boiling water and set the turntable in motion; as the barrel spun, streams of water squirted out, indicating leaks. I marked each spot and hammered in a wooden plug to stem the flow.

Most of the workers were related and had worked at the winery for generations. Glenn's eldest son, Peter, a massive bloke with rippling muscles à la Arnold Schwarzenegger, could throw full barrels of wine around like they were made of Styrofoam. On one blast furnace of a day, I helped him bolt on the sides of a high-sided truck to go into the vineyard and load buckets of grapes. I was barely able to lift one end of one side off the ground, but Peter waved me aside and lifted the whole thing into position on his own.

What can I say, I was a wimp... he wasn't.

Peter pointed toward a spanner lying on the ground. I wrapped my hand around it.

"Bugger...Bloody hell..."

I dropped it with a clang onto the concrete roadway and hopped around like a constipated kangaroo, shaking my hand in agony. The spanner was red hot. Peter grabbed my arm and shoved my hand into a bucket of water. When I pulled it out, skin was gone and my palm was red and raw. Peter didn't say much but I could tell what he was thinking.

I trudged "home" over the canal footbridge with shoulders slumped, wiping the sweat from my grimy brow with the back of my sleeve. A majestic wedge-tail eagle swooped down to take a look at me; as I approached the faded weatherboard guest house, the updraft from its red-tin roof sent the eagle soaring skyward and out over the surrounding orchards in search of a chicken or a rabbit for dinner. Under the red-tin roof, the baking sun had created an oven of what I hated to call my room. I flopped wearily onto the creaky bed, cradled my head in my grape-stained arms and drifted off to sleep with the window open.

Hours later, a frantic, low-pitched buzzing sound awakened me. I sat bolt upright and flipped on the lamp to see thousands of mossies, most involved in sucking the lifeblood out of me and the others getting in line for their turn. My naked body must have seemed like a buffet, a smorgasbord, a Thanksgiving dinner to them.

I swung my legs over the edge of the bed and grabbed a towel to swat them away. When my feet touched the patchy worn linoleum, I felt something crawling across my bare feet: cockroaches, hundreds of them, large and small swarming under the door, attracted by the bright lights of the bedroom. I went berserk, leaping around the room, flailing the towel at anything that moved, but it proved a total waste of time. Outnumbered and outgunned, I let out a guttural scream and collapsed exhausted on the bed, at the mercy of the insect army.

The mosquitoes had bitten me everywhere, even on my fingertips. My arms had changed shape from the swelling and my face resembled someone with simultaneous afflictions of mumps, measles and chicken pox. I took to spraying my room but as soon as the stuff dissipated the insect army returned in full force, cannons blazing. The nightly battle with the bugs drove me crazy at the time and the memory still sends shivers down my spine.

That first Friday night, I made my way to the Olympic swimming pool where the scent of eucalyptus and sheep dung overpowered that of the heavily chlorinated water. I stood poised on the spring board; there were no girls to impress this time, so I bounced up and down. Just before I hit the water, a voice rang out: "Giddai Johnno!"

I dived to the bottom and the cool liquid soothed my insect-ravaged skin. When I surfaced, I shook the water from my eyes and saw Ivan the Wonderful sitting in the shallow end. I swam over.

"How's the old witch treating youse?" He asked.

"I'm having more trouble with the night visitors!" I pointed to my splotchy torso.

"Jeez, man, you need to see a skin doctor!"

A fit-looking, clean-cut blond man about my age swam up to us. "Hey, Ivan. I race you to deep end?" He challenged in a thick German accent.

"Not me, mate. Ask Johnno here."

The German stuck out a hand. "The name is Fred. You want to race?"

"Alright… I'll give it a go… GO!"

I took off and got a yard start on him, but by the time I reached the far end Fred was a yard in front of me, heading back toward the shallow end, just a blur of spray, flashing feet and scything arms.

"He tried out for the West German Olympic team, you know?" Ivan announced.

I struggled to catch my breath. "Well, I don't feel so bad about getting a jump on him now!"

The German laughed. "You know Ivan cannot swim? An Australian that cannot swim… Ha! Ha! Ha!"

Ivan looked a little embarrassed. "I'm half Yugoslavian, mate!"

"Why did you challenge him to a race if you knew he couldn't swim?" I asked Fred.

"Vell… Jesus Christ should be able to valk on vater. No?" Fred raised his hand as if to hit Ivan but instead he swept his hand across the surface of the pool, spraying water into his face.

"Yes, mate. I could have once… but that was before I had these holes in me hands and feet!"

Fred pursed his lips and narrowed his eyes, but said nothing while Ivan and I climbed out of the pool and began to towel ourselves dry.

"Me and Fred are going to a dance at the town hall tonight. You wanna come, mate?"

"Yes… anything to get me out of that awful room!"

"The Echoes are playing. They're a local band but not bad."

An hour later, we stood in line to get into the hall. All the youth of the town were there. Many of the males were either farmers' sons or Jackeroos who spruced themselves up, drove into town, got tanked up at the pub, then invaded the dancehall.

We approached the ticket window.

"I'll shout youse blokes," Ivan announced. "I'm in a bloody

good mood 'cause I just got paid and I'm heading home to Sydney on Monday to see Mum and Dad."

He pulled a wallet from his back pocket, opened it up and looked inside.

"Christ… It's gone." He opened the wallet wider and felt down inside it with his fingers, as if that might make his money miraculously reappear. "I had sixty bucks in there… sixty. A week's bloody wages. It was there when I went to the pool. I know it was."

"Maybe you leave at guest house?" Fred suggested.

"No. No. I know I had it."

Behind us, the line stretched down the street. Someone shouted, "Hey can you lot finish your mothers' meeting and get a move on!"

"Youse blokes go on in. I'll go back and look for it and catch you later," Ivan told us.

Inside the auditorium, the girls lined up on one side of the floor, the boys on the other. The boys checked out the girls and the girls checked out the boys waiting for one to make the first move. It took some courage to walk across that dance floor and ask a girl to dance. Fred took the plunge and I watched Mr. Smooth choose the prettiest girl in the hall. She smiled and offered her hand, which he took, then whisked her onto the boards. He danced as well as he swam.

I waited until the Echoes played "Venus", a song that could make the dead dance.

She's got it,
Yeah baby, she's got it.
I'm your Venus,
I'm your fire and your desire…

I walked the gauntlet, but obviously I was nobody's fire or desire. Being turned down once was bad enough but twice was the kiss of death. I was unable to figure out why nobody would dance with me so I left Fred gyrating, surrounded by an adoring audience, and trudged home to the guest house. The mirror there reflected a swollen face that resembled the Elephant Man on a bad weekend. I started to worry if these mosquitoes carried malaria.

The next day, I visited the local Bush Nursing Association office, which was free. A nice old thing assured me that these were not the type of mosquitoes that carried malaria. She prescribed calamine as well as some ointment to heal my burned hand.

Things improved at the guest house. In a moment of weakness, Mrs. Maher moved me into a house she owned across the street. I must have come through some devious rite of passage. My new room had its own kitchen and shower room, but most importantly it had… fly screens! Three other men lived in the house: Ashmore Burford from London, Paddy Cascarino from Dublin, and Davy Heywood from the far west town of Broken Hill. Ashmore and Paddy were working their way across Australia from Perth to Sydney; the Wade Shire Council employed Davy as a clerk. The house itself was another nondescript weatherboard place with a red tin roof, much like the others on the street. It had a poor excuse for a garden, just dry patchy grass with a Hills Hoist in the middle to dry the laundry on.

I met the large oval-shaped man who inhabited the shack at the bottom of the garden early one morning as I was stumbling off to work. With a square jaw and short steely hair the texture of a Brillo pad, his piercing blue eyes were focused on a Kookaburra sitting on the top branch of a pomegranate tree in the front yard.

He pulled a pie from his jacket pocket, broke off a piece and placed it in the palm of his outstretched hand.

"Here Crusty…"

The Kookaburra swooped, landed on the big man's forearm and gently snatched the piece of meat pie from his dinner-plate hand. The big man broke off another piece and Crusty flew with it up to his pomegranate perch.

The big man noticed me watching.

"He knows he ain't gonna get any more so he won't hang about and beg." He thrust one of those large hands toward me, "Name's Cyril. I work nights at the bakery. Youse won't see much of me but youse'll see plenty of Crusty. He don't stray far from here."

"Crusty?"

"I calls him Crusty 'cause he likes me meat pies. Whenever youse feel a bit low, spend a bit of time with Crusty and he'll cheer youse up!"

Cyril was right about Crusty. The cheeky bird served as a cheerful but not-so-silent sentinel of the house. His Kookaburra laugh…*Oo oo oo aa aa aa ee ee ee*… sent me off to work with a smile on my face. My father always used to say, "Laugh and the world laughs with you. Cry and you cry alone." Crusty embodied that philosophy and served as a metaphor for the world that I found myself in as he perched, laughing, atop that pomegranate tree with its crop of sour acidic fruit.

Over the ensuing weeks, I settled into a rhythm, a rhythm of mostly hard work and exhaustion. Every morning I shifted tons of grape skins and seed from a sixty-foot aluminum silo, a backbreaking task for the two of us designated for this job. Opening a door at the bottom of the silo, we pulled the skins out with long-handled rakes into a trough with a screw in it, which then fed the mass through a press where the juice was extracted. Once this task was achieved we progressed to the next silo.

The final products of all this effort were excellent wines ranging from a Semillon Sauvignon Blanc, to a Cabernet Sauvignon, to Shiraz. It made me laugh when I overheard snippets of comments from the wine experts in the tasting room: "an aroma of tropical fruits and hints of fresh snow pea", "a hint of blackberry and blackcurrant with a touch of burnt toast", "the scent of cedar mingled with plum and prune juice." Nowhere did I hear, or have I heard since, a wine described as having "the delicate but unmistakable flavor of grape!" *Why is that?*

Another bestseller created here was McWilliams Oloroso Sherry, made from the Black Muscat grape; it had a raisiny color and fruity palate with a smooth, soft finish. I know this thanks to an old hand named Paul. Every afternoon Paul wandered past me, looked around to see if the coast was clear, and then disappeared behind a stack of sherry barrels not to surface again for hours. Observing me observing him, he nodded his head to indicate I should follow. I trailed him to the end of a row of barrels and around the corner to where nobody could see us. Paul pulled a piece of plastic tubing from the back pocket of his shorts, placed it in the bunghole of a sherry barrel and sucked. He handed me the end of the tube. I took a suck too. I swilled the sherry around in my mouth as if I knew what I was doing, and then swallowed.

"Ummm... very pleasant... very smooth!" I said.

The only words Paul uttered were: "Quality control, mate. Quality control."

The work got harder but life at "home" got better. My three companions in the house introduced me to the Ex-Servicemens Club, a large modern establishment at the end of town, where a WWII Fairey Firefly Fighter aircraft was mounted on a plinth across the street from the main entrance. Largely self-contained, the club housed a restaurant, a couple of bars, a snooker hall, a ballroom, and acres of poker machines. A subsidized evening meal cost about fifty cents and would typically include a roast with two veggies, mashed potatoes and gravy, followed by dessert and a pot of tea. I received a guest membership for the first month, which meant I did not have to cook at night. *What a deal!* My cooking skills were non-existent anyway and when not at the "Ex-Servos" (as the locals called it), I lived off cans of Irish stew and baked beans.

I yearned for home and to see my family again, but I was determined to prove to them and myself that I could make it on my own. It was still only March and just four months since I'd sailed out of Southampton Harbor. It was beginning to feel like a prison sentence.

ROUGH TIMES IN THE RIVERINA

Mrs. Maher moved in a young lad named Newt Parker as my room-mate. Newt was short and muscular with tight curly hair and a puggish face; from his squashed nose and cauliflower ears one might have guessed boxing had figured somewhere in his life.

Round one started well, when Newt invited all of the occupants of 176 Yambil Street for a Chinese meal. At the Café Beautiful, he informed us he had emigrated from Belfast and worked for a local dairy company who paid him a small fortune to make deliveries in a refrigerated van to various parts of Australia.

"Listen…" he said, "I've earned enough in six weeks to buy me a brand new Holden Monaro!"

With its sporty lines and powerful 6-cylinder engine, the Holden Monaro was similar to a Ford Mustang. I had worked about six weeks and couldn't afford a down payment on a bicycle. Walking home every night from the "Ex-Servos", I pressed my nose up against the window of the local auto-dealer's showroom and gazed at the sleek blue beast on display wondering if there would ever be a time in my life that I could afford such a vehicle.

Most of the boarders at Mrs. Maher's and other hostelries

were in town for the grape harvest and then the apple and citrus harvests. An eclectic bunch, some were "ten quid tourists" like myself, others were university students out to make a quick buck, but the majority were itinerant workers – Eastern Europeans, Greeks, Italians, some Aussies, some British – who travelled from town to town, from harvest to harvest, from grapes to apples, tomatoes to potatoes, flowers to sugar cane. Somewhere something in Australia needed picking, cutting, planting or digging up, so wherever this was, they were there. Some workers carried everything they owned in the back of a pickup, others had a fixed home but were on the road all year. Some were farmers who had walked away from their farms because of drought or bankruptcy and into this nomadic existence.

All of us had one thing in common – we sat at the bottom rung of the social ladder, in a love-hate relationship with the community. On one hand, the locals needed our money and services; on the other, they did not like us invading their town, stealing their women and filling up the pubs. They had a point, because although most fruit pickers were hardworking people who kept to themselves, a small criminal element did cause trouble… as I was about to find out.

Moving from one tough job to another at the winery, I thought that raking tons of lightly crushed grapes from a silo under a 100-degree sun was bad enough, but the next job was worse – far worse. Albert had me lined up for this from the day I arrived because nobody else wanted to work in the skin bin; the experienced hands knew better. The skin bin, reserved for seasonal workers, was a cast iron tank about twice my height into which the residue from the main crusher – seeds, skins and stalks – were blasted from an overhead chute. My job entailed spreading the stuff uniformly round the tank with a fork and rake before water was pumped into the mix and the "must" left to ferment for a couple of days. Then a large bung was opened in the floor and all the junk had to be shoveled down through the hole onto a conveyor belt that fed into another crusher to extract the last ounce of tannin and juice.

The remaining seeds, stalks and skins were loaded onto a truck and carted away for compost, mulch or bulk feed for livestock.

My days were spent filling one tank or emptying another while a blower blasted in fresh air to waft away the sulphurous gas, which had a nausea-inducing effect – or worse: It could kill you! When I casually jumped into a half-full tank and sank to my knees in the soggy skins, I knew I was in trouble because I could not feel the normal rush of cool air on my face. I looked around and noted the air blower was missing. I took a breath and my throat began to constrict, like a man on the gallows with a slowly tightening noose. I looked for the ladder. No ladder either! I was in too deep to pull myself out, and my oxygen-starved brain began to spin like the worst of hangovers. "Help! Help! Somebody help me!" My voice echoed off the iron walls.

What seemed an age was probably only seconds until an outstretched hand grasped mine and pulled me out.

I must have fainted because I regained consciousness on the lawn in front of the winery. Someone was slapping my cheek. When my vision cleared, I saw Phillip's boyish face amid a sea of other faces.

"That was a close one. Feels like you're drowning, don't it?"

"I don't know, I've never drowned before but I'll take your word for it!"

The other faces belonged to a party of tourists who were touring the winery at the time. One old man actually said that witnessing my rescue constituted the highlight of the tour!

I continued to work the skin bin by day, coming home exhausted, then stumbling off to the Ex-Servicemen's Club with the boys for a while before falling into bed.

One day I hobbled home from work early, because I had speared my foot with a fork. I took a shower and as I towel-dried my hair, I noticed my silver-backed hairbrushes were missing. Thinking I must have mislaid them, I went off to the club for dinner, but just the idea that they were missing troubled me. Uncle Johnny had won the hairbrushes at The Horse of the Year Show in London where the Queen of Spain presented him with a large silver cup and the hairbrushes prominently engraved with: *J. G. Olympia 1939*. My mother had entrusted me with the hairbrushes the night before I left. She must have thought they fit with the Boer War suitcase.

When I returned to my room, I asked Newt if he had seen the missing articles.

"Me wallet's gone missing too!" he said.

It seemed we had a thief about, but who could it be? We sat on the edge of our beds talking about possible suspects when Mrs. Maher arrived. She put her hands on her hips, thrust out her ample chest, her eyebrows joined in the middle.

"It can't possibly be anyone from the guest house because I only rent to nice boys!" She didn't hang around to hear more. She disappeared out the back door but the sound of her voice echoed back to us: "By the way, I've installed a new TV for you."

"Thank you, Mrs. Maher!" Newt and I shouted in unison.

"The old dear's gotta heart after all," said Newt.

However, the old dear had neglected to tell us that this TV came with a meter that took twenty cents for every twenty minutes of viewing time. *What a skinflint!* She already had a meter on the shower. Ten cents lasted about five minutes and the hot water would always run out before I had time to rinse off the soap. Just getting the gas water heater to work at all required a master's degree in hydraulics and mechanics. There were so many levers and switches that had to be pulled or pushed in the right sequence that the penalty for not doing so was either death by asphyxiation or death by gas explosion. It did not end there. She had also installed a meter on the water heater in the kitchen that blew out sparks and flames each time you lit it.

Sparks of another variety flew the next evening. Newt had pinned a note on the bedroom door: *I've found the thief. See you after work.*

"It's Fred… the German bloke," Newt informed me upon his return. "I stood behind him at the coke machine across the road. He didn't know I was there. He pulled out me wallet and used me twenty cents to feed the machine."

I shook my head in disbelief. "He was here last night watching TV with us… he even put twenty cents in the bloody meter."

"The bugger was casing the joint and when we was at work he snuck in and lifted whatever he loiked."

Newt pulled a damp towel off the rack outside the shower room. I stood by the door as he brushed past me into the bedroom.

"So what did you say to him?"

"Say? I didn't say a bliddy thing." Newt rolled the towel and swatted an imaginary fly crawling up the bedroom wall. "I bashed him up against the coke machine."

He shaped as if to swat me; I flinched but Newt was in another world. He shook his head from side to side as if to clear some blockage in his brain. His eyes rolled upward under the lids so that only the whites were visible then he swatted the wall so violently the towel cracked like a whip.

"I swear… I swear I'd have bliddy killed him if Jesus Christ himself hadn't turned up with a bit o'help from his two disciples…Bert and Gil!"

Bert and Gil were two older tenants of Mrs. Mahers. Bert did the garden and odd jobs and, I suspect, slipped Mrs. Maher "the beef bayonet" on occasion. Gil, a tall handsome man, had suffered permanent brain damage at the hands of the Japanese in New Guinea during the war. He was a gentle soul whose mind always seemed to be somewhere else. For all her faults, Mrs. Maher had given him a place to hang his hat.

"Did you get your money back?" I asked, slowly backing out of the bedroom.

"What was left of it. He confessed to stealing your stuff. He was scared, man. I took him on the milk round, made him do all the running for me then I beat the crap outta him."

While pretending to fill the kettle I shouted from the kitchen, "I don't think that was very wise."

"Taught him a bliddy lesson he won't forget."

The thin fibro walls shook as he cracked the whip again.

"You think so?" I yelled from the tamped earth footpath outside the back door. Ever since my school days I hated bullies like Newt, but I half agreed with him. I was angry that someone could socialize with us by night and rip us off by day. It registered as a major shock because I had led a somewhat sheltered life and believed the best of everyone. But suddenly I remembered Ivan's missing $60, and it all began to make sense.

"Mrs. Maher kicked him out. He won't show his face round here again," Newt said.

My frustration and resentment spilled over into the next day.

Albert had me in the skin bin as usual. The skins were being blasted in so fast I could not keep pace. I threw the fork at the wall and it made a loud clanging sound.

Albert peered over. "What's going on, mate?"

"Bugger off," I said under my breath.

"What was that?" he responded.

"I said, I'm getting a cough…. hhrrruumph…hrrumps…"

"You're going too slow. I've got another tank I need you to empty after this one."

How was I going to last? Southwater Brickworks had been a walk in the park in comparison. At least I could return to a comfortable home and Mum's cooking at the end of the day.

Hot, exhausted and soaked in sweat, I climbed down into the next tank and started shoveling again. Every half hour Albert would be around telling me to hurry up. Eventually he pulled me out and sent me out to mow the lawns. I smelled so bad that even the flies headed for the hills.

I stumbled off the bus and crossed the canal in a stupor. All I wanted to do was sleep but Newt was pacing the floor of the room. He had just returned from an overnighter to Sydney and noticed more of his things were missing. I looked around and saw that my transistor radio had gone.

Paddy Cascarino entered the room. "I saw Fred drive away in a taxi this afternoon… Burford's had a leather coat go missing and Mrs. Maher lost some paintbrushes."

"Fred's a painter isn't he?" I asked rhetorically.

Newt zoomed out of the room to return in half an hour. "I know where he is, fellers."

I had a queasy feeling as Paddy Cascarino drove Newt, Ivan and me up to the Griffith Guest House at the other end of town. Even before the car had come to a stop, Newt leaped out and disappeared somewhere into the motel-like compound.

In a few minutes he returned with Fred, twisting his arm behind his back.

"OK, yer fucker, what have you got to say for yerself? Speak up or I swear I'll kill you, you bastard."

He slammed Fred against the car. Fred could not say much because Newt was in the process of throttling him. He did not look such a smooth operator now.

Paddy Cascarino intervened. "Let him go. Let him speak,"

"OK, bastard. What do yers have to say?" Newt screamed.

Fred was shaking like a large blancmange on the San Andreas Fault. "About vat? Vat is you doing here?" he whispered hoarsely.

Newt slammed him against the car again and he fell to the ground.

Ivan stepped forward and tapped Newt on the shoulder. Newt jerked his head around and his eyes made contact with Ivan's.

"Leave him alone!" Ivan said softly.

"What?"

"I said leave him alone." Ivan's eyes did not waver from Newt's.

Newt stepped away, his body trembling with rage, but something about Ivan's calm countenance made him stop.

Fred looked up at Ivan, his eyes wet, his face red, all trace of Teutonic superiority gone. "OK. I take your money, Ivan. I take your stuff, John. Your hairbrushes. Your radio."

"Why?" I asked.

"I sell at pawn shop. I need money to pay rent… I have no money. No job."

"Why didn't you ask me? I would have lent you some

money, mate," said Ivan.

Fred just shrugged.

"You don't steal from friends," I commented – not that we were friends.

Fred started to weep. He tried to wipe his eyes with his sleeve. Newt, wild-eyed and almost deranged, knocked his arm away and closed his stubby fingers around his neck. This time Paddy and I could see that divine intervention was not going to work so we each took a hold of an arm and wrestled Newt away.

"If I were you, Fred, I'd leave town," yelled Paddy over his shoulder while attempting to stuff Newt into the back seat of his station-wagon. "You've made too many enemies here."

"Yeah… go. We don't wanna see your stinkin' face round here no more," Newt piped in. I eased my grip on his arm – he twisted and took another swing at Fred, who ducked behind the open car door. Newt's fist connected with the edge of the car door and bloodied his knuckles.

"Come on. Let's go," Paddy yelled.

Ivan helped us shove Newt, now in an almost trance-like state, into the car. I hopped in beside him. Ivan waved us away. Through the rear window I could see Ivan put an arm round Fred's slumped shoulders and help him to his feet. Fred stared after us, a lost and forlorn figure. I felt sorry for him.

Paddy eased his station-wagon to a halt outside the Area Hotel on Banna Avenue. "I don't know about you fellers, but I could use a pint!"

Newt mumbled something incoherent but joined us anyway in the crowded public bar. A couple of inebriated aboriginals wandered in and hustled Newt for money "ter buy some grog, mate!" Newt immediately wanted to fight them too. The atmosphere can only be described as akin to someone planting a bomb with a fuse so short you couldn't get clear before the thing exploded. To calm things down Paddy started to sing *Danny Boy*, a song that can bring tears to the eyes of men with the hardest of hearts. Most of the locals thought him crazy but a few joined in. When Paddy finished *Danny Boy* he launched into another Irish ballad.

And we're off to Dublin in the green, in the green
Where the helmets glisten in the sun
Where the bayonets flash and the rifles crash
To the echo of the Thompson Gun...

"Shut up. Shut UP... SHUT THE HELL UP!" Newt's face contorted into 57 varieties of hate. Steam was coming from his ears. "Don't ever sing that song around me. D'ya hear? NEVER sing that!" Newt's lips quivered and his eyes stared like pools in a black swamp. Paddy stood his ground and didn't blink. Finally, Newt averted his eyes, turned and stormed out of the bar, leaving the doors swinging in his wake.

"Bloody Orangeman," Paddy shouted.

I stood open-mouthed, more worried about what might happen next than what had just happened.

"What was that about?" I asked.

Paddy grabbed his schooner from the bar, tilted it to his lips and drained the contents. "Just testing the waters – and the fish were biting, it seems."

Newt did not return to the house but the incident spooked me enough to trigger one of my famous nightmares. This one seemed all too real. I was crossing a dark street when a bus barreled around a corner and almost hit me. The bus stopped. I stooped to pick something up. From the corner of my eye I saw a shadow in the headlights. Suddenly it was on me, pummeling me with clenched fists – a knife slashed at me and I felt it penetrate my stomach. I lay bleeding on the cold bitumen road, with the faces of Fred and Newt staring blankly down at me. I awoke shaking and drenched in a cold sweat.

Most dreams are usually forgotten but not this one. I had it in my mind as I shoveled in the skin bin. In fact it turned out to be a blessing in disguise because I turned my dark thoughts into thoughts of all the good things in life, which took my mind off the drudgery. I thought of Delia back in England and of how we had met and the cool times we had together. I thought about my family and the holidays we used to take. I thought about the horses I used to ride on Grampy's farm. I reached the point where I let no negative thoughts in. I daydreamed through the filling of the skin bin. I daydreamed through the emptying of the skin bin. I daydreamed when I stacked barrels. I daydreamed when I cleaned the presses and the conveyor belts. In an almost out-of-body state, my days passed in oblivion to the hard labor. I had inadvertently taught myself a lesson on how to take the mind off boring or unpleasant conditions, a lesson that I have used over and over throughout my life.

Back at Mrs. Maher's, things were moving fast. She had now installed a meter on the electric stove so virtually everything electrical or gas powered required money to make it work. I went over to complain, but before I got a chance Mrs. Maher started complaining to me:

"That Newt has disappeared. Do you know where he is? He owes me $12 in rent."

"I haven't seen him since we were at the pub last week."

Until then she had nothing but praise for Newt...*Yes. He's such a nice upstanding boy*... had been her mantra for him or anyone else who paid the rent on time. She scowled and slammed the door in my face. Newt materialized again when Ashmore Burford decided to move to Sydney; by way of an olive branch, Newt offered him a free ride. He loaded one of Ashmore's suitcases on the back of a pickup in the morning and arranged to fetch him from work in the evening.

At the end of the day I was surprised to find Ashmore sitting alone in the communal living room. He jumped up from the couch and seemed disappointed when he saw me.

"Oh, it's you, John. Have you seen Newt?" He wrung his hands and his eyes darted this way and that.

"No. I thought he was driving you to Sydney."

"Yeah, so did I."

"What, he didn't turn up?" I exclaimed.

"Right first time. He's got my bloody suitcase."

Paddy came through the back door. "I told him not to trust the bastard. I've just bin up to the milk depot where his nibs is s'posed to work..."

"Supposed to work?" Ashmore responded.

"The receptionist told me that Newt was not legally old enough to drive a truck!" Paddy pounded his fist into the palm of his hand, "What's more, they fired him for stealing money from the till."

"Jesus..." I filled my cheeks with air and expended it slowly. "So where is he?"

"Your guess is as good as mine, pal."

"I'm leaving," said Ashmore, "he can keep the bloody suitcase. There's nothing in it worth a damn anyway."

Paddy drove Ashmore to the railway station to catch the night train to Sydney leaving me to reflect upon the stories that Newt had spun. Suddenly they did not ring true. For instance, the brand-new Holden Monaro car he talked about. I never did see it. When I asked him about it he said, "Loaned it to one o' me workmates, a feller called Les." I never saw Les either. Other things did not add up. "I can get yers ninety-five a week delivering milk," he'd said. It seemed too good to be true at the time; I was doing slave labor at the winery for half that. It was too good to be true.

With Newt gone, I awaited a new roommate with some trepidation. Arriving home from work one night, I saw two suitcases sitting in the middle of the bedroom and heard the shower running.

A few minutes later a tall, bulky guy with a semi-Indian appearance strolled out with a towel wrapped around his middle. He bore a remarkable resemblance to Elvis Presley.

"Giddai. The name's Lou... Lou Muller." He stuck out his hand. I stuck mine out and introduced myself.

"Good to meet you mate... John ... Lou... Lou... John... something very lavatorial about that," he said.

We both laughed. He seemed to be a decent fellow but my guard was up.

"I'm a student," he said, "I've done a couple of years at the University of New South Wales but I'm taking a year off to earn some dough."

I did not see a lot of Lou at first because he found a job in a seed factory and worked at night, which was fine with me.

Coming home from the winery on Saturday, I crossed over the canal and ran into Mrs. Maher on the street. She seemed pleased to see me. For once she was out of her smock and curlers, adorned in a pretty pink two-piece suit and matching pillbox hat.

"Well, don't you look spiffy?" I said.

An elaborate mesh veil, dotted with mini blue butterflies, hung off her hat and covered the top half of the iron lady's face; on the visible bottom half flickered the beginnings of a smile that soon turned into a scowl.

"Get away with you. I've just come from my niece's wedding."

"Did you have fun?"

"Yes, I did, but I'm getting too old for all that frolicking about." She lifted the veil as if seeing the world through a sieve had suddenly become too much for her. "The Minister had some things to tell me about Newt."

I pricked up my ears at the mention of his name.

"He told me that Newt came to him for help when he first arrived in town."

Suddenly, the fancy hat had become too much for her as well so she removed the two long pins that held it on her head and yanked the whole thing off, leaving her already thin hair flattened against her scalp.

"Ah. That's better. Never did like hats anyway… So the minister said that Newt had apparently been to all the churches in town. Being Irish, you see, he had a fear of and a use for the church but the Minister also said that Newt had been in a sanatorium in Sydney. Now, the minister didn't know if he'd escaped, been let out or what but …" I knew instinctively what she would say next. "He seemed such a nice boy too… but what's more," she continued, "Fred came back to see me to try to put things right. He told me he was so scared of Newt that he'd confessed to stealing to save his own neck."

I waited for more information but she changed the subject: "How's Lou getting along?"

"I don't see much of him but he seems a decent bloke."

"Yes, he's such a nice boy."

With that, Mrs. Maher headed for the shops.

I rounded the corner of a hedge onto Yambil Street and stopped dead in my tracks. My upper palette went dry; I clenched my jaw and in the process bit my tongue. I could feel the blood trickling down my throat. A few feet ahead Newt stood, arms akimbo, glaring at me. He rotated his head, rolled his eyes backward, only the whites displayed.

I swallowed hard. *Christ! How much did he hear?*

He took a step forward, jerked his right arm as if to hit me but instead ran his fingers through his curly hair, turned away and crossed the street. Not a word passed between us.

I sprinted home to my room, slammed the door hard and locked it. Lou lay on his bed reading; he peered over the top of the book. "Bloody hell, mate, you look like you've seen a ghost."

"No ghost, someone very much alive."

Trying to catch a breath, I flopped on my bed and lay there, hands behind head, staring up at the ceiling, somehow finding inspiration from the streaks of faded yellow paint to explain the Newt story to Lou.

"There is something in his past. He got very touchy with Paddy over an Irish song he was singing. It's all speculation, but Paddy believes it's something to do with the troubles in Northern Ireland. He thinks that's the key."

"Jeez. Can't people come to this country and leave their bloody problems at home?"

Problems of a different kind were occurring at work. The harvest was at its height, the grapes were being delivered by the truckload in a continuous convoy, and I was toiling seven days a week. Albert was riding me hard – over the course of one weekend the winery crushed 400 tons of grapes and I had to empty three of the big silos on my own. Every day involved either filling or emptying a silo of some kind; there did not seem to be any job for me that did not entail a huge physical effort. I was probably the fittest I have ever been in my life, but that provided little consolation at the time.

After working three weeks without a day off, I ignored the alarm clock. *To hell with it...I'm staying in bed.* I ached from head to toe, so I rolled over and went back to sleep.

At nine o'clock I heard the sound of the vacuum cleaner, then a knocking on the door. Lou opened it.

Mrs. Maher, wearing a sort of pinafore and a headscarf tied at the front like an English charlady, said, "I've come to change the sheets and clean the room. Can you get up and come back in a couple of hours?"

I had picked the one day of the month she came over and cleaned house.

Bleary-eyed, Lou and I stumbled up to Banna Avenue and grabbed a cup of coffee at a milk bar furnished with 1950s-era varnished plywood booths and Formica tables. I had rarely been in town during the day and realized I'd not taken any photos of Griffith so I returned to get my camera from the wardrobe. It was gone. I searched everywhere but knew I would not find it. Newt Parker, ex-roommate, ex-mental patient, had struck again. What to do? This was the Las Palmas camera. My pictures of Canberra and Sydney were on the roll of film inside it. This was the last straw.

"I swear I will kill him. Psycho or not, I'm going to kill him."

I stormed around the room, picked up a book and threw it at the wall.

"Let the police handle it, mate," Lou said quietly. "Take a couple of deep breaths and calm down a bit."

Walking home later from the police station, I was overcome by a sense of unease... *What if the cops question Newt and he finds out it was me that told them?*

The plot thickened when Lou, Ivan and I attended a local event that had been advertised around town for weeks. We walked a mile or so along the canal path. In the distance appeared what looked like fairy lights hanging from trees. They *were* fairy lights hanging from trees, scattered around a large open space, partially illuminating a lot of people in various stages of inebriation. In the middle of the open space, a pop group bashed out what could loosely be termed rock-and-roll under a large banner that displayed the word *Canalival*. We had reached our destination.

A dozen barefoot and shirtless aborigines formed a line and danced rhythmically, corroboree style to the beat while two young men on horseback and stripped to the waist, galloped about in the half-light causing great swaths of the crowd to flee from their path, like schools of fish from a shark.

A spotlight flashed on the riders and a megaphone blared: "Would the two bloody riders please leave the park or else we'll call the police."

The two bloody riders ignored the warning. More of the throng began to stomp and clouds of dust obscured the stage. Fights broke out; people stopped dancing to watch the fighters. Young kids stole the light bulbs from the trees while the drunken horsemen galloped away in the moonlight, one with a half-naked aboriginal girl clinging to his back. The band played on and still there was not a policeman in sight. *What hope do I have of getting my camera back if the police can't even turn out for an event like this?* I thought as we trailed home alongside the canal. A lone streetlight up ahead silhouetted a small group of people walking toward us. I paid scant attention till they were upon us. Two aboriginal girls giggled but it was the two men they were hanging onto that startled me. The laughing stopped when Newt and Fred saw us. We passed each other in stunned silence.

Lying in bed that night, I realized that Newt and Fred had been buddies all along and had managed to pull off an elaborate sting against the residents of Maher's Guest House. I felt annoyed for not summoning enough courage to confront them. I did summon enough courage to inform the police that the perpetrators were still in town but as I expected, the long arm of the law displayed even less interest than the first time I filed a report.

Back at the winery, growers were delivering tons of grapes in an endless convoy of tractor-trailers, pickups and trucks.

Down in the skin bin, the skins were so warm and the gas so pervasive it made me drowsy. At lunch, like most of the workers, I found a quiet, shady spot to lie down and sleep. It was grueling work, even for the natives. Lunch consisted of sandwiches that Mrs. Maher had packed – for a not-so-small fee – and fresh peaches, citrus fruits and watermelons that growers donated to the cause. The watermelons were so large that eating a crescent-shaped slice left a pink stain from ear to ear.

Heavy rain blew in with its usual gusto; the ground softened, the red soil became a quagmire and put a halt to the picking. Tractors and trailers could not get into the fields to collect the buckets of grapes, everything slowed down – and we got the weekend off.

The Boer War suitcase and I went to Sydney. Only one of us would return. A letter had arrived from my half-Norwegian cousin, Tor Justad, who had just completed his two-year stint with Voluntary Service Overseas on a remote Fijian island and planned to return home to England via Sydney. He wanted to meet me during a brief stopover at the airport, not realizing that Griffith was five hundred miles from the airport. Following a cold rattling journey aboard the overnight mail train – which halted at every little town from Grong Grong Matong to Bong Bong, loading and dropping off parcels and mailbags – I arrived in Sydney in the early morning light, stiff and sore.

The last time I had seen Tor, he had just graduated from Cranleigh (the same English boarding school my father had been sent to at the age of five) and joined the merchant navy as a purser with the Union Castle Line. Then he was tall, clean cut and robust in a Scandinavian sort of way, but now at Sydney airport, I had to look twice because I did not easily recognize him. Thin and gaunt and sporting shoulder-length hair and a shaggy beard, Tor was dressed in a white safari suit and sandals. With a coconut mat rolled under one arm and a canvas hold-all slung over one shoulder, Tor seemed a bit nervy and unsure of himself, rather like a man living on a remote South Sea island for two years who is suddenly thrust back into the limelight. The phrase the Aussies use is "Gone Tropo." As I stuck out my hand, feeling a bit like Stanley finding Livingstone in darkest Africa, another hand clasped Tor's and shook it first. The hand belonged to an Old Cranleighan named Richard Hill who now resided in Sydney.

Tor's flight plans had changed and his altered schedule meant he had a whole day instead of a couple of hours. Richard drove us in to Sydney and deposited Tor and me in the heart of the city. Great aunt Mary was not up to a day's sightseeing so I became a surrogate tour guide, a case of the blind leading the blind. We visited Australia Square, which in fact is a circular building, unlike Circular Quay, which is u-shaped. At the time it claimed to be the highest building in the Southern Hemisphere, but now it is positively dwarfed by most of the buildings around it. We rode the bullet elevator to its top floor and lunched in the revolving restaurant, which garnered a spectacular view of Sydney.

A sleek hydrofoil ferried us across the harbor to Manly. In some ways Manly felt familiar to both of us because there were streets with names such as South Steyne, North Steyne and even a Steyne pub, all named after an area of Brighton in Sussex. A café on the Corso had the pretensions of a genteel English teahouse but appeared out of place amid the surfers and beach bums. Tor had no time for these trivialities as he was fast becoming a radical socialist, unshackled by the honky values of the English public school system. He had seen the other side of the coin in Fiji. I was seeing it for myself in Griffith.

Overjoyed to have Tor in her house, Mary prepared a wonderful teatime spread and wore herself out asking him questions.

"You two are the first relatives I've laid eyes on since my brother Charlie came to visit us in 1935…" Great aunt Mary actually knew more of Tor's history than mine because Tor's mother, my auntie Doreen, had been her only contact with

England. "…He weren't here long. I came down on the train from Newcastle to meet him at the docks. John was just a babe in arms then." She began to chuckle. "Charlie's mates on the ship gave him a hard time… they all thought I was his girlfriend and that John was a result of Charlie's last visit to Sydney! Anyway, Charlie hated it up there at the chicken farm. Wanted me to come back to England with him but…" There was a lengthy pause. The room suddenly seemed to shrink; it felt claustrophobic. "… but I couldn't."

"So what did you do?" Tor asked.

"We gave up the farm and came back to Sydney." Her eyes flickered.

We waited for her to continue, but it was John who broke the silence. "Dad got a job as a night watchman at the naval dockyards on Cockatoo Island then as a lift operator at GJ Coles department store in the city. He was sick a lot but Coles were good to him."

"Yes, they were a blessing. When John turned fifteen they offered him a job too, and the extra money saw us through."

"I'm still working at Coles," John added.

"When did Frank die?" Tor asked.

I grabbed a large chocolate-covered biscuit from a tray of goodies that Mary presented to us.

"About ten years ago. John had enough money saved for a down payment on this little place," Mary sat down again in her large overstuffed armchair, "and for the first time since I arrived on these shores we had some real security."

Both Tor and I wanted to ask the big question. I fidgeted and crossed my leg. My toe hit the edge of the tea tray with enough force to send the whole lot flying off the table and onto the cream-colored wool carpet. The strawberry jam gave it a nice pastiche effect and matched the color of my face. The ensuing laughter broke the drift of the conversation.

Richard Hill appeared at the front door and whisked the four of us out to Kingsford Smith Airport. Before Tor's plane departed we sat around a table drinking beer in a departure lounge full of sad, confused young soldiers being fareweled by their families and girlfriends; the boys were heading off for a tour of duty in Vietnam. This was their National Service – or Nasho as it was commonly known – and when the time came for them to leave there was much crying and emotion, which affected us all. We knew that not all of them would be coming back – and what is worse, so did they.

I had registered for the draft, a compulsory exercise in Australia and something that did not make me happy, given my antiwar feelings. Support for the war in Vietnam, never strong in the first place, was now almost non-existent in Australia, having seen so many of its sons killed in a war that for many had no point. Tor saw it as American imperialism and could not understand why Australia went along with it. I couldn't understand either.

I watched Tor's BOAC VC10 soar into the night sky and wished I could be going back to my homeland. I missed my family so badly; I could barely contain my emotions. Instead, I had to return to Mrs. Maher, Albert and the skin bin.

Leaving the Boer War suitcase at great aunt Mary's (wondering what memories of my grandfather it might evoke) I flew back to Griffith via Airlines of New South Wales on a Fokker Friendship aircraft.

The plane flew low over a patchwork quilt of canals interlacing hundreds of rice fields, vineyards and fruit orchards, then over some low, grassy, gum-treed hills where ahead lay two small wooden buildings that constituted Griffith Airport. The journey only took 80 minutes. I was "home".

I did not return to work on the Monday. I played truant, forgetting it was Mrs. Maher's cleaning day. A loud rapping on the bedroom door awoke me from my slumbers.

"Are you awake, John? I have some news on Newt," she declared loudly.

I was awake now. I pulled on my dressing gown and let her in. She flopped down on the end of my bed as I remained standing.

"I was speaking to the Minister again. He said that Newt came to him for a heart-to-heart… said he was sorry for all the problems he'd caused. The minister said he seemed conflicted because although his parents send him money, he can't go home again. Newt didn't say why, so the minister phoned his parents to get to the bottom of the story; they told him that Newt had to leave Belfast because of the troubles. Apparently, he got mixed up in the paramilitaries and killed someone."

I broke out in a sweat.

"Still, the minister said he left town so I think we've seen the last of him," she said.

"Don't be so sure. We saw him and Fred last week… together."

The color rapidly drained from Mrs. Maher's face. She covered the face with her hands.

"Are you OK?"

She muttered a few oaths then removed her hands and stood shakily. "I lent the German some money. He came round all apologetic and sweet-talking. I felt sorry that we'd given him such a hard time." She almost fell over.

I put my hand on her arm to support her. "How much did you lend him?

"Twenty dollars."

"Not a fortune then?" I responded. She narrowed her eyes to such an extent that, to all intents and purposes, they were closed. She departed without another word.

Lou came out of the shower. "And he was such a nice boy, too… until he had the impertinence to tap me up for twenty dollars!"

I would like to say that the saga ended in a dramatic confrontation, but reality is often very different from fiction. The fact is I never saw Newt or Fred again – but there is a slight twist in the tale:

One night I came home from work and did some laundry. While I was hanging out my clothes on the Hills Hoist, I noticed a brown grocery bag sitting upright in the long grass nearby. I did not remember seeing it there before so I went to retrieve it. Scrawled on the outside of the bag was one word – *SORRY*. Inside were the two silver-backed hairbrushes.

APPLES AIN'T APPLES

Above the earth, Apollo 13 developed a serious fault on its way to the moon so the astronauts nursed their crippled spacecraft home. On earth, Brazil defeated Italy to win the World Cup in Mexico. In Griffith, I was lying in bed one Sunday morning contemplating my navel, when I heard a loud rapping on the back door. Lou and I played dormant in the hope that someone else in the house would get up, but nobody did so we tried to wait each other out. This was a battle I was quite capable of winning. The rapping grew louder and more persistent. Thinking it was Mrs. Maher and she had lost her key, I crawled further under the sheets and pulled the pillow over my head but I could still hear Lou muttering expletives under his breath as he bumbled down the corridor. The door hinges squeaked then... "Holy Cow! What happened to you? Are you alright, mate?"

I ran through the kitchen and into the sitting room. Standing in the doorway was a skinny man, his head shaven; the upper half of his face, deeply tanned, and the lower half, sickly white from where a beard used to be.

"My God! Are you OK?" I exclaimed.

Those same blue-grey eyes that had stared down Newt now looked for an appropriate hole to crawl into.

"My number came up... I got drafted," Ivan announced.

Lou put a hand on his shoulder. "Jeez, man. I'm sorry to hear that. Can't you appeal that you're a conscientious objector or you've got flat feet or something?"

"Na. It's written in the stars, mate. I'm heading to Ingelburn to start basic training." Ivan ran the palm of his right hand over his almost-bald head. "I figured I'd save the barber some work! I've known for a while, but just didn't want to tell anyone."

I looked at this gentle soul, who even without the hair had an intangible aura. My heart went out to him.

"I suppose it might happen to any of us, but you're the first friend that it's happened to," I commented.

Ivan pulled a weathered baseball cap from his rucksack and planted it on his head, then walked away from Mrs. Maher's Guest House and on down the red dirt road for a date with destiny.

My own destiny was tied to the grape harvest. It came to an end, the work ran out and I found myself unemployed. I thanked Glenn McWilliams for hiring me sight unseen, but I think he had figured by then that I had no connection with his agent in England. He had got what he wanted out of me, but more than that I had got what I wanted out of him: some measure of self-sufficiency, a modicum of self-confidence and the knowledge that I needed to do something to secure a better job in the future. A career of any kind seemed light years away. And it was.

Lou's job at the seed factory came to an abrupt end when he was fired. His employers said it was because he could not lift heavy sacks, but I think it was because he took off too much time to visit his girlfriend in Sydney.

Lou and I were not unemployed for long, thanks to Cyril, our baker friend, who noticed us loitering around the house in the middle of the day.

"You blokes out of work?"

"Yes."

Cyril winked a couple of times, made a *cluck-cluck* sound

with his tongue, and beckoned us to follow. He did not tell us where we were going. We trailed him across town to a darkened room at the rear of a pub where a hubbub of conversation radiated from a group of men gathered around a snooker table. The crowd parted to let Cyril through, for in his hands he held the key to their being there: three large coins and a thin slab of wood.

"Place your bets gentlemen. It's Two-Up time!" The hubbub grew louder.

"I'm backing heads for ten dollars!" one man shouted. Another responded, "I'll see yuz for ten dollars!"

"Twenty dollars!"

"I'll see ya, mate!"

The wagering went on around the table for five minutes until all bets were laid. Cyril, the "tosser-in-chief", placed the three coins onto the piece of wood and tossed them into the air, where they spun until gravity took over and they came to rest on the green felt table top. Two of the coins displayed heads and one tails.

"Heads it is," shouted Cyril.

Half the group cheered, the other half jeered. Quickly, we got the idea of the game and joined in.

Our kitty of $9 rapidly swelled to $50, then to $100… before it reached a tipping point and started going south, a long way south. A lot of money flew around that circle; most of it flew out of out of our hands into somebody else's. I dug into my pockets and pulled out a grand total of $9.25. I voted we quit whilst still ahead. While contemplating a swift trip to the Gents to throw up, I observed a good-looking Italian man with long bushy sideburns enter the room, waving a thick wad of money in his hand.

"Ahhhh, Carlo, mio amico… we've been waiting for yuz," shouted Cyril.

Carlo flashed a smile and a quick one-finger salute.

"OK boys," he said, pushing his way through to the edge of the table, "Let's get adown to business. Let's get aserious here. I'll see asomebody afive hundred."

Five hundred. The man was serious.

In quick time Carlo doubled his money and kept on doubling his money. He was a born winner and he knew when to quit. He pulled a cash bag from his back pocket and stuffed it full of the winnings piled in front of him on the snooker table. But before he walked away with his thousands, and before I ran to the Gents to throw up, Cyril flagged him down.

"Hey Carlo. Me mates here are outta work. You got anything going?"

Carlo looked us up and down. He rubbed his thumb and forefinger down his jaw line, as though he was eyeing a couple of prime steers. "Yeah, I gotta orchard full of apples that needa picking. You wanna come picka for me?"

Carlo's farm, some three and a half miles from Griffith, consisted of a modern house with a Mercedes and a Land Rover in the garage and trucks, tractors and assorted machinery scattered around the squeaky-clean farmyard, all surrounded by orchards and vineyards that stretched as far as the eye could see. Sitting on a flatbed trailer, hauled by a John Deere tractor driven by Carlo, we headed deep into a vast maze-like orchard where he abandoned us with two ladders, two large canvas sacks and several wooden boxes. Hanging the sacks around our necks we climbed the ladders and picked Granny Smiths, dropping them carefully into the sack dangling in front of us. When it was full or too heavy we pulled a cord that opened the bottom end, and the apples tumbled out into the wooden boxes.

"You boys abe acareful eh... These are export apples. I donta want thema bruised, OK?"

"OK."

Just to ensure we did as we were told Carlo paired us up with two experienced pickers who were also Italo-Australians. They worked faster than us and never stopped chattering in Italian, but if we asked them a question they answered in broad Australian, without a trace of accent. "Non parliamo Italiano, mate? No worries... she'll be right." Seventy percent of

Griffith's population was of Italian descent and resentment percolated among some "white" Australians who felt that these "outsiders" tended to remain separate and speak only their own language. Carlo and his family were from the Calabria region of Italy, a mafia stronghold, and it was common knowledge that the Societa Honorata had a presence in Griffith. Most Italians had come to Griffith to throw off the shackles of poverty, and to create a better future for themselves away from intimidation, but I heard rumors of people having their homes burned down for failing to co-operate with these thugs.

At lunchtime Carlo took us back to the farmyard. The Italian workers went into the modern blond-brick house, leaving Lou and me confined to the tractor shed.

"Now I know how black cotton workers must have felt in the Deep South," Lou joked. I cannot say it was a form of discrimination, but then again, I cannot say it was not.

Carlo's mother, a widow dressed entirely in black, shuffled across the farmyard carrying two large steaming bowls, which she plopped down on the rear of a flatbed trailer. From the folds of her skirt she produced a bottle of Chianti that sparkled in the sunshine, as did her green eyes. She poured the clean bold Sangiovese red into two small pewter mugs and handed them to us. The wrinkles on her face came alive as she smiled a motherly smile and pointed to the bowls.

"Manja, manja… Bolognese."

It smelled deliciously tangy so we hoisted ourselves onto the back of the flatbed and with legs dangling, plates on laps, we sprinkled chunks of rough-grated parmesan over the sauce before devouring the steaming mass as if it were our last meal.

Soon we were back in the orchard, picking a variety of apples sold only for baby food. Evidently we were progressing too slowly because Carlo changed his payment method from a fixed daily rate to a contract of $4 for every box we filled. This new incentive motivated us to move faster and we crammed three boxes in quick time. Carlo seemed surprised – so surprised that he lowered our rate to $3.60, the bastard!

"My friend he says he only apay $3.60 a bin to his workers."

A likely story, but without any other gainful employment on the horizon, Lou and I stayed and picked all afternoon until Carlo appeared with his John Deere and we lay our weary bodies down on the trailer amid the boxes of apples. Despite the hum of the tractor, the potholed farm track, and the buzzing of gazillions of flies, we fell asleep bathed in the golden light of a sinking sun.

A murmur of conversation woke us. Peering over boxes, we saw the Italian workers, the brothers and their mother sitting in a circle in front of the farmhouse drinking mugs of a frothy brew. Carlo offered us a couple of beers for the road. We would have preferred the extra forty cents a box, but we accepted his generosity. Covered from head to foot in red mud, hands scratched raw, we headed home and fell into our beds fully clothed.

The whining of frustrated mosquitoes trying to find their way in through the fly screens and the sound of rain plopping through holes in the roof into tin buckets did not wake us. But all too soon the alarm clock did, signaling the itinerant workers back to the fields.

Driving out to some far-flung corner of Carlo's orchard, I looked skyward to see if I could spot the wedge-tailed eagle I had seen flying around the day before, a beautiful majestic bird with huge talons, the sort of bird poets write poems about. But unfortunately no poem would be written about this bird. Carlo pointed to it – nailed, spread-eagled, to the fence. Carlo had shot it because it took one of his chickens. He thrust out his chest, proud of his marksmanship, and then turned on the Land Rover's radio...

The Queen and Prince Phillip are to take part in the re-enactment of the landing of Captain Cook in Botany Bay today exactly two hundred years from when he first set foot on these shores.

Carlo switched off the radio and slammed his hand down on the dashboard. "Fuck the Queen. Fuck the bloody Queen."

"I don't think that would be the correct protocol," Lou joked, attempting to bring some levity to the situation.

I laughed. Carlo didn't.

"Why do we need a bloody pommie ruling over us?"

His vehemence surprised me. His contorted face scared me.

"Doesn't cost you anything does it?" I replied, remembering I was British.

"Ah. Fuck the Queen."

He jammed his foot hard on the accelerator and we sped away from the convoy.

Out in the orchard, the air felt much cooler. Winter was on its way and thousands upon thousands of apples begged to be picked. Lou and I threw ourselves into the work, but Carlo took the trailer away at lunch, leaving us without boxes to put the apples in. Hours dragged by and I sincerely hoped he had not abandoned us for the term of our natural lives. Maybe he had just twigged that I was a "bloody pommie."

While we ate our sandwiches I stared at the weed-strewn access to some of the rows of apple trees. The fruit already looked overripe and ready to fall.

"Those weeds need whacking. He'll have trouble hauling a trailer in there, won't he?" I said.

"They're not weeds and I don't think he intends to pick those apples."

I looked at Lou, not comprehending.

"Marijuana, mate."

"You're joking." I had never seen a marijuana plant. Somehow the swinging sixties had passed me by, but Lou had already figured that it was not apples that were making the family rich.

Carlo returned in a pickup truck. "That's it, maties. You're done."

Clearly there were thousands more apples to be harvested, but we did not argue. We had struggled to make $25 between us, barely enough to cover the rent and a round of drinks at the pub. Carlo invited us back for the following year's harvest, but I planned to be a long way from Carlo and his family by then. I heard a lot about them though – as did the rest of Australia.

In November 1975, Donald Mackay, a Griffith local councilor, received information about a multi-million-dollar marijuana plantation at nearby Coleambally. Distrustful of local police, he passed on his information to police in Sydney, for whom he had been a secret informant. They raided the plantation and arrested Carlo's cousins, who were tried and convicted in March 1977.

On the night of July 15, 1977, Donald Mackay disappeared. Bloodstains and three spent cartridges were found near his car outside the Griffith Hotel where he had been drinking. A $25,000 reward for information was offered, but none was forthcoming. His disappearance exposed the Griffith Mafia, earned the city the dubious title of Drug Capital of Australia, and resulted in the Woodward Royal Commission into drug trafficking. During the trial, a notebook was produced naming Mackay as an informant. The Commission stated: *It is probable that, inadvertently, Mackay's name may have been disclosed, and he became identified as the police informant whose information led to the raid.* His body was never found.

The scandal mushroomed, leading to high-ranking police officers and to the owners of the Nugan Hand Bank, money launderers with known ties to the CIA. Frank Nugan was found dead with a rifle beside him in January 1980. Ken Nugan was convicted and served a jail term.

A TURN FOR THE NURSE

Winter arrived and cold air siphoned onto my bed through a slatted window which was permanently rusted open. Beside the bed, a fireplace that Mrs. Maher had boarded up still admitted cold air through the cracks. To keep warm Lou and I huddled around the burners on the electric stove until Cyril lent us a two-bar heater with a long extension cord that we hooked up to an electrical outlet in the kitchen. Mrs. Maher appeared in our doorway one morning, the extension cord dangling in her right hand. Her bemused expression mirrored that of Alec Guinness in *Bridge on the River Kwai*, when he discovered the detonator cable to the explosives that would blow up his beloved bridge. In this case it was Mrs. Maher that blew up. As soon as she saw the heater, her considerable bulk became rigid, her curlers stood at attention; without turning around, she jerked on the cord and the plug flew out of the socket and slithered along the corridor like a snake on speed.

"I told you no appliances! I don't mind you using my power for a few minutes before you go to bed or before you get up but I don't want it on all night, understand."

What a cheapskate. In 1970, it would have only cost her about 70 cents a week if we had it on 24 hours a day. About the only thing we did not have to pay for was the toilet – and if she could have figured out a way to connect a meter to that, she would have. If a meter broke, she rushed over on the double to replace it, though the nozzle on the shower had been broken for months, two doors did not shut properly and there was a severe leak in the roof to which her indifference was laughable.

"I'll send Bert over to fix it," she'd say, but Bert never came.

Unwilling to feed any more of his hard-earned money into Mrs. Maher's meters, Paddy Cascarino decided to join Ashmore Burford in Sydney, but before he departed he struck a blow at the heart of Mrs. Maher's tightly controlled financial empire.

Getting fed up with the television picture disappearing every twenty minutes unless we fed the meter promptly, I voted we boycott the thing altogether.

Paddy rose abruptly from his armchair. "I've been thinking," he said before disappearing into the kitchen, to return a few seconds later with sticky tape. He tore off two strips then attached them either side of a twenty-cent piece, and lowered the coin carefully into the slot at the top of the box. When the time expired it did not drop so we were able to retrieve it, thus enabling us to reuse the same coin over and over. I laughed so hard that I cried. This was one in the eye for the old tightwad.

Paddy offered me his job at the frozen chicken plant. Guillotining live hens as they rolled along a conveyor belt was not part of his career plan. It wasn't part of mine, either, so I also started to make plans to leave. I laid out a map of Australia on the living room floor. Where to go next? I traced a route due south across southern New South Wales and Victoria to Melbourne, but I'd already been to that sprawling city as a port of call on the SS *Australis*. I kept my finger moving west along the Great Ocean Road towards Adelaide, a reasonably sized city where I might have a better chance of picking up work.

"Do you want to come to Adelaide with me?" I asked Lou.

"No, mate. I gotta get back to Uni in the spring. My Dad wants me to find another job first. He doesn't want me coming home penniless."

"But there is no work here!" Several futile visits to the Commonwealth Employment Agency had convinced me of that.

"I know, but try telling that to my father!"

Against the odds, Lou did find a job as an assistant wardsman at the Griffith Base Hospital. He soon realized why he had been the only applicant. A young motorcycle crash victim was admitted, barely clinging to life. The doctors desperately tried to save her but she had serious head injuries and died. When Lou returned home next night, his face resembled the Incredible Hulk with a bad case of food poisoning.

"What happened to you?" I asked.

"I assisted with the post mortem, that's what happened. We had to dissect her body."

I handed him a glass of Alka-Seltzer. He looked at the fizzy water but the sight of it made him gag, and he waved it away.

"How did you cut up the body? What did you use?" I was eager for the gory details.

"Just a regular bow saw with a sharp blade, the same type of saw you'd use in woodwork. The coroner directed the head wardsman and me, so we did his dirty work. We sawed off the top of the patient's skull, removed her brains, then used another type of saw called a gigli to slice her down the middle."

I wasn't feeling so "gigli" myself at this point. "I think I've heard enough."

"I haven't finished yet… After the coroner left, we had to clean up the mess. There were bits of bone and brain splattered all over the floor. I had to pick the stuff up and get rid of it. There was blood everywhere and…"

"OK. OK." I raised my hands in surrender.

Davy poked his head in the doorway. "You blokes want to go up the club for dinner? It's Chinese night!"

Lou grabbed a pillow and threw it at him.

Half Sri Lankan and half German, Lou was wholly Australian with more than his fair share of charm and good looks. Despite being the lowest form of life in Griffith, the hospital job raised Lou a rung or two on the social ladder, at least as far as the nurses were concerned. The house was suddenly filled with them. How they did not show up on Mrs. Maher's radar is still a mystery. The nurses cooked our breakfast, cooked our dinner, did our laundry, and best of all, invited us to parties.

There were even two nurses on our beds when we came home one night. A buxom lass named Sharlene, who had been chasing Lou since the day he set foot in the hospital, was on his bed. The girl on my bed was her friend, a sexy curvaceous brunette named Bindy Cant – only she *could*, but I was too young and naive to take advantage. I was smitten though, more for the fact she was willing than any rational feelings. I delayed my plans for moving – immediately.

The *Virgin Soldiers* was playing at the local cinema so I asked Bindy along on a date. It all went downhill from there. Taking our seats in the circle, I noted that the wooden sides of the theatre were opened up like giant shutters, allowing fresh air to circulate around the barn of a place. Halfway through the film a westerly wind blew in clouds of ochre-colored dust from the outback, partially obscuring the screen – an effective touch if *Lawrence of Arabia* had been showing but *Virgin Soldiers* took place in the jungles of Malaya. More annoying though was the sound created by hard candies called joojoo balls being rolled down the parquet aisles of the theatre by local adolescents. The noise reverberated like marbles rattling around inside a giant wooden drum.

However, it didn't put Bindy off completely and she invited me to a dance in a cellar club under the local supermarket. As no girl had invited me to cross the street since I arrived in Griffith, I eagerly accepted; things were looking up.

Bindy and I gyrated on the dance floor to a disco beat. Why I suddenly launched into my funky chicken routine again I'll never know. I should have left well enough alone. It had not impressed Nina on the boat, and it failed to impress Bindy in the cellar. I made a note to never attempt it again – ever – when Bindy stopped dancing completely, her eyes fixed on a tall heavyset Italian male staring at us from the doorway. Her jaw dropped and she mumbled, "I'll be back in a minute!"

"Hey …" I started to follow but Lou pulled me back.

"I wouldn't, mate."

"Why?"

"He's bigger than you."

He was right about that. The big man and Bindy stood arguing in the doorway. There was much gesticulating and angry sidelong glances aimed at me; at one point she had both hands on his chest, holding him back.

Sharlene whispered in my ear, "They've been engaged for six months."

I displayed some mock indignation. My pride was hurt but not that hurt. A lot more could have been hurt had I not excused myself to the Gents. When I returned Bindy and her fiancé were gone.

After Bindy left my life, another nurse, Raylene Weed, came into it. She invited me as her date to the annual Griffith Hospital Ball, a formal event attended by everybody who was anybody in Griffith. I was a nobody without a car and without a job, so Raylene must have been really desperate. Sharlene, a girl with unpredictable mood swings had already asked Lou; she had known him for just a few weeks but was already "in love" with him.

We had to rent tuxedos for the big occasion. I could ill afford the cost but what the hell, you only live once.

A fussy lady stood by the door of the hall and shouted, "All debutantes and escorts must gather over here." She poked and prodded us into some sort of line as other guests entered the hall. I was somewhat in the dark as to what was going on but Raylene, dressed all in white, and looking like something out of *Pride and Prejudice*, informed me that all the girls were debutantes and this was their coming out.

"Coming out of what?" I asked.

Raylene gave me a severe look. I could see she took it very seriously. Even in society England this tradition represented a leftover anachronism from a bygone age.

After a long time standing around in the cold, the fussy lady waved the first couple through the door. We followed, arm-in-arm up the middle of the hall on a red carpet to a dais where our names were announced and the girls were presented to the President of the Wade Shire Council.

I whispered to Raylene afterward, "So are you out now?"

She gave me another look and said nothing.

Everyone brought their own booze in large coolers known as eskies (short for Eskimos) but Lou and I, unaware of this tradition, had arrived empty-handed. Luckily the nurses liked Lou so were happy to share their beer and wine with us. The band struck up and we hit the dance floor. There were a lot of jigs and reels where partners changed and dosey-doed.

Our caller, a rather overweight gentleman in an ill-fitting tuxedo with a bulging velvet waistcoat called for a drum roll. "OK. Now's the moment youse've all been waitin' for, the highlight of the night, the piece of resistance, if you like… yes, it's…" He cupped one hand around his right ear.

The crowd, on their feet, bubbling with anticipation cried, *"The Gay Gordons!"* The word gay back then meant lighthearted and carefree but that's not exactly how I felt as Raylene and I faced each other. Raylene insisted she should be on my left, but I disagreed. Although I have consistently belabored my dancing skills, the *Gay Gordons* was a dance I actually knew. I grabbed her by the shoulders and positioned her to my right. She didn't like that, and pouted.

"Alright, most of youse know the steps, but for those that don't, I'm only gonna say them once and then you're on yer own! Let's have you facing in an anti-clockwise direction with ladies on the gentlemen's right, please."

I pretended not to gloat.

"Couples join hands … don't be shy now. We're going to be a little different this year and try the… progressive version."

Oh good. I liked this version. You got to change partners, and I had been ready to change my partner hours ago. The silence around the hall was palpable.

"What! You must be joking!" a large lady behind us shouted. "We only know the traditional version."

"Instead of the allemande hold, you use the varsovienne position," the caller informed her. "It's a bit more jolly and energetic than the Scots version!"

She was neither jolly nor energetic, and gave him a look designed to put him in his place.

"Now, this is how it goes, ladies and gents: You take inside hands. Jump towards each other, then jump away from each other, but still holding hands. Gentlemen, pull the lady in front of yers and let go, then swap places. Take inside hands. Jump towards each other. The gent spins the lady under the left arm with his left hand. He then takes hold of the lady in front of him in the Gay Gordons hold and you're ready to start the dance again. Got it? Of course you have. Let's have a trial run."

Raylene stood with her mouth hanging open. The band struck up something that sounded like Scotland the Brave and we were off and running.

"Just follow me," I announced with confidence.

The caller's yodel-like voice rang out: "Forward, 2, 3, 4…Turn back, 2, 3, 4…"

So far so good.

"Not bad. Not bad. Now let's see how lively we are tonight. We'll do a pas de basque… now, spring towards, spring away, pull the lady across. Jump towards; swing the lady under your arm. Start again with a new partner."

For once I seemed to be getting it right while many about me were getting it wrong. This was a new experience. Eventually I got around the hall to Raylene again. She looked like she had crawled through a hedge backwards. Her hair was a mess and her dress askew; her body, decidedly lopsided, which could be due to the fact that one of her high-heeled shoes was missing.

She glanced sheepishly at me. "I'm sorry. I am not very

good at this."

I raised a hand. "You don't need to apologize to me. Look, this is about the only organized dance I know; we used to do it at local farmers' dances back in Sussex."

Raylene inclined her head to one side to ease a crick in her neck, which caused her already severely tilted tiara to fall off. I caught it before it hit the ground and handed it to her. The lower lip came out again. She had had enough.

"Do you want to split?" She nodded toward Sharlene who lay sprawled on a chaise nursing a sore shin, looking like she had been through the same hedge.

I walked Raylene home in the wee hours. It was a long walk – a couple of miles in fact. The awkward kiss goodbye on the doorstep told me that this was another first-and-last date. Can't say I blame her. I would not have gone out with me either, if I'd had a choice.

Lou would have liked Sharlene to have been a first-and-last date too; he had done nothing to encourage or lead her on. When I got back to the house they were arguing in the living room.

"Look, I told you I didn't want a serious relationship. I told you about Pamela back in Sydney who I *am* serious about. Why don't you get it?"

At the mention of Pamela's name, Sharlene's face turned pink, her lips began to quiver and her eyes flooded with tears.

"I knew you didn't love me, I just knew it but..." sob... sob... sob...

Lou put a consoling arm around her shoulder, but she brushed it away.

"... I hate you!" She stormed out of the house.

But like a well-thrown boomerang Sharlene was back the next morning.

The sound of sizzling bacon awoke me. Through the kitchen door I saw her breaking an egg into the frying pan.

She smiled sweetly as though nothing had happened. "Breakfast in bed?

"Um... that sounds good."

I woke Lou and informed him that she was back. He just rolled his eyes. I hopped back into my bed and heard Crusty's familiar alarm...*Oo oo oo aa aa aa ee ee ee*. I knew Cyril did not work on Sundays so I ran to the kitchen and beckoned Sharlene into the bedroom. She didn't need much encouragement. Lou stashed her in the wardrobe while I took over the bacon-frying duties and nonchalantly whistled *Zippity doo dah...*

"You've got a woman in here. I can smell a woman." Mrs. Maher's prominently veined feet were tapping the linoleum at a rapid rate.

"No. No. It's just Lou's new aftershave..." I said as she whizzed past me into the bedroom.

Waiting for the sound of fury, I only heard the sound of silence. I poked my head around the corner. Lou stood in the shower doorway stark naked.

"Excuse me, Mrs. Maher. Is there no privacy?"

I did not think the iron lady capable of blushing, but she did.

Sharlene was incapable of blushing and proved next to impossible for Lou to shake off. Lou and I were feeling a bit worse for wear that afternoon, lounging around in deck chairs soaking up some winter sunshine in the scrubby front yard when a car pulled up at the front gate. The driver's side window slid open and Sharlene's head poked through.

"Hey! You blokes want to come to Hillston with us?"

The Queen hadn't asked us for tea that day so we went along for the ride. I sat in the back with a nurse named Kay who looked considerably older than the rest of us.

The fading sun made the red dirt redder as we drove through a region first explored by John Oxley in 1817, who wrote in his journal: *Country uninhabitable and useless for all purposes of civilised man!* That uninhabitable country was now fertile farmland dotted with small townships like Tibidda, Goolgowi and Merriwagga, all dominated by huge aluminum wheat silos that had been emptied by an inconvenient plague of mice.

Hillston, about sixty miles from Griffith, was a dusty place consisting of one main street with a milk bar, a petrol station, a pub, and not much else.

We pushed through the swinging doors of the pub. Heads turned – some with black eyes, others with busted noses – all were male and looked like rejects from the movie *Deliverance*. Most were dressed in blue singlets, khaki shorts and desert boots while Lou and I were in a semi-hippie stage, sporting longish hair, bell-bottoms and flowered shirts. Apparently the natives had seen nothing like us before.

"Who's the Sheila in this lot?"

"Forget your purse, darl?"

"No Sheilah's allowed in this pub…"

We were not sure if they objected to Lou and me or the fact that Sharlene and Kay were women and women were frowned upon in pubs, or if they just didn't like the general appearance of any of us, but instantly we decided that discretion was the better part of valor. We did not hang about to debate the merits of flower power or the new era of feminism sweeping the world, but rather made a swift but dignified exit. Some of the good ol' boys followed, heckling and jeering us as we walked toward the car. We casually walked faster, but so did they… then we started running – not so casually, dived into the mini and locked the doors. Sharlene fumbled with the ignition key, which fell to the floor; her shaking hand retrieved it while other hands shook the car from side to side.

I thought, *I've had a good life really – such a shame it's all going to end here.*

Sharlene's hand shook so much she could not get the key in the ignition. A yokel squashed his nose against the windscreen and made pig noises. Lou grabbed the key, inserted it in the ignition and turned it. The engine cranked into life. Sharlene jammed her foot to the floor and the little car accelerated away, sending the good ol' boys diving for cover. The boys were drunk, of course, but it didn't help knowing they might be regular people when sober.

Rankin Springs made Hillston look positively up-market. Without explanation Sharlene pulled up in front of its police station and Kay went inside. I assumed she wanted to report the incident in Hillston. I assumed wrong, as usual.

"Kay grew up on a sheep station 'round here. She knows the head cop," Sharlene explained.

Well, that was good news, to have a cop on our side for a change.

"They've bin having a long-term affair, but he's a pervert. I've bin trying to get her to break up with him, so Kay's decided now's the time to give him an ultimatum: it's her or the wife!"

Lou and I sat there like stunned wombats until Sharlene suggested we adjourn to the milk bar across the street. The milk bar felt eerily quiet so Lou coughed loudly a few times.

A woman's voice called gruffly from the back, "What do you want?"

"A Coke please," I responded.

"It's in the bloody freezer," she snapped.

I strode over and pulled the bottle out of the freezer, but still no sign of the woman.

"Do you want me to pay for it or is it on the house?" I yelled.

The woman shot into the room like a world class sprinter leaving the blocks, her hand out to receive the money. She gave me a look that would melt steel. I was not in the mood so I tossed some coins onto the counter and walked away.

"Bastard!" she screamed after me.

What a great day this was turning out to be!

As we left the milk bar, Kay was leaving the police station, her face white, her body vibrating so much she resembled someone permanently attached to a jack-hammer.

"Let's g…g…get out of here," she stuttered.

I could not agree more but a large person emerged from the corner of the police station and blocked our path.

"Who are these galahs?" he said, looking us up and down. Paunchy, greying at the temples and wearing civilian clothes, the policeman looked old enough to be her father.

"Oh. Just a couple of hitchhikers," Kay responded.

"They're trouble, that's what." The milk bar maven shot across the street while pointing at me with a long gnarled finger. "This one tried to leave without paying."

"That's not true and you know it."

The paunchy policeman glared at Lou and me. "Hitch-hiking's illegal, you know? I can't abide hitchhikers and if I were on duty, I would throw youse both in jail and fix youse."

Lou, who had remained silent to this point, rose to his full height of six-foot-two, and said, "We know where your missus lives."

The policeman took a step back. Lou walked by him and calmly opened the door of the mini. He took the keys from Sharlene and nodded for the two girls to hop in the back. I dived in the other side but not quite so calmly. Before the door closed, Lou jammed his foot on the accelerator and the mini roared away from Rankin Springs.

On the way home I realized that the whole thing had been a setup from the start. We had been mere pawns in their game. Kay had needed some heavy artillery, some backup while she dealt with her ex-lover, the creepy cop.

The road trip to Hillston marked the end of the road for Lou and Sharlene, at least as far as Lou was concerned.

A classy nurse named Thelma asked Lou out on a date. When she arrived at the house to pick him up, he had just wandered up the street to get a bottle of wine for later. While we waited for his return, Sharlene marched up the garden path. I shuffled Thelma into the kitchen before I let Sharlene in. I am a bad actor so she figured something was up, and tried to push past me.

"I'm sorry, but Davy's using the shower back there and Lou's not here," I told her.

"I need to talk to him... NOW!" Sharlene stared hard, hands on hips, waiting for my response. She looked dangerous, a bit like the bipolar Evelyn Draper in *Play Misty for Me* who becomes obsessed with Clint Eastwood's character then stalks and attacks him with a butcher knife after he tells her to get lost.

"Um...You do. Well Lou…" My eyes flashed left and right, avoiding contact with her blazing coals. At a loss for words, not sure what to say I blurted out, "He… he had to go to Sydney unexpectedly." Immediately I realized he would be back at any moment.

He was back at any moment. He came whistling around the corner carrying two wine bottles. Sharlene looked at me and took a swing, slapping my face… hard! Storming down the garden path she turned on Lou and slapped his face too. As we stood there swaying, reeling and seeing more stars than usual for that time of night, Thelma roared out of the house mumbling about having "never been so humiliated in all her life." She did not stop to sympathize.

A MOUSE TOO FAR

When the word got around the nursing community that Lou and I were just another pair of good-for-nothing, fly-by-night fruit pickers who could not be trusted, the heady days of nurses invading our house came to an end… to be replaced by something far more sinister!

The ravening hordes that devoured the wheat silos around Hillston were now descending upon Griffith in their millions. The rodents invaded our refrigerator, took over our pantry, and chewed the wallpaper off the wall; anything remotely edible was history. Lou strategically placed a bucket of water at the end of the kitchen counter with some cheese teetering on the edge. Watching TV in the next room, we could hear the plop-plop sound of mice falling into a bucket of water. By morning the pail was full of drowned mice.

It became too much to take when the rodents invaded the warmth of our beds. I awoke with one scampering across my face. Enough was enough, emergency measures were required. At the local hardware store we bought all the traps they had left; demand was rapidly outstripping supply. We surrounded the perimeter of our beds with traps, placing them end-to-end until no crack was left for a mouse to squeeze through. Lou and I stepped over the mice Maginot Line and deployed to our beds, lying on our backs, wide-awake in anticipation of what was to come. We did not have to wait long. As soon as the lights went out, there was a loud CLICK, then another CLICK, then another… and another. Our strategy worked. It worked too well. The sound of those damn traps snapping shut kept us awake half the night. The mice experience ended as soon as it began. The little buggers overpopulated and simply ran out of resources, perhaps a lesson that humankind should heed.

Following on the heels of the mice plague was an invasion of locusts, but I was one step ahead of them… I left town.

Lou went first. Receiving a letter from his "true love" Pamela back in Sydney he decided on the spur of the moment to return to her. I did not blame him. We were just treading water in Griffith, but I envied him returning to his family and girlfriend – oh how I envied him! I was going to miss him.

Lou's absence left a big vacuum to fill. Mrs. Maher moved in a new roommate. John Christiansen, hailed from Western Queensland, where areas that once had good grazing were now barren wastelands; just ten inches of rain had fallen since 1956. Thousands of sheep and cattle had perished, farm owners laid off men by the hundreds, and whole townships just packed up and moved away. In desperation at not being able to sell his farm, John Christiansen left his wife and children up in Queensland and walked off the land, drifting into Griffith to find any kind of employment.

All my friends had departed Griffith. I felt empty and nagged by self-doubts. What was I going to do with myself now? I became extremely depressed from fear of the unknown ahead and my dwindling funds. I could have written home to my parents to ask for money but stubborn pride prevented me from doing so. I started selling what little I had left of value. I stayed up half the night reading a faded copy of *David Copperfield* and slept every day till noon, frittering away the afternoons waiting for the mailman to come with any news from home. It soon became obvious that I was only wasting time. I had dithered about as long as I possibly could.

My stay in Griffith had been a memorable one. I turned

nineteen in Griffith, lost my trusting nature in Griffith, gained a measure of self-sufficiency in Griffith, but in the end it was all of questionable value. In England I'd had it cushy, my mother and father were always there for me and I never had to work too hard. We had a nice home and lifestyle but it was my parents' home and their lifestyle, not mine. I had always defined myself by their achievements, their successes. They gave me status in the world, but here in Australia, my background and past life counted for naught. I had to become a person in my own right. It was tough. I was starting from the bottom – rock bottom – and the immediate future would hold many unexpected twists and turns.

Davy and Cyril, my remaining friends at Mrs. Maher's, treated me to dinner at the Ex-Servicemen's Club the night before my departure, as the club had long ceased to renew my monthly "guest" pass. I borrowed twenty dollars from Davy to leave. I had about forty dollars of my own, roughly the equivalent of thirty English pounds – the Bingo money from the *SS Australis*. No wonder I was worried.

On Wednesday, September 20, 1970 I locked up my room and said goodbye to Davy and Cyril, and with Crusty's laughter ringing out from his lofty perch in that pomegranate tree, I crossed the street to farewell Mrs. Maher.

She stood in the doorway with a smirk on her face. She moved her right hand from behind her back and dangling from her stubby fingers was a long piece of sticky tape with a 20-cent piece on the end. Indeed, it was time to be away. I shook hands with Bert and Gil, swung my rucksack onto my back and trudged off down the red dirt road.

I could almost hear Mrs. Maher say "He was such a nice boy too… until he tried to beat the meter."

THE ROAD TO NOWHERE

Alone on the Sturt Highway just outside Darlington Point, a small isolated town on the banks of the Murrumbidgee River, I observed plenty of sheep and cattle, but not much in the way of human life for company. I tried to thumb a lift, but the few cars sped past me on the narrow asphalt strip that bisected the undulating grazing land that stretched from horizon to horizon.

A catchy song of that year rang over and over in my head:

A thumb goes up, a car goes by
It's nearly 1 a.m. and here am I
Hitchin' a ride, hitchin' a ride
Gotta get me home by the morning light…
Ride, ride, ride, hitchin' a ride…

The upbeat tune by *Vanity Fare* seemed incompatible with my reality. I trudged about seven miles with one of my leather boots pinching my right little toe; by the time a blue Holden hauling a camper came into view I was hobbling and fatigued. I raised my thumb high and waved it like a man possessed.

The driver pulled over and put his head through the window. "You won't get a lift like that! You must be a pommie." When I nodded, he opened the back door. "Hop in."

I scrambled in with my rucksack and sat next to the driver's five-year-old daughter. His pretty blonde wife dressed in jeans, and a tee shirt, sat with him up front.

"The thumb up in Oz is the same as the two-finger-salute in pommie land: means fuck off," the driver explained over his shoulder.

His wife dug him in the ribs.

"Oops. Sorry dear."

The family drove me the sixty-five miles to Hay, a town midway between Sydney and Adelaide, established originally as a river crossing for flocks of merino sheep. They deposited me at a road-house where several big rigs were parked. My inhibition had long been vanquished by desperation, so I entered and went from table to table: "Is anyone going to Adelaide? I need a ride."

Most of the tough-looking hombres scattered around the cafeteria ignored me.

"Yes. I'm heading that way," responded a fair-haired man in his thirties who startled me with a posh-sounding English voice. He beckoned with his knife toward a chair opposite. "The name's David Lloyd. Take a seat. I won't be a minute."

I watched him chow down on his lunch of chips and gammon garnished with a slice of pineapple. My stomach rumbled and my taste buds salivated but I sat waiting patiently for him to finish. The word IPEC was emblazoned on the pocket of his blue short-sleeved shirt and prominently displayed on the side of his big rig. For the next 570 miles, I would be traveling with David, courtesy of the Interstate Parcel Express Company, a leader in the Australian haulage industry. Leaving behind Hay and its grand Victorian buildings – a reminder of its wool boom years – the big yellow truck headed out onto the Hay Plains, some of the most bleak, uninhabited country I had ever seen and one of the flattest areas on earth; for mile after mile the scenery remained changeless and desolate.

Freckled and black ducks ventured into view from the Murrumbidgee, out of sight to our north. The river bisects the plains westward from Hay to Balranald for almost 170 miles and irrigation canals poach so much water that rice is grown in parts of this semi-desert. Mobs of wild emus kept pace with the big rig, while flocks of parrots with beautiful pink and grey plumage known as *Galahs*, flew ahead and did not deviate left or right. Thousands are killed each year by motor vehicles, so the word *Galah* is synonymous with someone who is none too bright!

I did not feel so bright myself. My own desperate thoughts mirrored the words of Charles Sturt, who traveled through the region from 1828 to 1831, tracing the course of the Murrumbidgee to its junction with the Murray: *The dreariness of the view … the plains are open to the horizon, but here and there a stunted gum tree or a gloomy cypress seems placed by nature as mourners over the surrounding desolation.*

Sturt's account of his boat trip down the Murray and back to his base camp at Pondebadgery is a compelling example of the ever-present dangers for early explorers: the possibility of accidents, the likelihood of running out of food, and the constant threat of attack by Aborigines making their first contact with Europeans.

Leaving the Hay Plains and its emus behind, Mungo Jerry's *In the Summertime* blasted out on the truck radio. By quirk of fate David just happened to be driving near the lunar landscape known as Lake Mungo, a prehistoric dry lakebed bounded on one side by a fifteen-mile line of ancient, crescent-shaped white sand dunes known as the Walls of China. This mysterious landform, sliced by the wind into hills and gullies, contained the bones and relics of native people who lived around the lake for tens of thousands of years.

"Lake Mungo is one of Australia's richest aboriginal artifact sites," David told me. "Just last year the place was swarming with archaeologists. They discovered some human remains said to be 27,000 years old. They called her Mungo Woman."

"How they could tell it was a woman?" I asked.

"Probably from the width of the pelvis or something. I don't suppose a penis would still be intact after 27,000 years, but I could be wrong!"

Following a standoff between Aborigines and scientists over the length of time the bones of Mungo Woman and Mungo Man were kept in Canberra, the remains of Mungo Woman were returned to the local Aboriginal community in 1992, while study of Mungo Man continues. (As for Mungo Jerry… whatever happened to him, anyway?)

We came to the little town of Piangil, population 196, two dozen miles northwest of the wine town of Swan Hill. Another IPEC big rig awaited us by the waters of the wide brown River Murray. The driver had a BBQ underway, groaning with sausages, T-bone steaks and lamb chops, which he generously shared with David and me. It had been many weeks since I had eaten so well. Those last days in Griffith I had survived on mini-packs of cheese puffs called Twisties and pomegranates from Crusty's tree in the front yard of the house on Yambil Street.

The truck passed through the Swan Hill wine country, crossed the Murray at Murraybridge, and entered the South Australia hills as the day was dying. The hills above Adelaide rewarded us with a spectacular view of the city lights.

David, a decent fellow, put me in the way of accommodation at a guesthouse in the suburb of Glen Osmonde, close to the IPEC depot. Marburg Lodge was owned by Mrs. Schick, a German lady; it was clean and orderly – and definitely up-market from Mrs. Maher's. I had a good night's rest in a comfortable feather bed, and checked out early the next morning.

I hit the streets, rucksack on back, and trudged around the city all day pursuing job leads. I decided in no time that I did not like Adelaide – not because of the city itself, for it appeared a bright sunny place with spacious parks and substantial buildings – but in my state of mind, I felt the whole world had conspired to put me in the predicament of having neither job nor money. It was my own fault, of course, but when you are down so far, it's easy to blame others for one's misfortunes.

Even the birds were against me. Wandering through one of

the many parks, I felt a rush of wind around my head, then another rush of wind a lot closer, then something actually pulling at my hair. Several birds that looked like magpies were circling above me. One swooped in attack mode. I darted toward a cafeteria but failed to make it before the magpie raked its claws across my scalp, and I staggered in clutching my head.

The doughnut-munching girl behind the counter was laughing so much that masticated gunk flew out of her mouth and across the counter.

"They're good for business, them birds," she said. "You're about the third person come running in 'ere this morning."

I massaged my head with my fingertips. "Are you breeding them for the specific purpose of drumming up customers?"

"That's not a bad idea, but they don't need any help from us."

She informed me that for most of the year this Australian version of the magpie, called a Currajong, is not aggressive but defends its territory vigorously for four to six weeks during the nesting season. People walking past are seen as invaders, prompting the magpies to fly low and fast, clacking their bills as they pass overhead.

Just my luck to pick these four to six weeks to come wandering by.

She handed me a flyer put out by the National Parks and Wildlife Service explaining what to do to if attacked by one of these pesky birds:

- *Magpies are less likely to swoop if you look at them. Try to keep an eye on the magpie, at the same time walking carefully away. Draw or sew a pair of eyes onto the back of a hat, and wear it when walking through the area. Try wearing your sunglasses on the back of your head.*

- *Wear a bicycle or skateboard helmet. Any sort of hat, even a hat made from an ice cream container or cardboard box, will help protect you.*

- *Carry an open umbrella, or a stick or small branch above your head, but do not swing it at the magpie, as this will only provoke it to attack.*

- *If you are riding a bicycle when the magpie swoops get off the bicycle and wheel it quickly through the area. Your bicycle helmet will protect your head.*
- *Attach a tall red safety flag to your bicycle or hold a stick or branch as a deterrent.*

If only I had known, I would have worn my sunglasses over a pair of eyes sewn onto the back of a hat (made from an ice cream container) and carried an umbrella while riding a bicycle backwards, all the while looking the magpie straight in the eye and shaking a big stick – simple, really!

Another lonely night at the Marburg Lodge convinced me I did not want to be in Adelaide, and another fruitless day of job hunting while growing ever more depressed sealed the deal. An inner voice bade me return to Sydney. I trudged to the Marburg Lodge at the end of the day and found some IPEC drivers relaxing in the lounge.

"Is anyone going to Sydney?" I inquired. "I need a lift."

None of them were but one driver slowly lowered his Lebanese newspaper and looked me up and down.

"No Sydney. I go Brisbane?"

I thought about it for a few minutes. My mother had a cousin in Brisbane whom she had wanted me to visit. Brisbane it was.

Heading back along the same route I had traversed two days before, I slept fitfully. When I awoke, the awesome sight of the sun rising over the Hay plains filled the windscreen. Soon we were back in Hay again – where driver Wally, who spoke little English, branched off onto the Newell Highway. Clouds of locusts blotted out the sky and smashed wholesale onto our windscreen, forcing him to pull over in a small town to clean off the mess with a squeegee. We remained there for a while so he could get some sleep.

I soon realized that the town was Rankin Springs. I huddled in the corner of the cab, cold, lonely and uncomfortable, keeping a lookout for the local policeman who'd once told Lou and me he would "fix" us. He did not like hitchhikers and here I was hitchhiking through his town. I poked Wally in the ribs; he started the engine and steered the big rig north away from Rankin Springs, while I breathed a sigh of relief.

In limbo with no job, no money and nobody to converse with, I sat quietly with my dark thoughts while the truck rolled across the center of New South Wales through small towns such as Forbes, Parkes, and Dubbo toward a cousin whom I had never met and who was unaware I was coming. My parents did not know my whereabouts; I could have been on the moon.

Near the Warrumbungles, a twisted mountain range that looked like the moon and poked out of a billiard table plain, Wally took a shortcut on a wide dirt road through a vast eucalyptus forest. Our load of toilet seats rattled in time with the bumps in the road while the forest closed in oppressively and so did the night.

There is a general rule in the outback that you avoid driving after sunset because of the danger of hitting kangaroos, but Wally did not follow this rule. Kangaroos kept popping out of the trees and crossing the road in front of us... hundreds of them. The truck smashed into one and its blood spattered up onto the windscreen. Wally squirted the windscreen washer a few times and kept going. In the cotton town of Moree, he pulled over and had another sleep while I wandered about the town, wasting precious dollars on a T-bone steak at a milk bar. It tasted good, but cardboard would have tasted good after two days without food.

When Wally headed out again along another isolated dirt track, I realized he was taking this alternate route through the bush to avoid the eight-hour sleep breaks required by law; he would pull over to catnap for an hour, but no more. The truck rattled north across the Queensland border, where skeletons of cattle lay by the roadside, and then crossed the Great Dividing Range via Cunningham Gap, which links the pastoral country to the west with the coastlands.

The Toilet Seat Express rumbled into the IPEC depot on

the outskirts of Brisbane. After 1400 miles behind the wheel, Wally looked a wreck, with a three-day growth and dark rings under his eyes. It had been kind of both Wally and David to take me because I discovered later that IPEC rules forbade their drivers from picking up hitchhikers.

Broke, homeless, and unhappy, I caught a bus to the inner-city suburb of Highgate Hill, named for the suburb of London where, coincidentally, the original owner of the Boer War suitcase, Samuel Holman, was laid to rest.

I approached a large two-story house. The bottom half – an open area that allowed cooler air to circulate in the hot Queensland summers; the top half – of timber construction with a wrap-around verandah. I climbed a flight of steps to the front door, knocked and waited. No response. I felt nervous but I knocked again, louder. Still no response.

I did not know what to do so I walked over to the house next door and rang the bell. The door opened to reveal two smiling little old ladies dressed in their Sunday best. To their credit, they did not flinch at the site of a smelly, long-haired Englishman on their doorstep, and also to their credit, invited me in and offered me the use of their shower – an offer I gratefully accepted.

Afterwards, the ladies informed me that the family still had not returned. "Would you like to stay for tea, dear?"

I was famished so they fed me and I fell asleep on their couch. Around eight that evening the ladies gently shook me awake and told me that their neighbors were home.

This time the door opened. An attractive slim redhead smiled when she saw me.

"It's John isn't it?"

"Well yes, but…"

"I'd have known you anywhere. You look so much like your mother. Come along inside and meet my son Ted; Rudi will be home later. I'm so glad you've come. We've just been to friends for dinner, but you must be starving."

"Well… um…."

"Of course you are. Come and sit down. I'll make you a

sandwich. Your mother wrote to me and said you were in Australia so we expected you to make an appearance one day. I love your Mum."

I strode into a large open plan living room with cathedral ceilings where an athletic-looking young man a few years older than me sat on a loosely covered couch strumming a guitar.

"Ted, this is your cousin John, from Sussex!"

He jumped up, smiling broadly. "Giddai, John. Mum said you might turn up one day. Welcome to Brisbane. I don't think we've ever had a cousin here before!"

"I'm glad to be here. Sorry I didn't give you any warning!"

Joy Cais, who looked much younger than her fifty years, ushered me toward a small bedroom where I dumped my rucksack.

"We've always got a bed made up ready for any of Ted's college mates who might want to spend the night. Come along; I'll make you some supper."

I had not the heart to tell her that I had eaten at the neighbors, so I tucked into a large ham sandwich and a tumbler of 4X beer. I filled them in on my journey to nowhere while Ted entertained us with a virtuoso performance on his 12-string.

Around midnight, Ted stretched and yawned. "Sorry, mate. Gotta get some shuteye. I've a chemistry lecture at 7:30. Some visiting pommie – sorry, English professor. I think he must be on Greenwich Mean Time, but I'll see you tomorrow arvo, take you out on my new bike, show you the sights, if you like?"

"Yeah, that sounds great."

"I'm afraid I have to be up and away early too, John," Joy said. "You don't have to go to bed. Make yourself at home. Get up when you like. There's bread, eggs and bacon, cornflakes for breakfast?"

"Thanks. I think I'll stay up for a bit. Could I watch the news on the telly?"

Joy smiled, almost sympathetically, "Oh, we don't have a television here, dear. Rudi won't hear of it."

"No TV!" For someone who had been weaned on the

BBC, I found her statement hard to comprehend. "Don't you feel out of touch with world events, the news, and sport?"

A man appeared at the front door. "Ah! We have a visitor!" He spoke with a distinct European accent.

"Yes Rudi. This is John, my cousin Diana's son. Do you remember her?"

Rudi was a man of robust build and ruddy complexion, an older version of his son with pugnacious jaw, high cheekbones, wide forehead, and neatly cut steel-grey hair going white at the temples. Instead of shaking hands he gave me a bear hug.

"Of course I remember. So that makes John second cousin to Ted. Come, you like a glass of vino? Of course, you would…"

He beckoned me to follow him to a room under the house where he flipped a switch that illuminated a wall lined with bottles. I had not seen this many bottles since McWilliams winery. He pulled out a dusty red and uncorked it.

"Sit, sit…" He pointed toward a faded leather armchair. He plopped down in another opposite me and poured two large tumblers and handed me one. Through the window behind him I noticed a yellow taxi parked in the driveway.

"There are many things better than TV, John." He raised his glass. "And wine is but one…" He pointed to another wall lined with books. "This is my office, my escape hole. Now John are you interested in science – of course you are…" He reached over to a shelf and pulled out Darwin's *Origin of Species*. "Have you read this?"

"No." I was embarrassed to say.

He tossed the tome onto my lap. "You read while here." Then he proceeded to discuss the concept of space in fifth dimensions. "You need to look at size," he said after we had polished off the bottle of Barossa red, "the first dimension contains the ultra-small, which are atoms; then the next dimension, the small, such as molecules and the earth; and then we get to third dimension, the large, which are the Universe and galaxies." The next two dimensions had something to do with infinity, and beyond my conception, but

I drank more of his wine and pretended I understood. Rudi fell asleep and I went in search of my room.

The following afternoon, I found Ted in the open area under the house. His brand-new Kawasaki 750cc was in pieces spread out on an old sheet.

"I couldn't resist pulling it apart," he told me.

"Is there something wrong with it?"

"No! I want to see how it works, how it all fits together!"

"Oh!"

"No worries. I'll have it back together in half an hour."

True to his word, Ted blasted off the Kawasaki from Highgate Hill toward downtown Brisbane. We arrived in one piece at the car park of a barn like pub. In the crowded beer garden Ted introduced me to his lovely blonde-haired girlfriend, Kirsty, and a large coterie of college friends with whom we drank a lot of ale. Surrounded by these bright intelligent creatures from the University of Queensland, I began to have a sneaking suspicion that I had been missing out on something.

Ted's friend, Mark, a good-looking business student from Southport, said, "Ted has three passions in life: Kirsty, rock climbing, and motorcycles – not necessarily in that order! He started climbing in 1962 and was a sort of protégé of a bloke called Albert Salmon, who pioneered the golden age of Australian climbing back in the 1930s."

I replied, "I'm sorry to say I know very little about my Brisbane family or climbing but I'm learning."

"Good on yer. Well, Ted has been sort of single-handedly responsible for introducing the sport to the rest of us – a new generation, if you like!"

When we got back to Highgate Hill I noticed photographs of Ted's climbing exploits heavily featured on the walls.

"Ted develops his own photos and has his own darkroom." Joy informed me.

I was not surprised!

I sat on the verandah pondering this unplanned but

fortuitous trip to Brisbane while observing a bold red sunset over a Brisbane skyline mercifully free of high-rise buildings. Joy, Rudi, and their gifted son Ted were just the ray of sunshine I needed at this time in my life. They were quite the most original family I had ever met.

My head was spinning from the beer when the same yellow taxi I had seen the previous night pulled into the driveway. From the driver's side emerged Rudi, dressed in white short-sleeved shirt, navy blue shorts and long white socks. He climbed the stairs toward me.

"You, surprised I drive taxi?"

"No, not at all, I just…"

He raised a hand and plopped down on the wicker couch next to me. "Don't worry. Everyone surprised, but that's the way it is. Listen, I tell you story." He scuttled into the kitchen and returned with a frosty bottle of Reisling and two glasses. "You see, I was engineering student in Prague before war. I did not finish my degree because Nazis invade and I escape to England. I join tank regiment in Peterborough."

Joy drifted in from the kitchen. "That's where he met me!"

"I didn't know that." My stomach felt queasy from too much beer so I pretended to sip the glass of wine.

"I'm not surprised. The family would have kept quiet about it. You see, I was married to someone else at the time. They thought it scandalous that a married woman should take up with a bohemian Czech!"

Was I the only one in my family who had not moved to Australia to flee a scandal?

Joy continued, "I married too young. It was a loveless marriage… then Rudi came along. He was fun. A great dancer. He charmed me with his continental joie de vivre."

I laughed, then said, "My mother once said that the main reason she married my father was because he was good at parties!"

"Ah, your mother – how I miss her!" Joy commented.

Rudi topped up my glass. "Come along, drink up. So after war we move back to Prague, but now the communists have me on list. They want me go to Moscow and work for Soviet government. Of course, that is out of question. Ted is just baby when we escape and return to England."

Joy wiped a tear from her eye. "But my mother and father did not like Rudi, my 'foreigner' husband; it was awkward being with them. And Rudi did not like the class system and the British climate, so we headed south to exile in Australia."

Rudi's eyes narrowed. "We should have gone to America." He gazed toward the darkening horizon, brooding over a perceived lost opportunity while I perceived a found opportunity to pour my glass of wine into a nearby potted plant.

"Maybe so, but Australia was easier for us to get into," said Joy. "Life was hard at first. It was largely an agricultural economy in the early 1950s and jobs were scarce especially for someone with Rudi's intellect, so we had to take what we could get. Rudi found employment on a cattle station in Western Queensland at a town called Cloncurry and I worked as a cook. I actually liked it there. Ted had the run of the property. The snakes, lizards and kangaroos were his friends. His love of the outdoors comes from that time in our lives."

Joy reminded me of the Deborah Kerr character married to Robert Mitchum in the Australian outback movie "The Sundowners." Rudi did not remind me of anyone; he was unique. At some point he must have given up on his own ambitions, to put all his efforts into his son.

"So John," Rudi turned his attention to me, "Do you have plans to go to university?"

I was taken aback. "Well, the English public school system rather dampened my enthusiasm for things academic."

"Buggery and buffoonery, aye?" Rudi said.

"That's about right."

"You should see about getting a degree, John. You need degree these days to get good career. Ted will get his PhD next year. You think about this. Think about one of the sciences. It is most important."

At age nineteen, the idea of spending four years cloistered

in a university, studying for a degree in who-knows-what was anathema to me; now I understand that I was just deluding myself and Rudi was right. I did realize that nine months of toil in Griffith had gotten me absolutely nowhere, so I vowed that my next job would not entail any form of hard labor.

The trim petite figure of Joy Cais cooking bacon and eggs in a modern kitchen in Brisbane seemed far removed from hard labor in the Riverina but although Joy, every inch the English lady, had done her time in the outback, she had never quite adapted to life in Australia. Over breakfast, after Ted and Rudi had departed and before she left for her own toils, Joy told me how much she yearned for the green fields of England and to see her sisters again.

"And your mother, of course. She was my favorite cousin. Oh, how I miss her. I'll always remember that she was so kind to us when we returned to England from Prague."

Joy and her wonderful family welcomed me into their midst, restored my confidence and enabled me to recharge my batteries in readiness for the next phase of my journey.

The evenings took on a pleasant rhythm. Ted finished his studies and we listened to what was called underground music in those days: Cream, Blind Faith and Lou Reed. They liked Jimi Hendrix, who had just died. I could not imagine my mother or father being able to relate to Jimi Hendrix on any level. Ted, with the ability to hear a chord and immediately play it, copied the riffs on his 12-string while we sang along to *All Along the Watchtower.*

I would chat with Joy about the family. Rudi would come home and engage me in marathon chess games or discuss books while I sampled more of his wine. One night he cooked a 12-course meal and between each course served a different bottle of vino. *Ah, this was the life!* Joy wanted me to stay in Brisbane. I was the only relative that had ever come to Australia. Rudi wanted me to stay because I made Joy happy. Ted wanted me to stay because he was about to marry Kirsty and move to America.

But something pulled me back to Sydney. The need to find

a job in a hurry was the most pressing reason, but there was something more than that, something indefinable, something almost spiritual, as if some guardian angel were guiding me. After three happy weeks in Brisbane I had to tell Joy I planned to head south. She understood but I did not tell her that I had to use all my remaining money to purchase a ticket on the overnight train to Sydney.

In the chill early hours I lay stretched out on a vinyl-clad seat in a maroon colored carriage shivering, fretting and trying to sleep. Around sunrise, when we were nearing Sydney, the solid *clickety-clack clickety-clack* sound of iron wheels above compacted gravel gave way to a more echoing sound of train wheels on a bridge. I lifted my head off the seat to see the train traversing a wide estuary. A sign flashed by: *Hawkesbury River.* The carriage was almost empty, save for a group of young people at the far end. They had been quiet for most of the journey but now I detected raised voices.

"You're what, Dan?"

A tall girl stood and gazed down at two individuals necking on the seat facing her. Dressed in T-shirt and bell bottomed jeans, she had a roundish face with blonde hair cut in a pageboy style. A blue backpack spilled its contents out into the aisle. "Dan, you're doing what?" She had an American accent.

Dan pulled away from the girl attached to him and rose to face the American girl.

"I said Colleen and me are getting a place together. You'll have to fend for yourself."

The American girl narrowed her eyes as she clenched and unclenched her fists. "Colleen, you never said anything about this before we left Surfers Paradise. What would your parents think?"

Colleen clung to Dan's arm. "Well, they aren't here, are they?" Colleen also had an American accent. She stood and I could see she was much shorter than the other girl; she pulled down on her rumpled mini-dress. "And they're not going to find out, are they?"

The taller girl stared out the window at some distant fishing boat on the river. Without turning round, she said, "Colleen, you and me planned this trip together for so long. It's our big adventure."

Dan fastened the buttons on his flannel shirt. "And I come along and spoil it all?"

"No Dan. I didn't mean it that way."

"Look," said Colleen,"I didn't tell you because I thought Ross would be coming too and the four of us could share a place…"

The tall American clenched her jaw and her fists. "You thought wrong, didn't you?"

"Why?"

"Because… look, I get it OK? Three's a crowd. You guys do what you want!"

She stuffed the spilling contents back into her backpack, swung it over her shoulder and walked down the carriage toward me. She shook her head slowly and rolled her eyes.

She had the most beautiful blue eyes.

THE MAGIC BUS

I arrived back in Sydney on October 17, 1970. Great aunt Mary came to the rescue and offered me shelter; I would have been on the streets otherwise. Fortuitously, a tax return check for $60 from my toils at McWilliams Wines had arrived ahead of me. I gave half of it to Mary before descending on the Commonwealth Employment Office.

Taking my place at the back of a long queue, I realized I had been under the false assumption that I was the only one in Sydney looking for work. A middle-aged counsellor, her blue-rinsed hair shaped like a beehive, sat in a booth and rang a bell to signal when the next-in-line should approach her desk.

After about half an hour, I reached the front of the queue. A plate on the desk revealed her name as Rose. I hovered in anticipation of the bell, but Rose lit a cigarette, stuck it in the corner of her mouth and commenced to file her nails. I gently placed my hand on the bell, which gave a sort of half-ring. Rose glared at me.

A short, one-eyed old man, his hair askew, grey stubble covering the lower half of his face, shuffled up and blew her a kiss.

"Ah, what's in a name? That which we call a rose by any other name would smell as sweet." His recitation had no effect on Rose so he rotated his head toward me and winked. "The name's Sid." He proffered a small hand clad in a fingerless mitten; his long, dirty fingernails dug into my palms. "If she's unmoved by the words of the Bard, she's a hard woman, that's for sure – but she sure is sexy!"

A wave of laughter erupted from the job-seekers around us but Rose's demeanor remained unchanged. She handed me a slip of paper. It directed me to report to the manager of a carwash in the ritzy suburb of Edgecliff. Situated on a busy road, cars lined up from dawn to dusk and my job description required that I dry the cars as they rolled out of the washer.

So much for the plan to avoid manual labor!

On a particularly hot and steamy day, cars idled bumper to bumper around the block. People seemed edgy; impatient drivers honked their horns. I towel dried one car after another in an endless blur, my sweat mixing with soap and grime. At lunch, I staggered over to Rushcutters Bay Park, inhaled my sandwiches, then fell asleep on a grassy bank overlooking the Cruising Yacht Club of Sydney. When I woke up, I realized that less than a year had passed since I sailed into the harbor aboard *SS Australis* and watched Edward Heath preparing *Morning Cloud* for the Sydney-to-Hobart yacht race, just offshore from where I now sat. It seemed a lifetime ago.

The start of my shift seemed a lifetime ago, too. Near the end of it, a white Mercedes emerged from the washer. I grabbed some dry towels from the bin and rubbed the beauty until she positively sparkled. I waved a towel in the air to attract the attention of the owner, a rather haughty-looking lady being fawned over by the manager. She waddled over to inspect the car and I noticed she bore a remarkable resemblance to Mrs. Maher.

"Excuse me, madam, but do you have a sister in Griffith who runs a guesthouse?"

She stuck her nose in the air and said nothing. Instead, she found a speck of dirt on the bumper that a normal person would have needed a powerful microscope to see. She stared sternly at the manager – who, in turn stared sternly at me. I wiped in the general vicinity of where she was pointing. Then she pointed to a speck on the windscreen so I took a bottle of Windex, sprayed it on and wiped but, she was not done yet. She managed to locate a pinprick of grease on the hubcap and pointed to it.

I handed her the rag, turned on a heel and strolled off into the sunset.

Back at the unemployment office, old Sid was ahead of me this time but he saw me coming through the door and saved a spot in line. He nodded toward Rose, who was applying a heavy layer of rouge to her pockmarked cheeks.

"You're just like me – can't get enough of the sexpot!" He sidled up to Rose's desk. "But I do love thee! And when I love thee not, chaos is come again."

Rose totally ignored him. Sid moved to ring her bell, but she beat him to it and shoved a slip of paper into his hand. As he passed the long line of unemployed, a wry smile lit up his face.

"I am not fooled by her cool exterior. She holds within her heart a secret desire for my body!" He rapidly rubbed his mittens together in front of his face and shuffled toward the door. "I will be back, my dearest one!"

Unmoved, Rose casually applied more rouge to her plastered cheeks. I stepped up to the desk. She looked me up and down, then vanished into another office for a few minutes, returning with a sheet of paper which she shoved toward me.

This time I found myself in the not-so-ritzy suburb of Redfern at the western end of the city, an area so ugly that the authorities screened it off when the royal train came through on the Queen's first visit to Australia. I expect the powers that be had decided to shield her from the poverty-stricken indigenous people who flocked to the suburb in search of factory work.

My new job was with an outfit called Auto Sprinkler Fitters or some such name, learning how to install automatic fire sprinkler systems into big buildings. Indeed, the Redfern warehouse was a big building that required two floors be retrofitted with hundreds of yards of pipe and thousands of sprinkler heads. The foreman, Ted, an always grumpy fellow in his late fifties, his Brylcreamed hair polished so buff you could see your face in it, did not like pommies – and especially did not like me. Ted expected me to make his tea twice a day. There was a pecking order; I was at the bottom, Ted was at the top. I can see that now, but I could not then. I was going through one of my rebellious stages and flatly refused.

"Who do you think you are… think you're too bloody good for this outfit….blah blah blah…"

I never did make the tea and my job ended much sooner than expected as it turned out.

While Ted scrutinized a set of blueprints I sat atop a tall ladder, screwing sprinkler heads into pipes in the ceiling

"Last one, Ted!" I shouted.

"Let's check her for leaks. Bruce, turn her on… slowly now…" Ted shouted.

Bruce, a dopey rail of man, turned the main valve. We heard a loud knocking, vibrating sound emanating from the wall, then the whoosh-and-gurgle of water flushing through empty pipes in the ceiling. All looked shipshape until, inexplicably, the strip lights went out – which left us in total darkness in a windowless warehouse in Redfern.

I felt in my pocket for the lighter that Ted had given me to light the portagas cooker to boil the water to make the tea that I never made. As I look at it now, it was all Ted's fault: He never should have given me that lighter. I flicked it on in front of my face and shoved it up toward the ceiling to see what was going on.

There was a loud noise, a swooshing sound of… well, it was the sound of hundreds of sprinkler heads going off simultaneously. Just as suddenly as they went off, the lights came back on to reveal a not-so-pretty sight. I was drenched. Bruce was drenched. Ted was drenched. What's worse, his blueprints were drenched as the water continued to fall like a thousand showers. I felt like I was in the engine room of the sinking Titanic.

Ted advanced toward me, his face as purple as a baboon's backside. The last words I remember were "Fucking pommie git" and then something about "not bloody good enough to make the tea."

Despite the fact I was busy trying to break the world record for the 100-meter dash at the time; I got the gist of it.

I went back to the unemployment office, alone and depressed. The fact that *she* was on duty did not help. And old Sid was not around to provide some light entertainment.

"Next!" Rose cried dutifully.

I approached the counter; she looked up and immediately slammed down a sign which read *Closed for Lunch*. A faint flicker, which I half-assumed to be a smile, crossed her lips. "Ah… parting is such sweet sorrow," she said.

I had not the heart to tell great aunt Mary that I had lost another job, so I didn't. I ate the breakfast she made me, left the house at the normal time and headed for downtown Sydney.

An old childhood friend, Donna Mills, had recently arrived from England and found a job as a waitress in the coffee shop at the up-market Wentworth Hotel. She had arranged an interview for me with the manager, so I entered the restaurant and made my way through the jumble of tables and chairs to where Donna stood behind the counter making coffee.

"Hello Donna," I said. No response. I tried again, but still no response. "Donna… hello…?" I repeated, a little louder this time.

She spun around. "Oh, John! I'm sorry, love; I was miles away." Lifting a flap in the counter, she shot through the gap and gave me a hug. "How are you then?" Sussex people always added then to the end of a question or statement. "You look great. You're so tanned and fit-looking. Australia seems to be agreeing with you then?"

"I'm fine, Donna. I'll be happier when I get a job."

Donna looked tense. Five-foot-nothing, blonde hair, blue

eyes, but her normal bubbliness was missing. "Fancy a cup of coffee then?" she asked.

"Yes, thanks."

She popped back behind the bar and poured a mug of fresh brew, then came around to my side of the counter and handed me the mug. "It's on the house, love." She hoisted herself onto a tall barstool. "That's better. I've been on my feet for hours!" She chewed on her lower lip. "You know, he's just asked me to marry him."

"Who has?"

"Wesley – that American marine colonel I've been going out with."

"He didn't waste much time, did he? You've only known him a couple of weeks," I said, hoisting myself onto the barstool next to her.

"Well, that's the problem – and he goes back to Saigon next week. He's much older than me, but I really like him. He's a real gentleman," she responded.

"Do you love him?" I asked.

"I'm not sure really. We need more time and he doesn't have it."

"I suppose if he's serious he'll come back. No sense rushing a big decision like that." I sounded like I was an expert on affairs of the heart, which I categorically was not.

"I know you're right. I don't want to make a mistake but…" Her words drifted off as did her attention.

"Hey! What about this interview?"

"John, I'm so sorry. The manager's sick and didn't come in today. Why don't you give me a ring tomorrow and we'll try and fix something up then?"

I tried to hide my feelings but they must have showed.

"Don't worry, love, you'll have no problems getting a job here."

She looked toward the front door where a large group of office workers in suits and ties were entering. She slid off the stool, lifted the flap in the counter and returned to her post.

"They can't keep people in the restaurant business, always

jobs opening up. You can come and bunk with Krishka and me for a while if you like."

"Thanks, I might take you up on that. I'm wearing out the welcome mat at great aunt Mary's."

I left the restaurant and wandered aimlessly through the crowded concrete canyons of downtown Sydney, the blue harbor a shining light in the distance. I felt in my pockets and pulled out the last $20 I had left in the world. A graffiti sign scribbled in chalk on an underpass at Circular Quay said *Jesus Saves*. I thought to myself, *Well, now is a good time to save me, mate.* Somebody else had amended it in a different colored chalk: *Jesus saves — at the Commonwealth Bank.* Somebody else had inserted an *h* before the a: *Jesus shaves — with Gillette razor blades.* It made me laugh.

I approached the Quay and was pleasantly surprised to see the *SS Australis* in port making ready to sail. A brass band played *Auld Langs Ayne* and hundreds of people threw streamers, cheered and waved their loved ones goodbye. The old girl weighed anchor and the colorful spectacle made me both sad and homesick. She pulled away from the dock; the streamers gently tore apart like dozens of fragile umbilical cords being cut between home, family and friends.

Reflective and motionless, leaning on the railings, I watched the tugs maneuver her out into the main shipping lane. When she had gone, the ferry wharves of Circular Quay were exposed, sticking out like stubby fingers into Sydney Cove. Gazing at the green-and-yellow painted wooden ferries buzzing in and out, the deckhands throwing their ropes and a myriad of passengers arriving and departing, that invisible guiding force, that silent traveling partner emerged and pushed me toward those ferry wharves.

"Excuse me," I said to a fiftyish but attractive female ticket seller with pink hair and light blue uniform. "How do I go about getting a job on one of these boats? Are there qualifications?"

"Not for deckhands or wharfhands, son. You learn on the job. You need to go and talk to the union over at the Rocks, just across the way." She pointed in the general direction of the office. "They should be able to help you."

I trotted across to George Street and up to the 2nd floor of a sandstone building where my last $20 was halved to $10 when I became a fully paid-up member of the Firemen and Deckhands Union.

They sent me back to interview with the tall, spare figure of the head wharfinger, Hughie Frawley, who asked me if I had any experience with boats.

"I used to sail with my Dad on the Sussex coast," I lied.

He tested me with a few nautical questions, to which I gave a few hapless answers.

He gnawed at what was left of the nail on his little finger and said, "Bullshit."

I thought I had literally "missed the boat after I had bought the ticket" until: "You can start on Monday morning at seven. Meet me at the office on number six wharf."

Eureka! I was in. That's the way things worked in Australia: Union first, job second.

Great aunt Mary could barely contain her delight that I had found another job; she knew I hated the sprinkler job. She did not smile a lot so I could tell she felt genuinely happy for me. I worried about her health and her worrying about me did not help.

That night I perused the *Property to Rent* ads in the *Sydney Morning Herald* and circled a small bedsit in the neighboring suburb of Bondi Junction that appeared to be within my soon-to-be-budget. I rang the number and made an appointment for the following day.

The following day began with an invigorating swim at Bondi Beach. Losing all track of time, I missed my bus connection to Bondi Junction. Missing that bus, not only changed the course of my journey, but the course of my life.

Furious with myself, I accosted the nearest bus conductor.

"Calm down, mate. There'll be another one along in a minute!" He directed me to a bus that took a slightly different route, via Curlewis Street rather than the quicker Bondi Road route.

I hopped aboard and as it chugged along Curlewis Street, I gazed vacantly out of the window on the right-hand side of the bus. If I had sat on the left and gazed vacantly out that side, the rest of my life would have followed a completely different script. Such are the details that lives hinge upon.

The bus had travelled no more than two hundred yards before I spotted a smart two-story Federation-style building surrounded by a lush tropical garden. A neon sign next to a wooden gate displayed the name *Nyah Lodge* and below that *Rooms to Rent*. Maybe it was that invisible guiding force again, who knows, but for some reason I jumped off the bus at the next stop, ran back and knocked on the door and waited until it opened.

A tall, shapely, athletic-looking girl, with long brown hair emerged. "Giddai. Can I help youse?" She had a nasally accent.

"I'm looking for a room to rent."

"Youse've come to the right place. Youse need to speak to Peter or his Ma, and they're out till tonoit."

"Should I come back then?"

"You can if youse like, but they mostly rent to girls."

A house full of girls. Now, here was a novelty; Mrs. Maher would turn in her grave – if she were dead.

"I'll come back later. Do you like it here?"

"It's beaut. Most of us are from the bush and we're a fun crowd, if I do say so meself. I'm sure youse'd like it." She gave me a smile that warmed my soul.

"I'm sure I would. What's your name?"

"Glynis. Glynis Graham."

That evening, a tall bearded man of about forty opened the same door. He introduced himself as Peter Hodgens.

"Sorry. We've no vacancies at the moment…"

I could not hide my disappointment, especially when I looked past him down the corridor and saw young women of my age bustling in and out of rooms, some only clad in skimpy swimwear. I slowly turned and walked away.

"… but I do have a small apartment in the building, which

a friend of mine rents. There's a spare bed in there. We can see if he doesn't mind sharing."

Peter Leder, in his late twenties was also tall and bearded, and a native of Switzerland. He and the landlord could have been twins. He stiffly shook hands. After I filled him in on my life thus far he said, "I think this arrangement could work. I travel frequently in my job so it would be reassuring to have someone around to look after the place. Plus..." he looked with a sly grin toward Peter Hodgens, "my rent will be less, yes?"

Peter Hodgens said not a word. Was this to be a male version of Mrs. Maher? Peter Leder and I shook hands again. I was in.

I moved into the small two-room flat on the ground floor of Nyah Lodge on the same day I started work with the Sydney Harbor Ferry Service. Life was sweet. One of two guys among thirty girls!

With the rural and industrial phase of my life in Australia well and truly over, the nautical phase was about to begin.

FERRY TALES

Ferry services have existed on Sydney Harbor since as early as 1789, the first steam service began in 1842, and as the population grew and spread to Manly and suburbs along the Parramatta and Lane Cove Rivers, the ferry service expanded to a fleet of seventy boats. The impact caused by the opening of the Sydney Harbor Bridge in 1932, combined with the rising popularity of the automobile resulted in a major downturn in the number of people using the ferries, so by 1951 just fifteen boats remained. In the mid-1960s they made a comeback with the introduction of new streamlined boats and hydrofoils, which were faster, more comfortable and carried more passengers than the old ferries. This, combined with an increase in tourism and the growing inadequacy of the bridge to handle large volumes of traffic, became a major factor in their renewed popularity. Rather than commuting to the city in a hot, smoggy traffic jam, one had the better option of commuting on the deck of a ferry enjoying the sunshine, salty air and magnificent scenery.

Hughie Frawley, the head wharfinger, didn't care about the magnificent scenery. A blustery sort of man, always in a state of agitation, all he cared about was that his beloved ferries departed and arrived on time. After some thirty years in the service, he should have known that things did not always run according to plan. They did not run according to plan on my first morning with Sydney Harbor Ferries because the P & O's big liner, the Canberra, had arrived in town, and access to the ferry wharves was blocked while the little tugboats maneuvered her across Circular Quay toward a berth at the Overseas Terminal. Hughie's fingernails were chewed to the quick, but he gnawed on the stubs as he paced the wharf, his carefully planned schedules thrown into disarray.

I hung around for half an hour, twiddling my thumbs and waiting for instruction. All of a sudden he noticed me. He looked at his watch and said, "I don't put up with unpunctuality."

"But I was here at five minutes to seven!"

He ignored my comment. *This was a good start!*

"I want you to go to number four wharf. Make yourself known to Willy Ackroyd. He'll be retiring next month so we want you to learn what he does."

Willy Ackroyd, burly, bald-headed and reminiscent of a bull terrier, taught me more about avoiding work than about how to actually do any. If Willy saw Hughie approaching, he would attempt to hide somewhere; if that proved impractical, he would pick up the nearest broom and pretend to be sweeping. Once the coast was clear, he'd discard the broom and return to his card game in the mess room at the foot of the wharf. Having me around made it an easier month than normal for Willy because I did all his work.

Willy's patch, wharf number four, was one of six wharves that thrust out into Sydney Cove between Bennelong Point (where the Opera House stands) and the old Rocks area, the so-called birthplace of Australia. Willy had clocked decades on the harbor, as had many of the older deckhands who had been around when the Sydney Harbor Bridge opened. Some of them were originally employed as stokers on steam-driven ferries, requiring them to shovel coal into furnaces that fired the boilers, an uncomfortable and backbreaking job.

My main duties were not so backbreaking. I tied up the ferries, shoved on the gangplanks, ensured the passengers embarked and disembarked safely, kept the wharf clean and tidy, threw drunks off ferries and threw drunks onto ferries. The first few weeks on the job proved more eventful than I could have imagined. Constant antagonism existed between Hughie and the younger wharfhands – and at age nineteen, I was *the* youngest wharfhand. Hughie watched me like a hawk, ready to pounce on any mistake. And true to form it did not take me long to make one.

A ferry pulled in. The deckhand secured the forward end of the boat and pulled on the forward gangplank. I secured the rear end and shoved on the rear gangplank – the logical procedure, I thought. Not so, Hughie.

"Here, what do you think you're playing at, boy?" he yelled.

"Who, me?" I looked up with some consternation at the tone of his voice.

"Yes, you. I told you to put on that rear plank before tying up astern." He wagged his finger at me. "Haven't you learnt a bloody thing yet?"

"Yes, but the deckhands told me to tie up first and…"

"Don't listen to those bloody mongrels!" he shouted.

"But what happens if the boat drifts out before I get a rope on?" I should have kept my mouth shut.

He poked me in the chest with his index finger. "You listen to me.... remember this…"

"Yes Hughie." I took a couple of steps backward.

"The rear gangplank first, rope second – and be quick about it."

Later that day, the *Kooleen*, a ferry that looked like a cross between a green and yellow mini-submarine and a giant pipe with windows, surged in. The deckhand secured forward and pulled on the front gangplank while I rolled on the aft gangplank. Before I had time to tie-up astern, a combination of wind and the wake from a much larger Manly Ferry pushed the stern end away from the pontoon. The gangplank dropped into the drink and sank in a cloud of bubbles.

Steam could be observed coming from Hughie's ears, but not a word did he utter. Resisting the urge to say, *Na na na naa naaa*, I watched him kick over a garbage can and storm off the wharf. It would not be long before he stormed back onto it again.

One quiet morning, I forgot to shut the gates that separated those passengers waiting to get on the ferries from those getting off. Willy Ackroyd, leaning on a broom, telling me his life story, did not help matters.

"See this," he said, pointing to an indentation in his forehead the size of a US quarter, "I got it during the war on the *Prince of Wales* in the North Atlantic."

"I thought you said you were Canadian?"

"I am but I were stupid enough to join the British Navy. They'd take anybody in them days. Biggest mistake I ever made. If yer knows yer history you'll remember that *HMS Prince of Wales* and the Hood engaged the Bismarck in '41 at the Battle of Denmark Strait. The *Hood* got hit in the magazine. Bloody ship blew to pieces. Only three survived. The *Wales* took three shells, but lived to fight another day. I was one of the unlucky ones and got hit. Don't remember much about it but the doctors operated on me head and removed a two-inch piece of shrapnel. Lucky I had a hard head." He rapped his forehead with his knuckles. "When they took out the bone fragments from me brain, they had a hole to fill so they inserted a metal plate. It's still there." He pulled a spoon from his trouser pocket and placed it on his forehead where it stuck.

"Try and pull it off…"

I grabbed the end of the spoon.

"WAIT FOR ME!" a voice bellowed from the top of the wharf, "WAIT FOR ME!"

A well-dressed gentleman in a three-piece pinstriped suit and shiny black shoes was scrambling through the turnstiles. He came panting down the ramp, through the open gates, waving a rolled-up umbrella.

"Hold that ferry. I have an urgent meeting, must get to Kirribilli…wait…"

Moving fast, he reached the edge of the wharf where a ferry bobbed a few feet away. Without breaking stride he jumped. I covered my eyes with my hands. I heard a splash, followed by some curse words, cut off by a short strangulated gurgle. I peeked through my fingers. None of the man was visible, but enough bubbles ruffled the water to reveal where he had entered it. An agonizing hush descended on the wharf. Then an umbrella pierced the surface, followed by the rest of the soggy chap. His face wore an expression that can only be described as… well… the face of a fully clothed man who had just jumped into the harbor.

Gary Mackleby, the short, stocky young deckhand on the *Karingal*, tossed him a lifebuoy. The man grabbed it and Gary hauled him aboard and secured the ferry alongside the wharf.

The skipper, Georgie Ellis, a handsome man with a skinny physique and shock of curly brown hair, trotted down from the wheelhouse.

"That was a bloody silly thing to do, mate. Youse could 'ave got yerself killed. Youse needn't have troubled, you know – we were coming in anyways!"

Willy and I looked at each other. I didn't know whether to laugh at the man with a spoon on his forehead or the soggy man on deck.

"What are you bludgers playing at? Who left them gates open?"

My head turned so fast I gave myself whiplash. Hughie was blustering down the wharf, his face about to burst a blood vessel.

"Holman, you're up shit creek – without a bloody paddle this time." My facial expression changed instantly to one akin to General Custer confronting the inevitable.

"Fair go, Hughie. Give the kid a break," said Georgie Ellis.

"This wouldn't have bloody happened if he'd kept those bloody gates closed like I told him," Hughie yelled, his body an agitated mass, as though he had just drunk ten cups of coffee on an empty stomach.

"Ain't you ever made a mistake, Hughie?"

"Shut up, Ellis."

Georgie put his hands on his hips, shook his mop of curly brown hair and smiled. "Relax, Hughie. Worse things happen at sea, you know. Nobody got hurt."

The man had presence, no doubt about that.

Hughie glared at Georgie, his lips pursed so tight they were, to all intents and purposes, invisible, then turned on his heel and strode away.

Georgie winked at me. "You know what his problem is, don't you?"

I shrugged.

"His pork sword's bin stuck in its sheath too long."

"Uh?"

"He ain't getting enough."

Hughie was right, though: I should never have left those gates open. For my penance I worked a month of late shifts. I never forgot to shut them again.

My first pay packet coincided with Willy's retirement. Holding that thin wad of notes in my hand was a great relief but my initial elation was tempered when I totted up how much I owed for rent, how much I needed to live and how much I owed Davy back in Griffith.

Willy insisted I come to his farewell bash at a dockland pub called Monty's, well known as the roughest pub in Sydney. I rode to Pyrmont in a cab with Georgie Ellis, Gary Mackleby, and an English seaman with a checkered past who called himself Don Maple. Don had jumped ship in Sydney, taken a false identity and joined the ferry service as a deckhand. A mystery man, he was never forthcoming about himself, but from snippets of information he dropped while drunk, I gleaned that he and his wife had run a pub in Dover near some of the locations used in the movie *Battle of Britain*. The film crew drank in Don's pub and because of that tenuous relationship, he'd been offered the part of a red-haired aircraft mechanic who worked on Michael Caine's *Spitfire*. His fifteen minutes of fame lasted five seconds, but on the movie set he met Wanda. Because of Wanda, Don dumped his wife and the pub and worked his passage to Australia on a cargo ship, arranging for Wanda to fly out from England to meet him in Sydney to start their new life together.

Don said to me on the way to Pyrmont, "You're a virgin, ain't yer?" I did not know what to say so I said nothing. "Don't worry, mate. We'll get yer laid – tonight." Evidently, he saw the night as some kind of rite of passage for me.

One step through the front door of Monty's, I knew I was in the wrong place. The noisy bar stank of stale tobacco smoke, vomit and beer, and was full of large tattooed men in shorts and singlets, men and women of questionable sexuality, and a multitude of prostitutes, deckhands, dockers and other assorted flotsam and jetsam.

Georgie and Don poured down the beer as if there were no tomorrow. Some deckhands began drumming on the bar with the palms of their hands. Willy, already three sheets to the wind, wobbled a bit as he climbed onto a table. I casually helped myself to a bowl of peanuts on the bar as the drum roll reached a crescendo. Willy flipped a teaspoon into the air and it landed on his forehead and stuck, he flipped another and it stuck too.

He chugged down his schooner of beer without a pause for air, then wiped his mouth with the back of his sleeve. "I tell you, it's per… sychical powers."

Jeers and cheers resounded from the motley crew.

"That's why he gets all them headaches," someone shouted.

"Na. It's me missus causes them," Willy said, "The uva night she threatened to shoot through if I come 'ome late from the pub again. Bugger me if I didn't get home till 3:00 am."

"What happened, Willo?" asked an old deckhand on cue.

"She were still there … dammit."

The bar erupted in laughter, the vibrations causing Willy to rock back and forth unsteadily. His wild-eyed gaze fixed on me, then on his empty glass.

"Tide's gone out, mate?"

I slowly felt in my back pocket, knowing full well I didn't have any cash not already accounted for.

"Typical bloody Pommie. Wouldn't shout in a shark attack."

Nervously helping myself to the remaining peanuts in the

bowl, I tried to avoid the hostile stares.

A bellowing voice emanated from somewhere above my right ear. "Hope you enjoyed those?"

I turned to face a chest. Slowly looking up I saw a cross-eyed giant dressed in the grey uniform of a deckhand, glaring down at me through bottle lens glasses; a mop of curly, greasy hair covered a head too big for its body.

"Yes. Thank you," I gulped, "they really hit the spot."

He bent over and placed his mouth next to my ear. His breath smelled of rotten fish. "I'm so pleased you did, coz you can pay for 'em and then buy me s'more."

"What do you mean?" I squeaked.

He grabbed me by the front of my shirt. "I mean I bought them for meself, not you or your noisy mates. I goes out for a leak and when I comes back you've scoffed the bloody lot."

"Look, I'm sorry," I whispered. "In English pubs they put them out as a courtesy thing."

"This ain't bloody pommie land." He let go of my shirt.

Georgie stepped between us and calmly laid a hand on the big man's chest.

"Lay off, 747. There's a good bloke."

I straightened my shirt and stepped back a couple of paces. "Yeah. Lay off," I said boldly, relieved that Georgie stood between us. Don grabbed my arm. A scary-looking tattooed woman of indecipherable age clung to his arm.

"Johnno, Violet here is dying to meet you."

I just wanted to leave.

A husky voice barked out, "Don. It's time."

Don looked toward the door where his tall, thin girlfriend Wanda stood. He nodded and left the pub as meekly as a lamb. She obviously had Don's number.

I took this as my cue to leave too. If someone divested me of my virginity, it certainly was not going to be a Monty's prostitute. The giant shouted after me, "I'll give her one for ya, Pommie!" He grabbed the inside of his forearm and thrust his fist in the air.

I was waiting for a bus, contemplating my lucky escape and

thinking of the old Groucho Marx adage — *I've had a perfectly wonderful evening, but this wasn't it* — when Gary Mackleby wandered over. He nodded back toward the pub. "He's not a full quid, ya know?"

"Which one are you talking about?"

"The big feller, 747. He's a few bricks short of a load that one."

"What did you call him?"

"747." Gary flagged down a taxi. "Come on, I'll shout yuz a ride home."

I did not argue. We hopped in the back seat and headed off through the mean streets of the docklands.

"He's been on the ferries for years. He's on the *Lady Denman* one day, scrubbing the decks, when a plane flies low over the harbor. He looks up and yells, 'Hey, there's a 747 up there.' This was the first one any of us had seen. He stares at the bloody thing, walks backwards to get a better view and there's an almighty splash — he's fallen overboard. He's bin stuck with '747' ever since."

Gary rested his arm on my shoulder, rather like my father would have done before giving me some words of wisdom. "Georgie told me you were skint. You need some money?"

"Thanks, but I'll be fine."

The cab let us off in a back street in the old Rocks area near Circular Quay. Traffic noises from the Sydney Harbor Bridge muffled our footsteps as I followed Gary up a sandstone stairway until we reached a row of run-down terrace homes.

Two panes of glass were missing from a front door which opened to reveal a fat, unkempt woman dressed in a tent-like dress, a sadly defeated-looking cigarette drooping from the corner of her mouth.

Seeing Gary and ignoring me, she said, "Oh it's you. Got paid, did yer?"

"Yes, Ma." He reached in the back pocket of his gray King Gee work trousers and pulled out a small, yellow envelope and placed it in his mother's pudgy hands.

"Thanks, son. I was on me last pack of smokes." She

turned and shuffled off.

Gary beckoned me to follow him inside.

"How long have you lived here, Gary?" I asked.

"Oh 'bout five years."

"Really?" I glanced around the cold, damp living room. I imagined it as once part of the barracks for the soldiers who had guarded the fledgling penal colony.

"Yeah…" He paused reflectively, scratching the back of his head. "It's Housing Commission. Me old man was a seaman. Shot through like a Bondi tram when me sister was born. This is the best we could do."

"He never came back?"

Gary bent to pick up a record from the floor. "Never. Ma went on the game till I were old enuff to work. Now she just lies around all day, smokes and drinks and watches the soaps on telly. Take a listen to this…"

He handed me the shrink-wrapped cover of a Creedence Clearwater album and put the vinyl LP on a turntable. The needle dropped into place.

> *It ain't me, it ain't me,*
> *I ain't no senator's son,*
> *It ain't me, it ain't me,*
> *I ain't no fortunate one …*

Gary, no fortunate one either, gyrated to the rhythm and lip-synched the words. I sat on a red beanbag and perused the liner notes on the back of the album cover.

The music stopped and Gary nodded toward the cover, "What's it say?"

I started to read it aloud then handed it to him to read.

"No use to me, mate."

"Why's that?"

"I can't read nor write."

He never had time for schooling he said, because he was always hustling work and "looking out for me Ma."

I met Gary next morning at the deli at the top of the wharf. A slim Middle Eastern-looking woman, her long dark hair pulled back from an ashen face, was opening up. Seeing Gary, her face brightened.

"Layla, I want you to meet my friend, John," Gary said. I extended my hand across the counter. "Lay's married to Freddie Laponis. He owns this deli and another in the city."

I nodded toward the wonderful array of cakes and pastries in the window. "I've tried your baklavas. They're delicious."

Layla smiled wanly, "Thank you, kind sir. Freddie prides himself on his pastries."

Layla gazed longingly at Gary. Gary gazed longingly at Layla. I felt like the ham in one of her sandwiches.

"What's up with you and Layla?" I asked later when Gary hopped onto the deck of his ferry *Karingal*.

"I love her."

The ferry pulled away.

"She's married, though."

He just wound his rope into a neat, tight circle.

On the whole, life was good on the ferries – it was by far the most fun job I had experienced anywhere, not that there was much competition. Those first weeks on the wharf were interesting and I got to know all the boats and their crews. I loved the old wooden ferries that were now showing their age – wonderful boats of immense character with names such as *Kosciusko, Karingal, Karrabee* and *Kameruka*. Many started their lives in the 1920s, served on Sydney Harbor and finally were scrapped or sold off in the 1960s and 1970s. The crews of these old campaigners contained a cast of characters extraordinaire, a real cross-section of humanity.

The word *larrikin*, used predominantly in Australia, means a person who pays little attention to what others think of them, who breaks the rules of social convention and is prone to eccentric behavior. And that is about the closest I can come to describing Georgie Ellis.

Gary Mackleby fit the description of the "little Aussie battler" to a tee: a person who sits at the bottom of society yet perseveres through adversity, despite the challenges of low pay, family commitments and lack of personal recognition. In

Australia it is generally a term of respect and endearment.

I don't know if there is such as a term as "the little Canadian battler," but Max Van Geest would not fall into the category anyway. A rancher's son, he had traded driving herds of cattle across the prairies of Alberta for driving ferries across the waters of Sydney Harbor.

Jimmy Greenlees, a wharfhand from Glasgow and ardent Communist, was one of the few who actually attended union meetings. He saw a worldwide conspiracy in every political decision made by the Firemen and Deckhands Union.

"Listen, laddie. You should be going to meetings. You pays your dues," he said to me one evening as I waited for a bus home.

"I'm not that interested, Jimmy."

The bus pulled up and the doors opened.

"Remember laddie," he pointed a finger at my head, "you are the union! You need to remember that. You have to keep tabs on the delegates because all men are corruptible!"

The bus disgorged its passengers and began loading.

"Oh. I don't know…" I said, stepping onto the bus.

"A few years back they almost went broke supporting members like you."

"Really?

"They were out on strike for months for better pay and working conditions."

"I didn't know that."

"I bet you dinna. There's a lot you dinna know."

The bus doors closed, almost pinning his head, but Jimmy was right: I probably should have gone to union meetings. The money was good on the ferries. I made $62 a week, plus overtime at double-time on weekends, triple-time on public holidays, the most money I had ever earned. The union made sure that if management, skippers or engineers got a raise, so did the deckhands and wharfhands, plus whenever we took a vacation we received a 17% bonus in addition to our regular pay. *Ahhh…the land of the working man!*

Stan Castanedes did not attend union meetings either. An

immigrant from Greece and a deckhand on one of the larger old boats named *Kanangra*, he sat a lot because of a chronic bad back. Apparently he'd got wedged between a wharf and a ferry and several lower vertebrae got crushed. Stan and I were eating our lunchtime sandwiches on *Kanangra's* upper deck when he dug me in the ribs and nodded toward the top of the wharf.

"Just keep quiet and watch him."

Ambling down the ramp onto the pontoon came the giant, 747, furtively glancing this way and that. When assured that nobody was looking at him, he put his hand into a garbage can and came up with the remains of a discarded ice cream cone, which he proceeded to stuff into his sizable maw. Moving on to the next garbage can, he retrieved a half-eaten meat pie and devoured that.

I turned to Stan, stuck a finger down my throat and pretended to vomit.

"Takes all sorts, matey. He's gotta more money than you and me putta together."

"I can see why... he must save a fortune on food bills!"

Nobody ever used 747's real name so I never knew it, but his place of residence was somewhere near Taronga Zoo – some said it was in Taronga Zoo. His work hours were spent cleaning the zoo wharf and his after-hours with the prostitutes at Kings Cross.

"Bin up the Cross to see me girlfriends," he boasted, "They love me up there, they do, and always give me what I want. Yes, they do, always and all ways."

In those early days, Hughie had me delegated to work at Taronga Zoo wharf with 747 on busy Saturday afternoons. One of those afternoons, while watching two schoolboys swing back and forth on 747's outstretched arms, I heard a familiar voice.

"Hello John."

I turned to see Donna and her friend Krishka walking down the ramp onto the wharf.

"How are you then? Just come to check up on you – aye, Krish?"

Krishka, an attractive girl with big hair and big blue eyes said, "Donna's been worried about you. She feels awful that she let you down over the restaurant job."

"I'm actually glad it didn't work out. This is more my style – plenty of fresh air and sunshine. The money's good. I've almost saved enough for a trip around Australia."

"Your Mum and Dad must miss you. It's been over a year since you left, hasn't it?" Donna inquired.

"I certainly miss them." Although I wrote to my parents every week, hardly a day went by that I did not think of them. I swallowed hard and changed the subject. "What happened to your US Marine?"

"Wesley's got a posting near the Cambodian border. I haven't heard from him since he left."

"Hey you, get on with your work!" 747's booming nasal voice rang out. "You're not paid to chat up the birds, you know."

He lumbered toward me while leering at the girls. I raised my eyes to the heavens and ignored him. The girls wisely scooted up the gangplank and onto the ferry.

From the security of the upper deck Donna shouted, "Come by for supper, John."

"Can I come too?" 747 boomed back.

As the ferry pulled away, Donna leaned over the rail. "Give me a ring – and don't let that oaf push you around."

747 hovered over me. "Next time you chat up the sheilas on my wharf, you better introduce 'em to me or else."

"Or else what?" I asked.

"Or else I'll dob you in to Hughie."

"For what?"

His crossed eyes appeared to be looking somewhere else, but he was looking at me. "Don't you worry, oi'll think of somethink!"

One of my comedic heroes, Groucho Marx, would have removed the cigar from the corner of his mouth, wiggled his eyebrows and said, "People say I never forget a face, but in your case I'm willing to give it a try."

A handsome Maltese immigrant named Paul Dalli, who looked like Chico Marx, stood at the end of the pontoon, holding onto the end of a long fishing rod. Observing 747 trundling away, he placed a finger to his temple and rotated it until his attention became diverted by the swooshing sound of a ferry approaching. His attention was diverted even more when he saw who was aboard. On the lower deck lounged seven exceptionally gorgeous women in bathing suits; on the upper deck a banner read:

MISS AUSTRALIA BEAUTY PAGEANT CHARTER.

Paul, known as "the singing deckhand" because of his fine tenor voice, had developed a following among female passengers who clamored for a seat on his ferry just to be serenaded by him. This was a moment made for "the singing deckhand." His fishing rod clattered against the steel pontoon. He dropped onto one knee, spread his arms wide and began to sing:

Be my love and with your kisses softly burning
One kiss is all I need to seal my fate
And hand in hand...

Spontaneous applause broke out from the passengers crowding the wharf.

We'll find love's Promised Land
There'll be no one but you for me eternally
If you will be my love...

I shoved on the rear gangplank and hustled to beat Gary to the front plank, wheeling it in front of the waiting beauty queens, who sashayed down it. Paul stood at the bottom of the plank and kissed the hand of each beauty queen as she stepped onto the wharf. Two men followed, their necks adorned with Leicas and zoom lenses. One of them offered Paul his hand; in the spirit of the moment Paul kissed it too. The other man reached in his pocket for a light meter, examined it and put it back in his pocket. "Oh, this will be perfect, girls." He waved a floppy hand toward me, "Hey, you there! The name's Harold. Lance and I need you and your friends for some pickies. You'll add a touch of earthiness to these petals."

"Yes. A sort of beauty-and-the-beasts motif," said Lance gazing at the sky and back at his light meter.

"You're joking?" Gary said.

"We've spoken to Mr. Frawley. Just go over there and do as you're told." Harold started to shoosh us with open arms toward the beauty queens, as if herding sheep into a pen.

"What about me, then?" With his usual impeccable timing, 747 arrived back on the scene, broom and bucket in hand.

Lance put one hand on his hip and looked at Harold, his mouth hanging open in exaggerated fashion.

"I think he wantsa to be in ze picture," said Paul while 747 ogled Miss Queensland's ample breasts.

"You said you wanted someone earthy," I remarked.

Paul whispered in my ear, then cupped a hand around his mouth and shouted, "Hey, seven fours, we need your help. The loo, she is blocked."

"Won't it wait?"

"No! Hughie he leave orders for you to plunge, matey." 747 leered lasciviously at Miss South Australia.

"I'll be back, girls. I've got a lot of friends like you up at the Cross. They like me up there."

Georgie sauntered down the gangway. "Yeah, I bet they do, poor devils, having to fuck you for a living,"

"Up yours, Ellis…" 747 gave Georgie a middle-finger salute, shuffled aboard and made his way along the rail.

Georgie looked at the beauty queens. "Christ, there's more wildlife here than up at the ruddy zoo!"

When 747 disappeared into the toilet, Georgie sneaked back to the wheelhouse while I crept along the rail and wedged a broom under the door handle of the toilet. Gary removed the gangplanks and unraveled the ropes. I jumped ashore and as *Karingal* steamed away I could hear the muffled but unmistakable howls of a big man locked in a small toilet. Oblivious to thoughts of any repercussions my action might cause, I had my picture taken with Paul surrounded by seven beauty queens, one for each state in Australia.

OUT OF THE ASHES

While life on the ferries remained full of drama, life was positively sedate back at my new digs, Nyah Lodge. Being one of two guys in a house full of girls sounds idyllic but most of my energy went into eking my way out of poverty and putting money in the bank. I worked a roster of evening and early morning shifts; the hours were intolerably unsociable, so I think most of the girls were unaware of my existence.

My flat had a small kitchen – without meters – but I rarely used it; once a week I ate at great aunt Mary's and frequently I ate at a Chinese restaurant called *Jippys*. It had good cheap food but not many customers. It did not attract many customers because the owner scared people away. In his multiple roles of chef, waiter and chief bottle-washer, Jippy always wore a striped apron over a grimy white t-shirt, and a tracksuit bottom, with flip-flops. A dishcloth hung over his left forearm; in his right hand he wielded a chopping cleaver with which he waved patrons to their tables. I came in regularly, so he cooked special meals for me.

"You likee fish… I have good fish today. Slapper… Barramundee… John Daweeeee…"

Jippy would gather his plump wife and two cute children and hover around the table, watching while I slowly chewed on the first mouthful. My nod of satisfaction constituted the official seal of approval.

"You likee like. That's gooood!" Jippy would slap me gently on the back and away they went, happily chatting among themselves in Mandarin.

Jippy had formerly been a pro wrestler in Hong Kong. If wrestling was airing on the small black-and-white TV hanging on the wall, Jippy would be right into it; the dishcloth and cleaver his props. He forgot his customers, his eyes glazed over and he went into a trance-like state, mimicking every move played out on the telly, grunts and all. The dishcloth was twisted and torqued every which way and sometimes he'd thrash the floor with it. Customers would enter the restaurant, see him rocking and rolling and immediately depart.

One evening Jippy recognized a wrestler from his past life. His eyes became transfixed on the small screen; he rubbed his hands together with glee, then pointed.

"Mask Destroyer... He Mask Destroyer..." His eyes began to water from the sheer sentimentality of it all.

On screen two wrestlers faced off. The Masked Destroyer was dressed in black mask and a full body suit that attained tautness only in the region of the stomach; the Great Tabouli was dressed in turban and loincloth, resembling an Indian Fakir with a penchant for burgers and French Fries. Jippy circled my table as the Masked Destroyer circled the Great Tabouli, then pulled off a surprise move, lifting him off the ground and hoisting him at arm's length above his head. Jippy raised his arms and did a sort of pirouette, rather like one of those hippo ballet dancers in Walt Disney's *Fantasia*. The Masked Destroyer did a sort of pirouette too, milking applause with the Great Tabouli held aloft. Jippy banged his fist down on the table. The Masked Destroyer banged the Great Tabouli down on the canvas. Anticipating the climactic moment, Jippy wiped his eyes, curled his upper lip under his top teeth and his lower lip over his bottom teeth, his head bobbed up and down, his arms pumped like pistons. Unable to contain himself any longer he burst forth with a surprisingly squeaky laugh for someone so big.

When the Destroyer launched himself through the air and belly-flopped onto the Great Tabouli's head, I downed my last mouthful of Moo Goo Gai Pan and headed for the exit.

Jippy snapped out of his reverie. "You blingee your flends and famileee nexta time, OK?"

I never did. Well, once I did, but that comes much later.

My other eating place was the deli on number four wharf. When I entered Gary was leisurely perusing the *Sydney Morning Herald*.

"Anything interesting in the paper?" I asked.

"How should I know? Can't read the bloody thing." Gary twisted the newspaper into a crumpled mess.

"Well, why –"

Gary knew what I was about to say and already had an answer. "Because Layla doesn't know and she thinks I'm bloody smart." He nodded toward her through the window. She smiled a thin smile and waved.

"Why don't you take reading lessons? I know they have classes at migrant hostels and night schools."

He threw what remained of the newspaper on the ground. "Look, I don't want to be in some class full of wogs and illiterates."

"Suit yourself," I said as he left in a huff.

Layla waltzed through the door carrying a cup of steaming coffee, handed it to me and sat down opposite.

"I'm glad Gary has you as a friend." She said.

I poured in some milk from a metal jug and stirred in a couple of sugar cubes.

"He's a good bloke. I like him."

She gave me a mischievous look. "So do I." She glanced left and right then lent over the table and cupped a hand to my ear. "Gary's going to study for his skipper's license. They make good money. Good benefits. Better than we make out of this bloody place."

Rather startled by her bitter tone, I did not know how to respond. "Freddie works seven days a week…" Her knuckles shone white as she gripped the edge of the plastic tabletop. "…for what? A lousy deli? When Gary gets his ticket, it's goodbye deli for me!"

Suddenly she didn't seem so meek and mild.

An overweight dark-haired man who looked tired pulled up a chair and joined us. "Who's your friend, darl?"

Layla smiled sweetly, all trace of bitterness gone. "Oh, this is John, a friend of Gary's. John, this is Freddie, my husband."

"Good to meet you, mate. Any friend of Gary's is a friend of mine. He's one of my best customers."

As I left, I realized that Layla had it all worked out; I just didn't know if Gary did.

John Mellion, the Australian character actor, had not worked out how he could get his large cooler full of beer from the ferry to a waiting taxi so I helped him carry it up the wharf to the street.

"Looks like you're going to have quite a party," I remarked as we lowered it to the ground.

"I hope so, mate. Going to the SCG. The Ashes decider," replied the man who would later play Wally in *Crocodile Dundee*.

"Half your luck!" I responded.

The historic seventh test of the 1970-71 Ashes cricket series was underway. The sixth test in Melbourne had been washed out due to heavy rains, so both sides agreed to play an unprecedented seventh in Sydney to decide the fate of the Ashes, the holy grail of Anglo-Australian cricket. Tickets to the match were at a premium. I would have given my eyeteeth to be going with Mr. Mellion but instead I returned to the wharf, where another ferry disgorged its human cargo, most of whom were also heading to the Sydney Cricket Ground.

I sat on a bench, splicing a sisal mooring rope that had snapped in two thanks to an over-zealous ferry skipper.

"Mr. Holman, I presume?"

I dropped the rope and looked up to see the tall, lean figure of Graham Mellis, his chiseled face framed by golden locks, beaming at me.

"Graham! What the heck are you doing here?"

"Well, we're a bloody long way from *St. John's* that's for certain!" said Graham, referring to the school we'd both attended in Sussex.

"What an awful place that was." I responded.

Graham looked fit and tanned, instead of his normal English pallor. "But we survived." He clapped me on the shoulder. "You took some tracking down, you bugger. We left Melbourne and drove to Griffith; your formidable landlady told us you'd left there. We called in at your great aunt's place in North Bondi, and she said you'd moved near the beach, so we shot over there and met some nice young ladies who said you were here!"

"Yes, you always seemed to be one step ahead of us," interjected Graham's wiry traveling companion, Jonathan. He reached into his back pocket, pulled out some tickets and fanned them in front of my face. "We're going to the SCG tomorrow to see the Poms thrash the Aussies. Do you want to join us?"

My mouth hung open. "Do I ever!"

Fortune had shone on me for once but it was tempered by a raging toothache that kept me awake half the night. Just as I drifted off to sleep at dawn there came a rap on the door.

I stumbled out of bed.

At the door stood a tall blonde-haired, blue-eyed young lady, who smiled a smile as wide as the Pacific. She reminded me of Julie Andrews – at least until she spoke with a strong American accent.

"Hi. I'm Martha. I wonder if I could borrow –"

"Ahhrggh!" I put a hand to my jaw – not in embarrassment, but in pain.

"– a cup of sugar. Are you all right?"

"Toothache!"

My teeth ached when I did just about anything – like suck air, for instance. Having a phobia for all things dental, I had not seen a dentist since I left England.

"Let me take a look."

"What?"

"Come on, don't be afraid. I used to be a dental nurse back in the States."

I opened up and tilted my head toward the light.

Martha peered in and jumped back in horror. "You've got some mighty big cavities in there."

I barely heard the words, distracted as I was by a combination of toothache, her smile and beautiful blue eyes.

"You need to get them taken care of, pronto."

"I'm sure you're right, but I'm off to the cricket and …"

"Cricket?"

"Yes. It's the Ashes, one of the world's great sporting rivalries."

"Like the World Series in baseball?" she asked.

"Well, sort of. Except more than one country plays cricket. It's quite simple, really."

I bade her sit down at my small kitchen table and grabbed a dishcloth that had the classically confusing explanation of cricket imprinted upon it.

"You have two sides: one out in the field, one in. Each man on the side that's in goes out; and when he's out, he comes in and the next man goes in until he's out. When they're all out, the side that's been out in the field comes in, and the side that's been in goes out and tries to get out those coming in. If the side that's in declares, you get men still in, not out. Then when both sides have been in and out, including not outs, twice, that's the end of the match."

In the back of my mind was a story that British talk show host Michael Parkinson told of the time he was at a party, going to great lengths to explain cricket to an elderly American lady. He felt a sense of achievement when he thought she had got it until she responded with, "My, my, and to think they do all that on horseback!"

But Martha just smiled and winked. She knew I was kidding her.

I continued, "Seriously, it's been going on for nearly a hundred years. We taught our former colonies our game and now most of them are better at it than we are! In 1882

Australia beat England for the first time on England's home turf. This didn't go down too well, so some little old ladies got hold of the stumps from that game, burnt them and put the ashes in an urn to represent the death of English cricket. Those ashes are what they play for now. The urn is only about six inches tall but one of the most sought-after prizes in international sport." I felt like I was talking mumbo jumbo.

"Wow. That's really neat. I would love to go to the game," she said with another smile. Martha seemed to smile a lot.

"You would?"

"Yes, I would. I love sports."

This was unusual. Most girls I had known in England were totally indifferent to cricket or football. Either Martha liked me and was prepared to put up with six hours of boredom or she did, indeed, like sports – either way she was a breath of fresh air.

Somehow Graham managed to purloin an extra ticket, so eight-eight years after the first test that started the Ashes rivalry, three shirtless Pommies and a Yank (not shirtless) sat under a blazing sun on the bleachers below "the Hill" at the Sydney Cricket Ground, drinking beer out of plastic cups, a minority in a hostile crowd of rowdy spectators chanting abuse at "the Poms."

Spectators in Sydney are not a sedate lot and the noisiest barrackers used to sit on "the Hill" – literally, a grassy knoll at the eastern end of the SCG and the cheapest spot in the ground. Never dull, the hill mob made their own entertainment from wolf-whistling at girls in short-shorts, to throwing beer cans at the scorer's window, to cries of "AVAGOYAMUG" directed at some pedestrian batsman. The effects of heavy beer consumption and hot sun caused the place to heat up during the last session of play and *this* last session of play was no exception.

John Snow, a tall man with muscles rippling, shirt tail billowing, ran up and bowled a couple of bouncers (fast, head-high balls) that shook up the Australian batsmen. Umpire Lou Rowan pulled Snow aside and told him to cut it out but an angry Snow ignored the warning and took out his frustrations by bowling a bouncer at Terry Jenner, a tail-end batsman. There is an unwritten rule that you do not bowl bouncers to tail-end batsmen, but the bouncer was an effective tool in Snow's armory because batsmen did not wear helmets in those days. The ball reared up and struck Jenner on the temple. Jenner fell to the ground, bleeding from a cut over his ear. Umpire Rowan confronted Snow again and warned him that he was intimidating the batsman and breaking the rules under law 46. The England team captain, Ray Illingworth, protested, but by this time the partisan crowd was outraged – none more so than the Hill mob, who began throwing beer cans and bottles onto the field. Snow snatched the white sun hat that Umpire Rowan had been holding for him; a cacophony of jeering and abuse ensued. In protest, the England team sat in a circle in the middle of the pitch until the bottles and cans were cleared from the outfield and the restive crowd calmed down.

Martha dug me in the ribs. "Hey, he's coming over here."

His shock of curly black hair covered by the floppy white sun hat and his shirt sleeves rolled almost to the shoulder, Snow was returning to his fielding position below us.

"I don't think that's a good idea," Martha whispered in my ear.

"Neither do I."

The jeers and boos of the crowd started up again. Snow did not care. He pretended to conduct them like an orchestra.

"He's got a bit of an attitude. Good-looking, though," Martha said.

"Of course – he's from Sussex!"

She elbowed me in the ribs as the cans and bottles started to fly past our ears.

"Bloody hell, this is a bit serious," Graham whispered.

I began to worry that Martha would be rattled by the hostility, but she seemed to be enjoying it. Below us, some spectators shook hands with Snow but another grizzled-looking fellow, having imbibed too much amber liquid, grabbed Snow's shirt and tried to pull him over the boundary fence.

Martha jumped up and shouted at him, "You're an idiot, buddy!"

The crowd around us found that quite amusing. Things were getting out of hand. Anything could happen. The atmosphere was electric.

"Oh, what a jerk!" Martha shouted as he was hauled away by the police, which made the crowd around us laugh and eased the tension a bit.

Ray Illingworth, the England captain, did his bit by leading his players from the field in protest.

"You didn't know cricket was an audience-participation sport, did you?" Graham teased as he led us into the public bar of the Olympic pub across the street where a friend from the Lodge, Lennie, worked as a barmaid.

Lennie peered through a mob of customers, three deep at the bar, only her curly black hair and black horn-rimmed specs visible, she raised her hand above the heads and pointed to the corner of the room. Martha's roommates, Beth and Glynis, were sitting on barstools at a tall round table.

"Well, what did you think of it?" Glynis shouted through the throng. We squeezed in beside them.

Martha said, "I thought it was great. Most Americans would not understand why a game that lasts five days could be exciting, but it really is – or at least today was!"

"Bloody oath," said Beth, taking a swig from a schooner of beer. "A bloody Yank likes cricket – that's a first. Glynis and me can't stand the game, can we, Glynis?"

"Yeah. Too bloody slow for us!"

"It's a subtle game, like a game of chess," I said. "Sometimes it can be boring, sometimes exhilarating – there's a lot of tactics and nuance."

"Nuance is something we Americans are not very good at. We tend to see everything as black and white," Martha responded.

Graham returned with a tray brimming with schooners of beer, and plonked it down in the center of the table.

"What brings you to Australia, Martha?" Graham asked as he handed out the amber liquid. "There are a lot of us Pommies here, but not many Yanks – except the poor blighters in uniform, of course."

"My Dad always wanted to move here. I'd already been to Europe and wanted to go somewhere different, so I came out with my girlfriend, Colleen. We'd planned it since high school. We cruised out on the *Oriana*, went up to Surfers Paradise for the first six months and ..." She shrugged and said no more.

"What happened to Colleen?" I inquired.

"We parted company."

Beth, who had an attractive boyish face and closely cropped hair, would not let the story die. "Colleen met a Kiwi in Surfers and fell in *love*." She loaded the word love with noticeable sarcasm.

Martha laughed, "Yeah. Two was company, but three was definitely a crowd."

"Yep, Colleen did a bunk and left Marty in the lurch," added Beth.

"Bloody hell, Bethie, you do get to the point," said Glynis.

"Beth's right. They made me feel real uncomfortable," Martha said.

Something clicked in my memory. "You were on the train. I saw you on the train."

"Oh my God, you didn't!"

"Yes. I saw you arguing with your friends. I was at the back of the carriage."

"Oh my God!"

"I would have done the same thing! But it looks as though you're in good hands now." I nodded toward Glynis and Beth,

"These guys are so neat," Martha responded. "So are you. I feel real lucky to have found the Lodge."

"Me too." I downed the ice-cold schooner of beer and winced as sharp pains shot through my head.

Martha flashed me a sympathetic look. "You've gotta go see that dentist."

Conveniently, a dental office was located next door to Nyah

Lodge. To my surprise the nurse/receptionist was Nina, the Dutch girl from the *Australis* whom I failed to impress with both my diving and dancing prowess. She stood over me, handing the dentist his instruments of torture. I sincerely hoped this was not payback time.

"Have to save those buggers. Only ones you've got, right?" the dentist said.

I mumbled agreement. I was impressed. Mr. Bufton, an alcoholic and my so-called dentist in England, always wanted to pull them out. When he did, nitrous oxide seemed to be the only available anesthetic. I was often scared he'd give me too much and I wouldn't wake up. Afterwards, Bufton would be leering down at me, his breath smelling of stale whisky, holding a whale's tooth in his hand. "Had the devil of a job getting this one out. Ho! Ho! Ho! Ha! Ha! Ha!"

This Bondi dentist was a revelation – good and relatively painless. After two weeks of treatment he said, "Those are big fillings. Might last six months. Might last ten years. Only time will tell."

They lasted twenty-five years and gave me no pain, except in the initial stages. The initial stages were when I took leave from the ferries. With some trepidation I entered the office of Bill Anderson, the General Manager of Sydney Harbor Ferries to ask for time off. "Yeah. Go and enjoy yourself. You're only young once," he said cheerfully. Anderson had decently allowed me to extend my trip from a long weekend in Brisbane to a jaunt around Australia.

Setting off on the bus two weeks later, I did not feel so young. My jaw ached from the fillings and my nose was blocked due to allergies, but despite the initial pain, discomfort and random thoughts of Martha, this journey proved to be one of the great adventures of my life. I had money in my pocket and felt good about myself. My jaw complex was pushed into the recesses of my consciousness.

SPARKS IN PARKES

I spent five weeks hitchhiking and traveling by bus and train through the Australian outback, a journey of a lifetime, bookended by Ted and Kirsty's wedding in Brisbane and a visit with the Eliots in Canberra.

When I returned to the soggy edge of Sydney life, I discovered I had been given a promotion of sorts.

"I'm moving you up to deckhand status on the standby crew. You'll be doing the odd jobs, like filling in for crew who are late, sick, taking meal breaks or on holiday. You won't get bored, mate."

This was my first promotion anywhere, to anything, so I was excited: Hughie loved me after all.

The standby crew rarely knew what awaited them from one day to the next, and we seldom worked as a team, because a boat would normally require the services of just one. Although most ferries carried three crew members, each crew member was represented by a different union. The skipper, Arthur Roberts, a jovial, roly-poly character, was represented by the Ferry Masters' union; the engineer, Ernie Edwards a fastidious Lancastrian who kept the most spotless engines in the fleet was represented by the Engineers Union; and yours truly by the Firemen and Deckhands Union. In any given month, one of those unions would be on strike over some demarcation or wage dispute, and then the other two unions would walk out in sympathy, which meant I got a lot of time off. The silliest dispute came while I trekked around Australia: The boys of the Firemen and Deckos instigated a 19-hour blockade of the *SS Australis* as a protest against the new military regime in Greece. Of course, it had no effect on the right-wing military junta in Greece but Jimmy Greenlees felt good about it!

From splicing ropes to polishing brass fixtures to helping little old ladies aboard, it was a healthy, open-air job with plenty of variety. Every wharf had different characteristics: Some were pontoons that floated up and down with the tide, others were on fixed pilings – and some, like Long Nose Point could be a bear to tie up at with a running tide and strong wind, but others, like Mosman in a sheltered bay, were relatively easy.

Things had been relatively easy on the home front too – until my roommate Peter entered our small flat minus his normal upbeat personality. Shoulders slumped and head bowed, he tossed his leather briefcase onto our small kitchen table; papers and aeronautical magazines spewed onto the floor.

"I failed," he said.

"Oh no!"

"Yes. I am rather disappointed."

That was something of an understatement, given that Peter lived and breathed flying. He had been hitting the books hard and spending every weekend draining his bank account to pay for the rental of an aircraft in order to accumulate flying hours in preparation for his commercial pilot's license exam.

"Don't give up," I volunteered. "Try again?"

Peter was as precise and neat as a watch from his native country. He needed to be, as he made a living as an elevator engineer.

"No, John. It is not so simple. It is my eyesight. I pass on everything – theory, flying – everything but my eyes. I am extremely nearsighted and there is nothing to be done about that. I now have to think about a new career."

"But you have the elevator job?"

He paced the floor of our small kitchen.

"I hate job. I do it only to pay for the flying."

A knock on the door broke the tension. The landlord, Peter Hodgens, stood there dressed in shorts, singlet and running shoes.

"Come on, Pete, let's go; you need a release. Come with us, John. We're just gonna do a couple of lengths to blow away the cobwebs." I had studiously managed to avoid these nightly marathons up and down Bondi Beach, often stating that the imported American craze for jogging could do more harm than good. I didn't actually mean it; it was more my sheer laziness than anything else. So I just followed along as they streaked over Campbell Parade and down to the promenade. I managed to keep up for one length of the beach, then I started dropping back. As I staggered toward the south end of the beach, I met them jogging north, back toward me. Enough was enough.

At the south end was a saltwater pool that filled and emptied with the rising of the tide. I don't know if it was my sweat-filled eyes that made me miss the sign that said *Danger – No Swimming* or just my overheated thermostat, but I dived headlong into the pool, the cool seawater invigorating every part of my body. Through a watery film I could make out a group of people waving and shouting. I nonchalantly waved back. The waving became more vigorous, then the word 'shark' rang out loud and clear. Somebody pointed toward the other end of the pool, where a grey fin, slid through the water. I never thought it possible to leave a pool faster than one could dive into it, but somehow I managed the feat.

Standing there wet and shaking – not from cold, but from fear – I noted the shark was only about eighteen inches long, a Port Jackson, someone said. This episode only highlighted for me that jogging is, indeed, bad for your health.

A few schooners of Tooheys Draught at the Bondi Astra across the road did wonders for my recovery – and for Peter Leders.

"Look who is here!"

I looked up from the bottom of my beer mug to see Martha and her friends Glynis, Beth, Denise and Lennie – coming through the door. Peter stood up and beckoned them over. "Please to come and join us, ladies. I have news to tell of John's escape from jaws of man-eating shark!"

The girls gathered around our table while Peter scrounged for spare chairs. Then his shapely girlfriend, Anita, appeared and whisked him away for an evening of love and sympathy, leaving me to confess that the shark had not been an 18-foot Great White but an 18-inch Port Jackson.

The atmosphere changed as if someone had sucked all the oxygen out of the room with a powerful vacuum cleaner. Attempting to fill the vacuum, I ran through my repertoire of corny jokes; I really wanted to show them what an entertaining fellow I could be when tipsy.

"I saw a man walking along the street pulling a piece of string. I stopped and said, 'Why are you pulling that piece of string?' He said, '*Well have you ever tried pushing it?*'"

Denise rose from her seat and yawned, her long black hair seeming to stretch almost to the floor. The phrase "laid back" could have been coined with Denise in mind. Nothing seemed to bother her… except my jokes.

"I think it's time for bed!" She headed for the door.

"I went to the doctor the other day. I lifted my arm and said 'Doctor it hurts when I do that.' The doctor replied 'Well don't do that!'"

Lennie got up and left in a hurry.

"Two cannibals were eating a clown – one said to the other, *Does he taste funny to you?*"

Martha laughed and said, "I think you're funny" then gave me her All-American smile. She had perfect teeth, not one out of place – unlike mine, which were, in typical English fashion, bent and crooked and barely met but for a couple of places.

"You do?"

She seemed to understand my warped English sense of humor.

Beth yawned. "You wanna come to Parkes with us on the weekend, Johnno?"

I hesitated, knowing I would have to find someone to work my Saturday shift.

"Marty's coming!"

I hesitated no more.

"Yes, I'd love to. I was in Parkes last year!"

Beth looked surprised. "You were?"

"Yes… just passing through on a truck loaded with loo seats." For some reason Beth found that funnier than my jokes.

In an FJ Holden that had seen better days, we motored westward through the Blue Mountains toward the central plains of New South Wales. Driving the car was Beth's current beau, Dave, an amiable Hells Angel, his dark hair slicked back, his overweight physique covered in tattoos. Beth sat close to him on the front seat, her hand resting on his leg – at least, I think it was his leg. I squeezed into the back between Martha and Glynis, not an entirely unpleasant situation.

Dave turned on the radio and we sang along to a crackly *American Pie*.

"That's a great song," said Martha. "I've no idea what it means, but it's a great song."

"I read it's supposed to be about the death of Buddy Holly. The day he died, music died and all that," I said, attempting to impress her with my knowledge of American popular music.

"So how much farther is this one horse-town?" the Hells Angel interrupted.

Wearing a black beret on her head and with a glowing Disque Bleu in her free hand, Beth looked like a femme fatale from a French gangster movie.

"Couple of hours, mate," she replied.

Dawn broke. A ribbon of red in the east became a sheet of orange as we cruised through grassy plains filled with sheep.

The FJ Holden descended into the small wool town of Parkes, named for Sir Henry Parkes, Premier of New South

Wales for twenty years, and one of the movers and shakers of the nineteenth century who guided Australia to self-rule. Parkes has been called the father of Australian federation and in 1889 he declared that the time had come to set about creating a "great national government for all Australia"; although he died in 1896, before his vision could be realized, his contribution was not forgotten. His picture appears on stamps.

The FJ pulled up in front of a spacious fiberboard bungalow and even before we had time to alight, Beth's family erupted from the front door and surrounded the car: Her mother, Barbara, was a big boned woman, full of humor; her father Brian, was tall with prematurely white hair and a pale but sunburnt face; her younger brothers and sisters were noisy and gregarious.

Barbara ushered us indoors, where a large breakfast of lamb chops, eggs and toast materialized before our eyes. There was enough to feed an army.

"This is fabulous, Mrs. Anderson," said Martha, leaning back in her chair.

"Best breakfast I've ever had!" I said, and almost meant it. It ran a very close second to my mother's breakfasts, which warrant a chapter on their own.

"It's my pleasure. Besides, we've never had a visitor from America before."

"I wanna thank you so much for inviting us, Mrs. Anderson," said Martha.

"No worries, love, and please call me Barbara. We don't stand on ceremony 'ere, you know. You're a long way from home in a strange land."

"It doesn't feel strange to me," Martha said, "I love it here."

Beth sat next to her father warming her hands around a mug of steaming tea and staring fondly at him. "We all live too far from home," she said.

Her father nodded in agreement.

I chewed the corner of a piece of toast. "Hey, I'm farther

away than anybody."

"You're a Pommie. That doesn't count." Beth put her thumbs in her ears, wiggled her hands and stuck out her tongue in jest.

"Beth, be nice," said Barbara. "He's an Englishman. There's a big difference."

"It's lovely to see the house full of young people," Brian whispered. Beth gave him a hug. He appeared a troubled soul.

The family trotted off to the wedding of Francie Noonan (an old school friend of Glynis and Beth) to Terry Scurfield, an up-and-coming star of Rugby League who played for a top team in Sydney called the Parramatta Eels.

Martha, Dave, and I were not officially invited, so we went instead to the Parkes radio telescope, recently immortalized in the movie *The Dish*. The giant dish stood in a remote paddock ten miles north of Parkes, surrounded by leaping lambs – but just a couple of years earlier, on Monday 21st July 1969, it was one giant leap for mankind. An estimated six hundred million people, one-fifth of the planet, watched Neil Armstrong's first steps on the Moon. The signals were relayed to Mission Control at Houston from this very spot. Relating this remote location to one of the seminal moments of the 20th century boggled the mind.

The three of us motored back to Parkes to join the revelers at a post-wedding reception party in the local RSL club. The impressive building was filled with wall-to-wall poker machines, and we heard the strains of a local pop group bashing out the songs of the day. The Hells Angel, a fish out of water, headed straight for the bar.

There were many pretty country girls on the dance floor, including Beth and Glynis, but I had eyes only for Martha. We danced to fast numbers, we danced to slow numbers. I could feel a magnetism that I had never experienced with any girl before. When the slow dances ended I was reluctant to let her go and she seemed reluctant for me to do so. I think I fell in love with her that night.

We returned to the Andersons' in the wee hours. Barbara

made a pot of tea and handed out mugs of the steaming muddy brew. The country life proved too much for the Hells Angel, who passed out on the carpet, his tattoo-covered stomach exposed to all.

Martha sat close to me on the floor. "What a great day!"

The stereo was playing something by Tony Joe White, but Beth changed the record. "Leaving on a Jetplane" wafted forth.

Martha noticed a change in my mood. "You OK, John?"

"That song reminds me of home. They were playing it a lot before I left England. Makes me think of my girlfriend... ex-girlfriend."

"That's so sweet." She said it like she meant it. "Do you keep in touch with her?"

"No. Not really."

The next morning, when we assembled for the dash back to Sydney, Beth informed our group she wasn't returning with us.

"I have to stay. Dad's not well."

"What's wrong?" Martha asked.

"He's haunted by North Africa and what he saw there during the war. Sometimes he's with us, sometimes he's back there."

Martha put her arms around Beth and gave her a hug. "You need to look after him," she said. "My father died when I was 17."

"Beth's the only one who can reach him when he's like this," Barbara said as she emerged from the kitchen carrying a stack of sandwiches wrapped in greaseproof paper.

"My Dad was in Burma during the war. He saw some terrible things." I said.

"Yes they saw and did things that we can never truly understand," Mrs Anderson said with a sympathetic smile.

Now it would have been diagnosed as Post Traumatic Stress Disorder (PTSD) but then there was no diagnosis, so Brian Anderson and countless other veterans suffered in silence.

"Gee, I hope all of us being here wasn't too much for

him?" Martha asked.

"No, darl. He loves having younguns around. He wanted youse all to come. It takes him out of his self. I think it makes him realize what he suffered was worth it."

"That's so sad," said Martha.

"It is, love but it's life. I think sometimes he feels guilty about being alive while his mates died." She handed Martha the sandwiches. "For the road, love."

"Thank you so much." She spontaneously wrapped her slender arms around Barbara's shoulders and hugged her. "This is so nice of you."

"Please come and see us again!" We all knew she meant it.

The Anderson kids surrounded Dave's FJ Holden and raced it down the street until the car crested a hill and they disappeared from view. "Such great people," Martha said, speaking for all of us. "In this world, the ones with the least to give are often the most generous."

How right she was.

Somewhere near the Blue Mountains, I asked Martha, "Would you like to go out one night... to dinner or something?"

Before she dozed off with her head in my lap, she murmured, "Sure. I would love that..."

ALL THAT JAZZ

The sky grew dark and heavy as a storm busted in from the Tasman Sea, whipping the surface of the harbor into a frothy white cauldron. Ferries were blown away from exposed wharves and those deckhands unfortunate to be out in the worst of it were having a tough time.

I was on the *Karingal.* I gripped the guardrail, climbed to the wheelhouse and slid the door open.

"This is a bit dodgy, isn't it?"

"Na ... Just a blip on the radar, mate," said Georgie.

I was not reassured as the ferry was being tossed about like a cork in a bathtub.

"Georgie, can I ask you something?" A strong gust blew in torrents of spray.

"Yeah mate, fire away – but close that bloody door!"

I slid the door shut; the sudden quiet seemed almost cocoon-like. "Well, I've asked this girl out, her name's Martha. She's American and she's ... well... special, and I don't want to mess things up like I usually do ..."

"Come on, mate. I ain't got all day..." Georgie stared straight ahead into the gloom.

"Well, I'm not sure where to take her. You know... somewhere nice?"

"I'm the last person you should ask about wimmin – here, hang on to this." His hands didn't leave the wheel until mine were on it, then he opened the side door. A gust blew him back into the cabin.

"Jesus Christ! Gary, hold this bloody door open."

Gary grabbed the sliding door while Georgie stuck his head out and peered into the semi-darkness.

"His sheila's an Italian. She don't speak much English and he don't speak no Italiano," Gary shouted to me.

"Listen," Georgie said as Gary closed the door behind him, "There's only three things in life worth a carrot – eatin', drinkin' and bonkin' – and you don't need to talk to do any of 'em."

The creaking and straining of the rivets on the old wooden ferry drowned out the laughter.

"Get ready, mate. I'm gonna pull her in at Kirribilli." Georgie spun the wheel hard to starboard. "We'll ride the storm out there."

I put my yellow sou'wester back on, pulled the hood over my head and fastened all the buttons. The rain blew sideways as I made my way downstairs to the lower deck. I reached the exit gangway and pulled back the guardrail; in my right hand I coiled the flexible nylon rope that Hughie had issued to replace the regular sisal ropes that became hard and unbending in the rain – a "stiffie" in the lingua franca of the deckhand. The lights of Kirribilli wharf glowed ahead. Ernie cut the engine and *Karingal* swooshed eerily toward the pontoon. A strong gust ruffled the calmer water and stalled her forward momentum. I looked up to the wheelhouse. Georgie shouted something but his words were lost on the wind.

I heard the noise of Ernie cranking the engine, but the engine spluttered – and died.

Oh great… adrift in a leaky ferry in a cyclone! What a way to go!

Ernie cranked again and this time the engine erupted into life. Georgie circled *Karingal* through the driving rain. Lining up the bow with the end of the pontoon, he telegraphed for Ernie to cut the engine. The boat drifted in, but the swirling wind began to force her away from the pontoon again.

I stood in the stern gangway, swinging the loosely coiled rope back and forth, building momentum. The bollard slipped away…five… ten… fifteen feet abreast. I released the rope. It uncoiled fast, flat and long, and the eye snapped over the top of the bollard. I wrapped the other end around the t-bollard on deck. The nylon rope slipped through my hands, then tautened… fibers snapped and my hands burned; I feared the rope would break. But the ferry moved forward, swung inward and hit the wharf with a resounding thump that knocked me over. Picking myself up, I secured aft, then ran to secure the front end and put out a single gangplank. The passengers hustled down it.

One man patted me on the back. "What a relief…Roy Rogers couldn't have done better than that, son!"

Secure alongside Kirribilli wharf, Georgie, Gary, Ernie and I sat in the warmth of the wheelhouse and watched a waterspout sweep across the harbor, blowing small craft off moorings, capsizing others.

Georgie tipped his head sideways, smiled and winked at me. "Listen… you might try the Gap Tavern at Watsons's Bay. Wine her and dine her, mate. If she rejects youse after that, you can always end it all over the cliff there."

When my shift ended the following Saturday, I leaped ashore and strode briskly toward the top of the wharf, only to see the corpulent figure of Cedric Morganstern striding briskly toward me, his purple proboscis glowing like a beacon.

"You're working till midnight tonight," he said. He wasn't very polite about it. "Need someone to work the *Lady Edeline* with Merve Kramer and Ernie. The deckhand didn't turn up."

"Cedric, I have a date."

"Not my problem. You're on standby."

I wanted to say, "Bugger it. You'll have to get somebody else" but given the fact I had just returned from five weeks leave that I really wasn't due for, I kept quiet.

Cedric worked the evening shifts. An immaculate dresser,

he wore a grey three-piece suit, white shirt with Windsor-knotted tie and regulation white handkerchief poking from left breast pocket. Stashed in an inside pocket, he carried a silver hip flask that he took a swig from whenever he thought nobody was looking. The ferry crews had little respect for Cedric's authority because he was apt to panic in tricky situations; consequently, the law of averages being what they are, bad things tended to happen on his watch.

Martha sounded disappointed on the phone but accepted my apology with characteristic grace. Standing her up on our first date did not make me feel good.

Georgie did not look good. Arriving for work to take charge of the Jazz Boat, he appeared disheveled and unshaven and said barely a word as he climbed to the wheelhouse.

"What's up with Georgie?" I asked Don, the deckhand and skilled clarinet player who would have felt more at home playing with the jazz band onboard than at his paying day job.

"He's been drinking. Gary says his girlfriend left him because he drinks too much, so he drinks even more now. He'll be alright... if he doesn't drink no more."

The band struck up "When the Saints Go Marching in" and the Jazz Boat went sailing out, to be followed by the *Lady Edeline*, who for most of the evening ran back and forth to Mosman Bay, a picturesque inlet surrounded by old colonial and federation-style houses, gardens, trees and cliffs. On warm summer nights, the bay is laced with the sweet smell of frangipani and jasmine, but on this winter's night, the air was cold and damp and smelled of diesel fuel and blocked toilet. I sat above the engine bay with Ernie watching the crankshafts cranking and the piston rods pumping, trying to keep warm, hands clasped around a tin mug of tea frustrated at the way things were turning out.

"You'll be reet glad to to get home t'warm bed tonight, son," Ernie said with his thick Lancashire accent. "It's a miserable night to be out on the water. Neither one thing nor t'other. I almost prefer it when it's storming like it did the other night. Of course I saw some bad storms when I was in navy. I remember up on the South China Sea…" Ernie rambled on a bit, but I was in no frame of mind to listen. I just wanted to get back to the Lodge.

"Hardly worth doing this trip is it Ernie?" I interjected.

Ernie nodded toward a mound of shawls and headscarves rocking an old-fashioned 4-wheel pram at the rear of the cabin.

"There's only that old dutch. Aye, probably would've been cheaper to get her a taxi from Quay."

At Musgrave Street wharf I rolled out the gangplank for her. She struggled with the pram, so I lifted one end and helped her carry it ashore.

"Oh, thank you. Oh, I wish I didn't have to carry my babies up those steps in this weather. This thing is so heavy."

I looked at my watch; it was 11:30. "Hold on, Ernie. I'll be a couple of minutes."

A short flight of stairs ran up the cliff to a bus stop. I maneuvered the pram through the drizzle to the top.

"Would you like to see my babies, dear?"

I was cold and anxious to be away but in the hazy glow of a street-light, she peeled back the blankets to reveal several sets of green eyes staring up at me. There must have been six or seven kittens in there.

"How'd you like my babies, dear?" she asked.

"They're beautiful, Ma'am, just beautiful."

Bathed in the soft glow of the scaffold-covered Opera House, I coiled a rope by the rear gangway. I saw the Jazz Boat rounding Bennelong Point behind us. I heard the clang clang of the telegraph as Ernie slowed to half-speed, then to quarter-speed. The Jazz Boat drew alongside and overtook us. There was no clang clang from her telegraph. She was still running at full speed as she approached the wharf. *Lady Edeline* came to a stop on wharf number four, but the Jazz Boat did not stop. I watched in horror as she hit a wooden piling that served as a barrier to prevent ferries hitting the more solid concrete harbor wall rising behind it. The piling fractured and splintered, smoke billowed, the top of the bow caved in, passengers screamed.

Ernie and I ran across the wharf but could not see a

deckhand. We looked up to the wheelhouse and saw Don behind the wheel, not Georgie! The wharfhand tossed a line to a young woman and maneuvered a gangplank across the gap between ferry and wharf. Most of the passengers ignored the gangplank and leapt ashore.

Cedric Morganstern was in a state of total paralysis, his face gawping at the gaping hole in the bow while swirling around him was a maelstrom of flying trombones, trumpets, guitars and panicky passengers.

With his arm around Georgie's waist, Don staggered down the gangplank.

"What happened?" Ernie shouted.

Don shrugged. "Couldn't stop him boozing."

Georgie looked at us through rheumy eyes. "Ah go get fucked, you mongrels…" His words trailed off as Don helped him up the wharf toward a taxi.

Most of the passengers hung around to witness the demise of the ferry. Fortunately for Cedric it remained afloat; unfortunately for Georgie, one night of idiocy wrecked his career.

I was wrecked by the time I got back to the Lodge. En route to my room, I stopped and put an ear to Martha's door. Detecting no signs of life, I moved on and fell into bed, exhausted. But I could not sleep, I tossed and turned, fretting over Georgie's fate.

The next morning I rapped on Martha's door. When it opened, my mouth opened to speak but no words came out. I just stared. I had only seen Martha in jeans, but now she wore a mini-dress, her hair nicely done and wearing make-up. She looked stunning.

"Martha, look I'm so sorry about last night…"

Before I had time to complete my sentence a tall, muscular man strode through the door. Martha smiled at him too.

"John. I'd like you to meet Ross, a friend of mine."

I stuck my hand out, but Ross ignored it. I swallowed hard, rubbed my jaw and pushed back the errant cowlick.

"Ross and I met when I was living in Surfers."

Ross continued to ignore me. He took Martha's arm and whisked her away, leaving me staring in their wake. My world crashing around me, I felt empty and fragile and wondered if I had missed the boat with Martha.

I wish I could have missed the boat that Hughie had scheduled me for that afternoon. The harbor cruise, normally a cushy number, had the mood of a funeral on a wet day. Georgie, already suspended, awaited a Maritime Services Board tribunal. Most of us had already predicted the outcome.

Cruising through Rose Bay, I leaned over the prow and gloomily watched the streamlined 18-footers flying ahead of the wind, their crewmen hanging by a toenail out over the water. A canny skipper tacked right under our bow to gain an advantage over his opponents. Merve Kramer, our skipper for the day, gave him a blast on the horn, but he did not care because he had stolen an edge on the competition. Steam gives way to sail on the harbor.

Wondering how I could steal an edge on my competition, I saw steam of a different kind billowing up from the galley. The kettle was boiling. I went down and made coffee for Ernie, a man who always dressed immaculately. Never a drop of oil touched his pristine boiler suit, so white I needed sunglasses to ward off the glare. But when I handed him a mug of the steaming brew, the boat lurched to starboard and the contents of the mug spilled out. What is most remarkable is how none of it landed on the floor or me. It all landed in Ernie's lap. Ignoring his reaction, I bolted up the stairway to see what had happened. I looked port-side: Nobody in sight. I looked starboard: The decks were jammed with passengers staring at the shoreline.

Unable to see anything, I entered the wheelhouse where Merve was peering through a spyglass.

"What's going on?" I said.

"Lady Jane Beach, mate. Don't you read the papers?"

He handed me the spyglass, and in the excitement I peered through the wrong end, and couldn't see a thing.

Merve turned it around. "It'll work better this way, mate!"

He was right about that.

"They've just made nude bathing legal at Lady Jane... biggest tourist attraction in Sydney."

Through the spyglass, the beach appeared to be light on nudes but heavy on voyeurs. Every pervert in Sydney was armed to the teeth with binoculars and telephoto lenses, peering from behind rocks, hanging over cliffs, dangling from branches of trees and gawping from boats.

Ernie appeared on the scene. Not wishing to ruin his image, he had changed into another set of whiter-than-white overalls. "I suppose they're just airing their differences, aye."

"Keeping abreast of the times," I retorted.

Merve was disdainful of the whole thing. "Those that should, don't. Those that shouldn't, do." He folded his spyglass and steered the boat away from shore.

Times were indeed changing fast in Sydney.

I visited great aunt Mary after work. She could tell I was down. "Penny for 'em, son?"

I related the events of the past week at work and tried to explain my feelings about Martha. "I didn't realize how I felt about her till I saw her with this other bloke!"

"If you really like her, dear, let her know how you feel. If it don't work out, at least you've tried. Better to have loved and lost than never loved at all." Her words echoed back through the generations. She seemed to understand and always offered kindness when I needed it most.

So with her encouraging words, and my confidence boosted by a few cans of cousin John's ale, I walked the mile or so from her house in North Bondi to my digs in Bondi Beach. It started to rain halfway home. Soaked to the skin and with my shoes squelching, I passed Martha's open door. I glanced in. Martha and Ross were sitting close together on the edge of the bed talking animatedly. They did not see me.

I locked myself in my room, lay on the bed and contemplated the ceiling fan whirling above.

MRS. MACQUARIE'S CHAIR

Karingal glided through the early morning mist carpeting Mosman Bay. *Karingal* in aboriginal means "Happy Camp," but I did not feel like a happy camper. I sat on a life raft below the wheelhouse, feeling cold and sorry for myself watching a coxless four slide silently across our path.

I closed my eyes but the sound of swishing propellers jolted them open again. I jumped up and ran along the gangway in time to throw the rope, secure the ferry and pull on the plank. Through the gloom I saw Georgie, but not the happy-go-lucky face I knew. I ran down the plank ahead of the few passengers.

"Gosh it's good to see you," I told him.

"I knew you was on this run. Just came by to apologize and say goodbye."

"There's no need for apologies."

"Yeah, there is. Don told me what I said. A bloke should never speak to his mates that way."

"No offence was taken. What are you going to do?"

"I'm off home to Brisbane after the tribunal. Thanks for bein' a good mate."

"I wish there's something I could do."

Georgie looked sheepishly down at his feet. "Look mate, the tribunal's a witch-hunt. I've got about as much chance of

237

getting off as I have of pushing a pound of butter up a parrot's arse with a hot needle!" His eyes met mine and he grinned.

I laughed so hard, tears streamed down my face and mucous flowed out of my nose. It took me five minutes to recover.

"You alright mate? You wanna lie down for a bit?"

"I'm sorry, but nobody can make me laugh like you do!"

"You'll live a long life if ya keep laughing."

"I'll miss you."

"I'll miss you too – and all the other blokes – but there's no defense for being drunk in charge of a passenger ferry. I used up me nine lives on this job long ago." He winked mischievously. "Now it's time to start the next nine!"

He extended his arm as if to shake hands but changed his mind and hugged me instead, then he strode away and vanished in the mist.

My head was in a mist so after work, I walked through the Botanic Gardens and sat at a spot known as Mrs. Macquarie's Chair, a pile of rocks overlooking the harbor and favorite contemplative spot of the wife of one of the early governors of Australia, Lachlan Macquarie, who was known as the "father of Australia." From this vantage point one would normally see the familiar ferries ply back and forth, the sail-like roofs of the opera house and Pinchgut Island where 18th-century convicts were incarcerated on starvation rations. But I did not see anything. I felt incarcerated myself, trapped in my own body, a prisoner of my emotions. My brain kept telling me it was time I returned to England. I missed home and family, but mostly my mother's counsel. I always did when things were going south. She accepted me the way I was, no matter what.

I picked up a large pebble and hurled it over the rocks below. Narrowly missing the head of a Chinese fisherman, it splashed into Sydney Harbor and sank. I watched the ripples subside and the surface return to normal.

"Anytime you think you're indispensable or get a bit big for your boots," Mr. Tittensor once said, "stick your hand in a bucket of water. When you pull it out, see how big a hole it leaves."

Georgie and Martha had left a pretty big hole in my bucket and a veritable tidal wave of ripples.

I felt a tap on my left shoulder. I swiveled around.

"Hi!"

My mouth hung open for a moment. "How... how... did you know I was...?"

"I didn't," Martha said cheerily. "It's really weird, but for some reason, I don't know why, I was waiting for the bus, then I just started walking through the park. I've never been here before."

"Like some kind of guiding force?"

"Yeah, kind of, but I'm not into all that stuff."

"No. Nor am I, but I have to say I have had similar feelings since I've been in Australia."

We sat down on Mrs. Macquarie's very hard chair.

"What happened? I expected to see you last night," Martha said.

"Oh, I went to my great aunt's after work. I saw you with Ross when I got home, but you were deep in conversation and I...I didn't want to disturb you."

Martha looked mildly surprised. "Ross?"

"Yes. I saw you both sitting on the bed."

"Look, he turned up out of the blue; I had no idea he was in town – evidently, Colleen told him where I was. We had a brief relationship in Surfers Paradise but..."

"But what?"

"He was too possessive for my liking. He thought he owned me," she continued, "so I put him on the train back to Surfers. I think he got the message."

I felt a sudden surge of well-being dissipate my gloom. I grabbed her hand and pulled her up. We started walking.

"So should we try again? Where would you like to go? Same place?" I asked.

She kissed me on the cheek. "Sounds wonderful."

"I'll book it. Is Saturday OK with you?"

"Why wait? Let's go tonight."

I was flummoxed, unused to spontaneity. "Well, why not!"

We ate and danced at the tavern until the small hours of the morning. Then we walked up to the Gap, a rocky cliff overlooking the entrance to Sydney Harbor, where the wind nearly took us away. The waves crashed below against the jagged rocks where many a jilted lover had ended it all.

"My friend Georgie said that if I didn't make it with you, I could always throw myself over the edge here."

She laughed. "Well, you won't need to do that now, will you?"

I took Martha to tea with great aunt Mary and cousin John, studiously managing to avoid knocking the strawberry jam onto the creamy white carpet again.

I had never seen my great aunt smile so much. As we left the little suburban semi, she beckoned to Martha and whispered something in her ear, which made Martha smile too.

"What did she say?" I asked as we walked back to the Lodge.

"That's between your great aunt and me. I'll tell you someday."

Martha's smile could soften the hardest heart; she possessed a unique ability to radiate warmth and good feeling wherever she went. I had never met anyone quite like her.

I'd never met anyone who liked to sing first thing in the morning either. I'd be sitting in the breakfast room with the toast popping, the eggs sizzling and the Rice Crispies crackling, as Martha's voice wafted along the corridor well before she came into view.

Oh, what a beautiful morning,
Oh, what a beautiful day!

"Jeez," Glynis looked at me one day. "Are all bloody Yank's like Martha?"

"I can't answer that – she's the only one I've known."

Martha waltzed into the room, a smile on her face.

I got a wonderful feeling,
Everythings going my way…

"She's as happy as a clam every bloody day," griped Beth.

"Good morning, Sunshine!" Martha responded.

"We were all wondering how you can be so jolly first thing in the morning," Lennie asked, "…it takes all my energy to roll over and throw the alarm clock at the wall!"

"I dunno. My Mom and Dad were morning persons. My Dad always got up at 5:30 every day, so I guess I inherited it from them. It's my favorite time of day."

"I do twenty press-ups every morning," I said.

Martha looked at me with some skepticism. "You do?" She responded.

"Yes… and then I do the other eyelid!"

Martha laughed an infectious and robust laugh that complimented her smile.

For the first time since I arrived in Australia, I realized I was as happy as a clam too, assuming clams are happy. I'm not sure anybody has asked one.

One wet morning, as I ushered travelers off the *Lady Denman* following an upriver trip to Greenwich, I observed a well-dressed young man disembarking. I realized it was Jerome Duncanson, a wealthy neighbor from my village, West Grinstead. A vague flash of recognition spread across his face. After we exchanged pleasantries, he informed this grubby individual in oilskins holding the gangplank steady that he was on a world trip, a graduation present from his parents.

"No time to get together for a beer, old chap. I'm leaving for Fiji tonight… then Tahiti and the States!"

How the other half live.

Later Martha and I had tea at Vaucluse House, the historic home of the Wentworths who'd done much to open up New South Wales by finding a route through the Blue Mountains. As I stuffed a scone in my mouth and gazed into Martha's blue eyes, I thought: *You know, John, you are the lucky one. Forget the money, the lightning world tour. I doubt Jerome will experience what I have experienced in the last two years, nor be as happy as I am at this moment.*

Martha and I became inseparable. We rode the roller

coaster at the famous Luna Park fairgrounds, danced till dawn at the Texas Tavern in Kings Cross, breakfasted at the American Pancake House. I took her to see *Jesus Christ Superstar*. We swam at Bondi and Bronte. I burned the candle at both ends and developed a bad habit of turning up for work late – or worse, not turning up for work at all.

Hughie cornered me one morning and justifiably gave me the roasting of my life, then sent me round to talk to Bill Anderson, the General Manager.

I was mad, but more at myself than anyone else. I knocked on Bill's door expecting the worst.

"You'd better pull your socks up, mate. You've missed too many days and been late once too often. You used to be bloody reliable. What happened?" he scolded.

There was nothing I could say in my defense because he was right. Bill continued, "Too many blokes have had to cover for you. I'm moving you back on the wharf for a while." This was the ferry service equivalent of a hundred lashes. I did not know whether to laugh or cry. "I was gonna fire you, but Hughie put in a good word."

"Hughie did?"

"Yes, he did. He says you're a good deckhand."

"Hughie said that?"

Bill nodded. "That's praise indeed from him."

I was sweeping the wharf midway through my banishment when I spied Gary sitting on a bench, nicely dressed in a suit, reading a book.

"What are you reading?"

He lifted the cover of the book to reveal it was *Moby Dick*.

"I'm impressed."

"Yeah, mate, it's a great book. Steph passed it on to me. Don't understand all of it, but I can read it!"

"Who's Steph?"

"Stephanie. She's me… I mean *my teacher*! She's a pommie like you. We've bin seeing a bit of each other, like."

"What about Layla?"

Gary frowned. "She's history, mate."

"You're kidding."

"I'm not; she was a bloody gold digger. Ran off with a salami salesman, according to Freddie – he's well shot of her, too!"

Gary looked deadly serious and then grinned when he saw my bemused face.

"I'm a different man now, thanks to Steph."

Gary spun round as a ferry arrived. A plain-looking blonde-haired girl walked down the plank.

"Here she is now. We're off to the theatre. See you, mate."

Hughie arrived just in time to see Gary and Stephanie walking arm in arm up the wharf. "Who'd have thought that, aye?"

I just shook my head.

Hughie hovered over me. I waited for him to find fault in some minor detail in the way I swept the litter into my long-handled dustpan but instead he said quietly, "Did you hear about Georgie Ellis?"

I looked up. "No."

"The verdict's out. The Maritime Services Board have stripped him of his Ferry Master's license and banned him for life from skippering a boat on Sydney Harbor."

I wasn't surprised.

"You know," Hughie said, "no matter what these bludgers might think, I liked the bugger."

You could've fooled me.

Most of my daily thoughts were filled by Martha, who projected a strong independent spirit, a contagious, all-American confidence that was beginning to rub off on me. Confinement to the wharf turned out to be a lucky break because I worked mostly day shifts, so my evenings were free to spend with her now.

One of those free evenings, two new arrivals at the Lodge, Barry and Graham, invited us to play squash with them at an RSL club. Unimpressed with the jogging craze sweeping the world, I had taken up squash as a fun way of keeping fit. Only one court was available so while we waited, Martha and I wandered into a recreation room next door, ordered beers and started a game of table tennis instead. Attempting to impress her with my control of spin, I threw the ball high in the air and cut across it with the smooth rubberized face of the paddle. But instead of the ball flying back over the net, it flew up into the rafters.

Martha seemed a little detached and looked un-characteristically pensive.

Maybe she takes ping-pong a bit more seriously than I do? Perhaps Nixon's ping-pong diplomacy was getting to her.

When I went for the second serve, she interrupted me mid-flight. "John, I have something to tell you."

The ball landed, but flew by her to rattle around the legs of a snooker table.

"What's she doing 'ere?" An ancient, scrawny, semi-paralytic individual sidled over.

"Are you talking to us?" Martha said.

"Too bloody right. Women aren't allowed in 'ere, you know?"

"No, I didn't know." Martha's calm face reflected no outward signs of indignation.

"Not against the law, is it?" I said, rising to my full height of 5'9⅝". He pointed a gnarly finger at Martha, but looked at me.

"Well, it's a bloody unwritten law 'ere, mate. Blokes like to go somewhere to get away from the missus and the nagging."

"If you were my husband, I'd like to go somewhere to get away from you!" Martha quipped.

The old man's veins stood out on his neck.

"We're not interfering with you. We're just playing table tennis." I chipped in.

The reddish splotches on the old man's face melded into one big splotch and he began to hop around like a boxer waiting for the bell. "Just bloody well get her out of – HERE!" He spoke slowly, building up to the last word, which he said very loudly.

Martha fixed him with a concerned look. "Take it easy; you'll burst a blood vessel."

She smiled that trademark easy, warm smile, but the old man was too far gone, so it had the reverse effect.

Staggering toward me, his arms flailing like a demented threshing machine, he yelled, "Fuckin' pommie moron – get her out of here."

One of the flailing arms flailed in the direction of my head.

An embarrassed mate stepped forward from the bar, grabbed the old man by the collar and pulled him away.

"I'm sorry, love... he always gets like this when he's pissed. I'd like to buy youse all a beer by way of apologizing. Not all Aussies are like him."

"Gee, thanks. I sure hope he's all right," Martha replied.

She had taken no offence. She was like that; nothing much bothered her, and she always accepted an apology with good grace.

She looked at me, smiled and said, "Thanks."

Never comfortable with compliments, I shrugged and said stupidly, "For what?"

"For sticking up for me."

"What was it you had to tell me before we were so rudely interrupted?"

She took a breath, picked up her paddle and whacked a ball back across the net toward an invisible opponent, then she put the bat down.

"Oh... nothing. It can wait."

A few days later, Martha and Glynis were in the laundry, their backs toward me, piling their clothes into the washer. I was about to announce myself when I heard Glynis say, "Have you told Johnno yet?"

I stepped back from the doorway.

Martha did not reply.

Glynis continued, "Oh, like that, is it?"

The washing machine started to swish.

Martha said, "I haven't yet..."

I stepped into the doorway. Glynis saw me first, flashed a sympathetic smile, said, "I'm outta here!" and scooted from the room.

Martha turned. "Oh! John... I..." Her eyes suddenly became moist but she looked me straight in the eye. "... John, I'm going home."

"You're what?"

"I'm going home."

My measure of shock was akin to that of a man picking the winning lottery numbers and then realizing he'd forgotten to submit the entry form.

"Is it because of me?"

"No, no, it's just that my mother has sent me a ticket."

"When do you leave?" I managed to ask through the turmoil I felt.

"In two weeks. My Mom wants me and my brothers home for Christmas. I tried to tell you the other night, but..."

The washing machine was making gurgling noises. I nodded toward the suds emerging from the top. "You'd better take care of that."

"Oh shit." She ignored it and said, "Look, I'm coming back. I love it here and... I love you."

I took a deep breath and let it out slowly. I felt sick and words deserted me.

A gaggle of friends and acquaintances descended on Kingsford-Smith Airport and sat in the same lounge where I sent off my cousin Tor. Then it had been filled with sad-faced mothers and sweethearts farewelling their young men who were shipping out for Vietnam. Things had not changed much in a year and a half: another group of National Servicemen, another group of mothers and sweethearts. Same picture. Same war. One extra sad face.

After a blaze of flashbulbs, a mass of hugs, wet Kleenex and an awkward kiss goodbye, Martha's Pan Am 707 was winging through the air toward California, while all the air had left my sails.

I unlocked the door to my empty room at Nyah Lodge, fell

on the bed and buried my head in the pillow. At that moment, I did not know what to feel. I wondered if her mother might be unhappy that her beautiful, talented daughter had taken up with a long-haired deckhand on a Sydney Harbor Ferry. Martha did not possess a return ticket.

STIFF MEDICINE

Prior to Christmas 1971, thoughts about my future weighed above all others. Rudi's words came back to taunt me: "You need a degree to get good career."

A career in what? Tell me, punk!

I had no idea. The past two years in Australia had only taught me what not to do with my life. It had toughened me. It had taught me self-reliance. But now, some of the old doubts began to creep back and I retreated into myself. However, a couple of random events jolted me out again.

Hughie shanghaied me for a dawn run up the Parramatta River to Greenwich. Steaming under the harbor bridge, I stood alongside the skipper, Gerry Onions, a dour, humorless Kiwi whose conversation never amounted to much more than a one-word answer, or failing that, a grunt – oh, how I missed Georgie's irreverent jocularity. A police launch floated off to our starboard side.

"Another poor bugger whose had enough of this mortal coil," said Gerry dryly.

"What do you mean?"

Two policemen were hauling something out of the water. On closer inspection, I could see it was a naked body.

"Suicide jumper. Haven't you seen one before?"

It was the body of a young woman; her blonde hair streaked with seaweed, her face blue and puffy.

"No."

"You're lucky. On average there's one or two a month – I even had one land on the deck once, not a pretty sight. It's amazin' how the human body breaks up even if it lands in the water."

"Really!" I was unable to divert my eyes from the young woman. She looked at peace.

"Yep. It's like jumping into concrete from that height. Don't know what makes 'em do it in the first place, but there's no shortage of 'em."

A few days later, I stood in the pouring rain waiting for a bus in front of the Bondi Hotel. An ambulance pulled up, medics ran inside, then wheeled out a dead man on a stretcher, his weathered face staring blankly skyward. I read in the paper that evening his name was Jack Haines, a once-famous middleweight boxer; in the 1930s, Ambrose Palmer, a more famous middleweight boxer, had knocked the stuffing out of Haines and put an end to his career. Standing there with the rain dripping down my neck watching another stiff being carted away, my petty problems seemed just that – petty problems. Martha had often said, *It takes forty-two muscles to frown, but only eight to smile* (of course, it only takes four to extend your arm and punch somebody's lights out, but I opted for the middle ground).

With my third year in Australia approaching, I decided it was time to return to England. I missed my family and friends. I missed the familiar surroundings of home – the farm, the horses, the green of the English countryside – I missed them more than I had for a long time. I felt I needed to get some perspective. I had seen England only through the eyes of a child and an adolescent; now that I was an adult (or thought I was) I wanted to weigh my options vis-à-vis the two countries, although I felt strongly that Australia would play a role in my future.

I paid a visit to the offices of the Wilhelmsen Shipping Line in downtown Sydney to see about working my passage home.

A lanky, studious Dane said in precise English, "We do take young men as crewmen on our cargo ships but…"

He pulled out a large file and tossed it on the desk; pages spilled out, containing names of young men with the same idea as myself.

"…little chance of getting anything this year. Sorry!"

Time to put plan B into action – except I didn't have a plan B yet.

I did have a plan to meet Lindy Eliot. She'd sent me a letter saying she would be in Sydney for a brief visit to do some Christmas shopping; the gorgeous Elisabeth Mackay would be accompanying her. Maybe this was a sign from the Gods: When one door closes, another one opens.

On a steamy afternoon I waited for a bus at Circular Quay for the short ride up Elizabeth Street to St. James Station, where I had arranged to meet them. I crammed into the bus at rush hour, so it was standing room only.

The driver yelled, "Everyone move to the rear please, make room for those that's trying to get aboard."

I ended up wedged between a fat lady and a man whose garlicky breath left me in no doubt as to what he had eaten for lunch; the bus was so hot that the ceiling dripped with condensation from all the overheated bodies. As this sauna on wheels crawled up Elizabeth Street at a pace an arthritic snail would have had no difficulty keeping up with, I realized there was going to be a problem: How was I going to get off?

I could see the girls walking alongside the bus – in fact, they were moving decidedly faster than the bus itself. I yanked an arm free and pulled the cord, then fought through the mass of people who were not trying to get off. There were murmurings all around me: *"Bloody galah"* and *"There's always one isn't there?"*

When I reached the driver, he said bluntly, "Didn't you read the sign? This is an express bus; only one stop, at Kings Cross, before Bondi."

"An express?" It must have been the slowest express on earth. "Oh great. Can't you open the doors and just let me out?"

"Rules is rules, mate. If I get caught, I could lose me job. If I open these doors, there'll be twenty people scrambling to get on."

I saw his point but it did not help as I gazed out through the closed doors and saw the girls slowly slipping away. I waved but they didn't see me. I felt like Zhivago seeing his great love Lara from a bus and not being able to make contact. He ended up dying of a heart attack for his efforts, but fortunately that fate did not befall me.

I jumped off at Kings Cross and sprinted back down William Street to Elizabeth Street, but when I got to St. James Station, they were nowhere to be seen, so I missed Elisabeth on Elizabeth Street. Something mildly ironic about that, I thought.

Christmas 1971 was to be a lonely one as great aunt Mary and cousin John were flying to Melbourne. Just before they left I went round for lunch. John was at work and Mary was not her usual chirpy self – in fact she seemed unusually quiet. She sat opposite me spooning chokoes onto a plate filled with roast lamb and roast potatoes.

"Are you OK?" I asked.

"I'm worried about you, now that Martha's gone," she replied.

"Well, I'm trying to put a brave face on it but I really miss her."

She poured some brown gravy over the meat and handed me the plate.

"I know how it feels to lose someone you care about but…" She put one potato, a thin slice of lamb and half a choko on her own plate. "Come on, tuck in, don't wait for me."

The lamb melted in my mouth. Great aunt Mary was a wonderful cook. I would have probably starved without her and Jippy, the Chinese wrestler-cum-restauranteur.

"Don't give up on Martha, son. She's a wonderful girl!"

Aunt Mary played with her food, shoving the potato from

one side of the plate to the other, making a little trail through the gravy. When she looked up, I felt as though she was about to open her heart to me.

"My best friend just passed away," she told me.

"I'm so sorry. "

"Massive kidney failure, the doctor said."

"Had she been ill for long?"

"Yes. She'd been in and out of hospital. She were addicted to Bex powders, you see, and it eventually destroyed her kidneys." Mary smiled for a moment. "They used to say to stressed housewives – *take a cup of tea, a Bex and have a good lie down* – well, Doris did that for years, but when the doctors realized it were addictive and the massive doses of phenacetin these women had put into their bodies caused kidney disease, it were too late for Doris to do anything about it. Her kidneys had had it."

"So she knew her days were numbered?"

"We all knew she was just hanging on, but it doesn't make it any easier. She was my oldest friend here; we'd known each other for fifty years."

Mary looked away and sighed. Another sadness in a lifetime of sadnesses.

"Still, I don't suppose I'll be much longer for this world either."

"Don't say that, Auntie."

"Time's catching up with me so facts have to be faced. I'm 78 years old and not in the best of health. I'm not scared of death. The only thing that worries me is what will become of John. He's always had me to look after him."

The conversation upset me. Great aunt Mary lingered in my mind throughout that Christmas. I had grown to love and respect her since the day I turned up on her doorstep with the Boer War suitcase.

Like great aunt Mary, most of the residents of Nyah Lodge fled the city for the holidays, but I declined all invitations and elected to work a double shift. The triple-time on offer for working Christmas Day, Boxing Day and New Year's Day would go a long way toward an airline ticket home.

Skeleton crews manned a few ferries carrying a few passengers. The deckies brought along eskies crammed with beer; the ladies who manned the ticket booths supplied the food. Even Hughie was in a good mood – he ignored the drinking, something that normally would make him livid. In the evening, deckhand Reg Golding brought in some of his homemade wine – a migrant from Liverpool, Reg commuted an hour and a half on the train every day from Seven Hills. I thought it an appropriate place for him to live; being a good Catholic he had seven children – one for each hill! I supped on his plum wine, alcoholic content unknown, wishing I was anywhere but where I was when –

"John. Are you there, John? Does anyone know if John's working today?"

I hustled through the throng of late-night Christmas revelers heading home.

"Yes. I'm here Robert."

"Giddai, Johnno."

Robert Leman, a big man, always looked dapper in his off-white tropical suit and dark sunglasses. I gave him my arm and the crowds parted to let the three of us through – the other member of the party was Goldie, his faithful yellow lab, companion and guide dog.

Robert played the harmonica on television variety shows and the club circuit so he was something of a celebrity. Hughie had introduced me to him early on and designated me to help him negotiate the turnstiles and the gangplanks. Not that Robert needed much help, as Goldie did a wonderful job, but I think Robert liked the company. For all his faults, Hughie showed great kindness toward Robert.

There were only a few passengers on the *Lady Woodward* so I found Robert a prime seat on the foredeck.

"John, why don't you ride over with me? You'll be back in half an hour." Robert must have sensed Hughie lurking on the wharf. "Alright if John comes across with me, Hughie?" His powerful voice matched his size. "Goldie's a bit off today. I could use some help at Cremorne."

"Er…" Hughie's face contorted and he gnawed on what remained of the nails on his left hand. "Yes, we'll cover for him here."

Lady Woodward surged through the balmy night air, as streaks of lightning flashed around the harbor, illuminating the sails of the Opera House so it resembled some sort of futuristic pirate ship.

"That'll be quite a building when they get around to finishing it!" I said.

"I hope I'm still around to play in it," Robert replied.

I paid scant attention to his remark as I stared in awe at the magnificent building and realized how privileged I was to have it as one of the cornerstones of my workplace. They eventually finished it, of course – sixteen years after it was first designed, eleven years later than originally planned, and $100 million over budget. The Danish architect Joern Utzon quit before completion of the project and never saw the final masterpiece that became an architectural hallmark of the twentieth century. The Queen opened it in 1973. The final cost: $105 million, paid for by lottery money.

The wind stung my eyes but Robert liked the feel of the salty air in his face.

"So what have you done to get her back?" Robert asked, taking me by surprise.

"What do you mean?"

"Look, mate. Martha's been gone a month." He turned to face me. It felt like his blind eyes were burning through me from behind his sunglasses.

"Well, I've written her two letters saying how much I love her!"

Goldie lay on the smooth deck at his feet, her eyes darting this way and that, ever observant, ever looking out for her master. Robert felt for her head and gave her an affectionate rub behind the ears.

"Like I said, what have you done?"

"What do you mean, what have I done?" I began to get

mildly irritated. I stood up and leaned against the rail. It wasn't just the wind from a passing hydrofoil that rocked me off balance. "She lives 6,000 miles away. Short of going over there and banging on her mother's front door, I'm not sure what I can do."

Robert nodded sagely. Goldie lifted her head to look at me quizzically.

"I've been lost without her," I admitted.

"I know you have."

"How do you know?"

"Just because I can't see through these things," – he touched the dark lenses – "doesn't mean I'm blind. I've been in love too, you know."

I felt a little uneasy. A small crowd had gathered around Robert. Some who knew him were attracted by his ebullient personality; others, who didn't, were often drawn in by Goldie, but many just travelled on the ferry with him and enjoyed his company. This particular group seemed to be hanging on his every word.

"So what do you suggest?" I asked.

Robert pulled out a harmonica and blew the opening few bars to *Granada*. When he pulled the harmonica away from his mouth, little rivulets of spit ran down his chin. A lady friend dabbed them with her handkerchief.

"There is such a device as a telephone, you know. It's been around for at least seventy years. You know, you speak through one end and words come out the other end…"

The crowd laughed but I just cringed. Robert liked an audience. I hated it, but he was in the moment.

"John, I don't mean to sound facetious, but just give her a ring."

"But it costs about ten dollars for three minutes – that's a week's rent!" Instantly regretting what I had just said, I sensed some hostility from the crowd.

"So? Look… How much do you love her?"

I did not wish to divulge my most intimate thoughts to an audience, so I said nothing. That didn't stop Robert, however.

"Sleep on a park bench for a week. Do you know how many songs are written about love?"

"I have no idea."

Lady Woodward ploughed into the wake of a cargo ship causing a shower of spray to cascade over the bows.

"Ninety percent of all songs written about anything are about love, so as a musician, I think I am something of an expert. I'm not necessarily lucky in love but I do consider myself an expert nevertheless."

"So I give her a ring and then what?"

"Use your head. She knows you love her, but she needs that little bit extra. You know you don't want to be a deckie all your life – not that there's anything wrong with being a deckhand, but I sense it's just a stepping stone for you. You know that, but does she? Tell her of your ambitions, your hopes and dreams. Tell her what you aspire to in the future – and tell her mother too!"

The ferry pulled in at Cremorne Point, where the little white lighthouse cast a bright light over the harbor and illuminated the dark, tree-covered hillside above the point. Robert and his small crowd of admirers disembarked.

I hung back, a little embarrassed that he had exposed my innermost feelings for all to see.

Robert yelled back to me from the wharf, "You've got the picture now, Johnno?"

"Yes. Thank you Robert!"

He vanished into the darkness but his voice came drifting back: "I want a full report, Johnno! Oh, and have a very Merry Christmas!"

TELEPHONE BLUES

Thousands of people lined the harbor foreshores, many with picnic hampers filled with whatever was left from Christmas Day. They were waiting for the start of the Sydney-to-Hobart Yacht race, one of the world's great ocean races. The best place to get up close and personal was on the harbor and the ferry service provided a grandstand seat.

I crewed on the *Karingal* with Arthur and Ernie. The small ferry kept her distance from the eighty-nine big yachts jockeying for position behind the starting line. The cannon boomed and the fleet moved ponderously down the harbor while *Karingal* followed at a suitable distance, amid an armada of pleasure craft that far outnumbered the craft in the actual race. The forest of tall masts and colorful sails rounded South Head and out into the Pacific, where spinnakers were hoisted like Mum's laundry on a blustery day. The fleet headed south for Tasmania.

I headed south to a phone booth in Bondi.

In the 21st Century, distance is overcome with the click of a mouse or with a cell phone, but in the early 1970s the personal computer was at least a decade and a half away, and one had to book an international call in advance – and it *did* cost a week's rent. The alternative was to write a letter; from Australia, it took a minimum of one week to reach a foreign destination and, if the planets were aligned, another week to get a response. Luck rode with me that day because I managed to snag a three-minute overseas phone booking that someone had cancelled at the last minute.

My pockets bulging with enough loose change to sink a battleship, I stood outside the Bondi post office divesting myself of it into the meter of a pay phone.

"Hi! This is Martha." The identification was unnecessary as there was no mistaking that cheery voice.

"Martha, its John, I just thought I'd ring…"

"Oh my God, John, is everything OK?"

"Yes, everything's fine, but it would be a lot better if you were here. I miss you."

"That's so sweet. I …" *Crackle…crackle…hiss…*

"Martha listen, I want you to come back. I don't know exactly what I want to do about the future, but I know it will be a hell of a lot easier if you are with me… I just…."

Your three minutes is about to expire.

I glanced at my Timex. I had been on the phone for barely two minutes. "Hey, you're cutting me off too soon!"

Your three minutes is about to expire.

"Martha, I just want to say…"

"John, I've booked a call tomorrow for 7:30 pm your time. I have something to tell you and –"

The line went dead. "Oh, bugger!"

I slammed the phone back in its cradle, and stared blankly at the hordes of happy, smiley beachgoers descending from buses, lugging surfboards, boogie boards, picnic hampers and towels, moving en masse toward the already overcrowded sands of Bondi Beach.

Gary entered the locker room of number four wharf. "Giddai, mate. Did you speak to Martha?"

I hung my gray overalls in a gray locker and glanced at my watch. "She's ringing me in half an hour. I've got to run!"

"Well, good luck, mate. Hope things work out for yuz."

"I hope so too."

He patted my shoulder and departed.

I buttoned my shirt and pulled on a pair of jeans. I heard the *clicking* sound of the door closing, then the sound of a key turning in the lock.

Tap... tap...tap...

I looked up and saw a face filling the small glass window pane at the top of the door. It was 747 leering down, taunting me with a set of keys dangling in his left hand.

"Touché, peanut snatcher."

I fumbled with the door handle. "You bloody idiot, 747, let me out!" 747's face disappeared, his departing footsteps echoing off the worn out boards of the mess room floor. I heard the outer door slam shut. I thought of an old Mae West line: *His mother should have thrown him away and kept the stork!*

"Somebody let me OUT!"

The skin on my knuckles grew red and raw from banging on the door until I heard more footsteps, then the key turning in the lock.

"What the bloody hell happened here?" Hughie wore his usual scowl.

"747 locked me in. I've got to go!"

Hughie's scowl turned into a grin, as I shot out the door and sprinted up the wharf, but his voice pursued me: "Listen, mate, never do unto others that you would not wish done unto yourself."

Hughie's message had sunk in by the time I reached the taxi rank, but I had no time for self-examination. This was Christmas week in the height of summer and Circular Quay swarmed with holiday makers, all seemingly standing in line to get into the one or two token taxis that emerged now and then from the steaming, teeming jungle of uptown Sydney. A bus looked like my only chance of getting back to Bondi before the beginning of the next ice age so I climbed aboard. Once again, it was standing-room only and slower than "molasses in January" as Martha would have put it.

Already an hour late for her phone call, I was two hours late when I jumped off and ran the two-hundred yards from the bus stop and burst through the front door of the Lodge. Normally bustling with humanity, on this night the Lodge was as quiet as the grave. The silence from the phone was deafening.

1972 began and many of the gang at Nyah Lodge departed in something resembling a mass exodus. Peter had inexplicably imposed a curfew at 10:30 pm, which meant all guests had to be off the premises by then. One of the first to go was Beth; a beautiful person, a rebel with a heart of gold, she lived life under a lot of stress and had a knack of choosing the wrong guys who ended up breaking her heart; consequently, she chain-smoked and drank too much. She hated Peter's rules and regulations. In truth most people hated the rules and just ignored them, but Beth was the one who got caught escorting another soon-to-be-ex-boyfriend to the front door long after the curfew ended.

Not too unhappy about being kicked out, she immediately found a house just a couple of miles down the coast in the suburb of Waverley. Glynis, Noeline and Lennie decided to move with her. Beth asked if I would like to move in too, but I declined. Nyah Lodge had been a good place for me.

On a gorgeous Sydney Sunday afternoon, filled with brilliant blue skies and brilliant blue water, I took a solitary stroll along the cliff path from Bondi to Tamarama to try and sort out things in my head.

"Have you given it any more thought, Johnno?"

I shaded my shades with my hands; the intense sunlight sparkled on the ocean like a carpet of diamonds. A silhouetted figure sat on a rock, arms hugging legs, chin resting on knees.

"No. Not really, Beth. I'm happy where I am for the moment."

Beth picked up a pebble and cast it out over the rocks. I watched it skip a couple of times across the surface of the Pacific Ocean.

"Your rent will be a lot less," she pointed out.

"I've honestly never considered moving."

"I know mate, but don't forget all the new rules and curfews that Peter's put on the place."

A fisherman reeled in a Snapper onto the rocks below. The big fish wriggled defiantly on the hook. The fishermen hit it on the side of the head with a solid piece of wood. It flopped about a bit on the flat-surfaced rock before the fisherman tossed it into a large wicker basket already half full with other dead fish.

"Come over. Check the place out and see what you think."

The fisherman baited his hook and cast his line.

I cast mine for Bondi Post Office and once again unloaded the contents of my sagging pockets into a public phone.

"Hallo!"

"Hello, who is this? Martha?"

"No! It's Betty, Martha's mom."

"Oh! Hello. This is John, ringing from Sydney."

Crackle...crackle...crackle... "Who?"

I flattened my hand over my left ear while pressing the phone hard against my right.

"It's John, Martha's friend." *crackle... hiss.*

"I'm sorry, Jaahn, it's a bad line. Martha's not here; she's out with..." *crackle...* "Sam..." *hisss...* The line went dead.

The Australian mint would have to increase their output of coins for me to continue making long distance phone calls to America.

I sat in my flat, alone and restless, aimlessly pushing the salt and pepper shakers around my little kitchen table while wondering who the heck Sam was. Martha had never mentioned his name before. The last time she had said the words *I have something to tell you*, she told me she was going home. Maybe Sam was the real reason she went home? Maybe Sam was part of her mother's plan to lure her back for Christmas. I sighed and opened a book, read a couple of pages, put it down and turned on the radio.

We'll go walking out
While others shout of wars disaster.

I turned the knob to full volume.

Oh, we won't give in,
Let's go living in the past.

I failed to notice the knocking on my door until the door started vibrating like a San Francisco temblor. I jumped up and opened it for fear it would come off its hinges.

An unsmiling Peter stared at me. "Hey, are you deaf or something? Ma's in bed upstairs and can't get to sleep because of the noise. Turn it down, will ya?"

"It's not noise – it's Jethro Tull!"

"I don't care if it's Turnip Townsend, turn the bloody thing down!"

He slammed the door in his wake, leaving me impressed with his knowledge of the 18th century agrarian revolution in Suffolk.

All good things come to an end. No living in the past for me or Jethro Tull. I packed up my room. There was little to pack: a few clothes, some books and a transistor radio. I closed the door on Nyah Lodge and another chapter in my short life. When I'd moved in, my confidence had been at a low point with ever-present nightmares. Now, as I prepared to move out a year and a half later, they were coming back in the shape of 22 Gipps Street, Waverley.

The house, although solidly enough constructed of red brick and red tile, did not exactly fill me with enthusiasm, due to the peeling paint, threadbare carpet and rising damp. My new room wasn't a room at all, just an open space between the kitchen, laundry and bathroom. Obviously, as the last one in, I had drawn the wooden spoon of rooms.

THE BONDI BREAD VAN

Hughie chewed on his fingernails, more vigorously than usual and stared pensively at the upper girders of the Sydney Harbor Bridge.

"Are you alright, Hughie?"

He continued to stare skyward. "Just thinking about Robert Leman."

"What do you mean?"

"He has lymphatic cancer. Didn't you know?"

"No I didn't. I haven't seen him since Christmas but he never said anything."

"No, he wouldn't. He's very private that way."

I suddenly found the girders interesting too as I tried to come to terms with the news.

"How can God, if there is one, let someone like Robert suffer blindness and then burden him again with cancer? It doesn't make sense." I did not really expect an answer.

"I'm not much for religion myself, but a true believer would say that God moves in mysterious ways," Hughie responded softly, "but in my humble opinion there's too much believing in this world and not enough thinking. Religion puts all that thinking energy in a box."

Surprised that Hughie could be such a philosopher, I

realized I really did not know him at all. I watched him spit out a sliver of fingernail into the murky waters lapping the wharf then fix his gaze on me.

"What do you want to go and bloody well quit for?" he said, returning to his more normal persona. "We were just making a bloody deckhand out of you."

"Hughie, I have other things I want to do with my life now. I'm going home to England for a while."

"Listen, mate." He always said "listen" before launching into a tirade but this time was different. "I know I can be a bit of a bastard, but you've bin alright. I don't want any hard feelings between us." He sounded surprisingly sincere.

"No hard feelings, Hughie. I've enjoyed working here and with you." I meant it. I was going to miss the old bugger. I was going to miss Gary, Georgie and a cast of thousands – even 747, bless his heart.

So that's the way it ended with Hughie, not with a bang but a whimper. The shifts had been taking their toll and at the end Hughie was using me to train new deckhands. It felt too much like a real job. Time for a change. After two years on Sydney Harbor I bid my shipmates adieu. I picked up my pay packet, turned in the uniform and union card and walked away from one of the best jobs I ever had.

My nautical days over, I hit the streets looking for a higher paying job without shifts and compulsory overtime, but I soon discovered that I had made a big mistake and unskilled people were looking for work in droves. Once again, I had not planned ahead. I think Mr. Tittensor would have thrown in the towel at this point.

A gardening job with the City Parks Department looked a possibility, but when I arrived at the office, a line of men and women stretched down two flights of stairs and almost around the block. There must have been a hundred people ahead of me – for two jobs! Disillusioned, I wandered around Sydney in a daze. It felt like déjà vu. I passed a travel agent, where a poster in the window caught my attention. It displayed a

Greyhound Bus traveling through the majestic peaks of the Canadian Rockies; emblazoned across the top in large red letters, it read: *Travel anywhere in the United States and Canada for $99*. I went inside, but all the agents were busy, so I sat and perused the employment section of the *Sydney Morning Herald*. I saw a job for a bread van salesman advertised, no experience necessary. That was me, Mr. J. No-Experience. Unsure if the job entailed selling bread from a van or selling bread vans, I used the travel agent's phone and arranged an interview with Cobbity Farm Bakeries.

The interview, conducted by the manager Ken Harrison, a jovial, redheaded gentleman in his mid-forties, turned out to be a mere formality. The fact that I did not have a valid driver's license did not seem to be an issue; he never asked to see it.

"You'll be getting your own route..."

"Route 66?" I quipped.

"No – route 52. It's part commission and part salary, so you won't starve."

I could not believe my luck when Ken took me out on the first day and I discovered that route 52 took me all around North Bondi, Bondi Beach, Rose Bay, Vaucluse and Dover Heights, an area I knew better than any other in Sydney. My van was the oldest in the fleet; known as the Cobbity Comet, it stalled a couple of times in traffic and nearly reversed over an old woman in front of Franklin's Supermarket in Rose Bay, but Ken laughed it off. I must have hidden my nervousness or he just didn't notice.

After a couple of days with experienced drivers around the route, Ken let me loose. I started at 5:30 am from a cavernous garage underneath the bakery where thirty-plus bread vans were parked. Stacked beside each van were hundreds of still-warm loaves, ready to be loaded. The fleet of vans emerged from the cavern into the early morning light and dispersed to the four corners of Sydney to dispense their fresh cargo.

Things progressed well enough. Fridays were the busiest days, as we had to deliver enough bread to last the weekend. Mondays were busy too, because I had to deal with the weekend returns of bread that had not sold. It became obvious that the run managers were loading me up with more bread than I could possibly sell. Eventually I began to tweak the loads so that we ended up with increasingly fewer returns. Once I had the loads balanced, I began to gradually increase them again – but now it was as needed by the store managers, rather than the wishful thinking of our run managers. Pay and benefits were good and the incentives on offer, such as an all-expenses-paid weekend for two in Surfers Paradise for the top salesman each quarter, encouraged me to work hard and sell more bread, which vindicated my decision to leave the ferry service.

I became a member of the Bread Carters Union. Our delegate came around the first of every month, cap in hand, for his dues, which I paid diligently. I had learned enough in Australia to keep on side with the unions. They had a lot of clout and quite rightly so. Someone had to stick up for the little guy and stand up to those right-wing generals in Greece!

Midway through my daily round I delivered to an old Victorian pile circa 1856 called Strickland House, located on the harbor foreshores in the exclusive suburb of Vaucluse. It had been many things in its lifetime but at that time it housed a women's convalescent home that looked and felt much like *St. John's* transposed 12,000 miles to the south. Indeed, the kitchens where I delivered two dozen farmhouse whites every day had the same dank, dark stone walls and ancient cooking equipment. But there the similarities ended. The ladies who cooked meals for the patients were much nicer than the staff at St. John's. They always had a cup of coffee, bickies and a kind word ready. One Friday before a long weekend, I had to do two rounds because the sheer volume of bread I needed to deliver wouldn't all fit in the van, so I did not arrive at Strickland House until the afternoon. Instead of being irate at my late arrival, one of the kitchen staff, dressed in a white pinafore and white cook's hat, said, "Come and sit down, dear! Would you like some roast beef?"

"Yes, that would be lovely."

She ushered me into a wooden chair at the end of a long rough-surfaced oak table and proceeded to carve slices off a huge roast. Accompanying the roast were boiled potatoes, cabbage, runner beans and Yorkshire pudding covered in lashings of gravy. Before I had finished the roast beef, a hand pushed a bowl in front of me, containing a mound of treacle pudding smothered in custard.

"Just for the road, dear."

I turned to thank the voice. An elderly lady smiled down at me. She wore a neat white uniform like the other staff and looked vaguely familiar.

"Do I know you?"

She smiled. "My name's Ada Benson. I never forget a face. On a cold and damp night; you helped me with my babies!"

"Oh my goodness! I had no idea…"

"That I was a normal person?"

"No, of course not. How are the kitties?"

"Just fine, son, but they're not babies any more. I've found homes for nearly all but one. Perhaps you know someone who would like a lively little Siamese?"

I thought about it a moment. "I don't know, but I could ask my great aunt – I'm heading her way right now."

The route back to the bakery took me past the top of Mary's street and once a week I would drop off a loaf for her. Before I had alighted from the van, I saw Mary standing on the lawn waving to me. She came over.

"Have you heard from Martha, dear?"

I let out a long breath as I stepped onto the street. "No, but I think she's going out with someone else. I spoke to her mother and she said she was out with some bloke."

"Well, it could be her brother, dear!"

"No, her brothers' names are Mark and Eric. His name was Sam."

"Look son, come along inside. Use my phone and ring her now!"

"Are you sure?"

"Of course I'm sure. We won't tell John. You stay on as long as you need to."

I followed her down the short corridor, past the two small bedrooms and into the living room. She sat on the edge of her overstuffed armchair and watched as I dialed an operator who put me through to California. It seemed to take an inordinate amount of time for anyone to pick up.

"Hallow," said a man's voice

I hesitated. "Um... is Martha there?"

"Just hang on a minute... I think she's out with Sam. Hang on..."

I took a breath, dreading what was to come.

"Hi!" It was Martha's voice.

"Martha, it's me, John!"

"Oh my Gaad, I've been trying to reach you. I called the Lodge and Peter said you'd moved on. He didn't know where."

My palms were sweating and so was my forehead.

"Yes, yes, I moved out with the girls, but we don't have a phone. I wrote to you with the address."

"Well, I didn't get your letter. I was worried about you. Sam, Sam, just behave... go away...I'm sorry, John, he's just being a pain but – oh shit, just a minute."

I heard the noise of a phone being dropped on a table. Silence.

"What is it, son? Everything alright?" inquired great aunt Mary in response to my expression.

I shrugged. I heard the phone being picked up.

"Oh my gaad, John, I'm so sorry..."

"What happened?"

"He just peed on Mom's carpet."

"Who did?"

"Sam."

"Sam did? Who is Sam?"

"You know. I told you about Sam – Sam and Digger."

"No."

"My Mom's dogs! I swear I told you about them. They're so cute."

I put my hand over the phone.

"What's up, son? Good news?" said Mary.

I raised my free hand while attempting to hold back a wave of laughter.

"I'll tell you in a minute."

"Are you OK, John?" Martha inquired.

"Yes, never better. Listen. I miss you. I am planning go to England in September. I thought I would do the $99 Greyhound bus trip."

"The what?"

"Never mind, but I'd like to come and visit, if that is OK with you and your mother, of course."

"Like it. I'd love it but I called the Lodge to tell you that I'm coming back to Sydney. I've been missing you so much —"

"What? When?"

"Next month. Is that OK?"

"Next month. Of course, it's bloody well OK!"

I looked at Mary, who was grinning from ear to ear. Even her little blue and white budgerigar "Peter" began to chirp happily, reminding me that there would be no room in this small house for Ada's Siamese and the budgie!

A welcoming party that would have done justice to the arrival of a movie star waited at Kingsford Smith Airport. Martha breezed through Customs wearing a pretty, pale yellow mini-dress. Despite a 17-hour flight from Los Angeles via Hawaii and Fiji, she appeared as fresh as a daisy, looking gorgeous. Four months vanished in an embrace. Had it been only four months? It seemed like four years. I had booked a table for that night at a fancy restaurant called the Martinique in Edgecliff, just a few yards up the road from the hellish carwash I walked away from a year and a half earlier, but I cancelled the reservation when I realized there was really only one place I could take Martha.

"Ahhh, Johnny. You bling flend this time?" Jippy's bulging eyes almost popped out of their sockets.

"Yes Jippy. A very special friend."

"I cook you special dinner then. Velly special dinner."

Jippy ushered us to our table. As usual, there was nobody else in the restaurant. He lit a candle, opened our bottle of wine and left us alone. I poured from the bottle of McWilliams Sauvignon Blanc vintage 1970 and raised my glass.

"It's great to have you back."

Martha raised hers. "It's great to be back."

"To the future…"

We chinked the glasses together.

"To the future, wherever that will lead," Martha said before taking a sip. "Wow! This is lovely wine."

"Yes. A lot of sweat and tears went into that bottle."

"What do you mean?"

"I will tell you sometime." I touched my glass against hers again.

"It's really quite exciting when you think about it," Martha commented, "two different people from two different countries, living in a third country. I wonder what the odds are of us making it."

"It'll work if it is meant to work." I said with some confidence.

"So you had enough of old Tricky Dickie, did you?" Lennie asked Martha as we sat around a table in the kitchen, a kitchen that consisted of a scratchy linoleum floor, an electric cooker that hadn't been cleaned since the turn of the century and a refrigerator that had long forgotten it was designed to keep things cold.

"Yes, and the war, and the Watts riots, and the assassination of the Kennedys, and Martin Luther King. It just got to be too much. I wanted out as soon as I left high school, but the trip home just reinforced why I left in the first place. Come on, I'll make us some breakfast."

Martha mastered the decrepit stove and cooked an omelet stuffed with corn, ham, cheese, peppers, onions and parsley. We had never seen such an enormous omelet. She delicately flipped the thing over.

"Well, we're glad you saw the light, Marty," said Beth. "Johnno hasn't been the same since you left!"

"I always intended to come back. I told John that when I left but somehow our communication got all screwed up." She plonked a steaming mug of instant coffee in front of me. "You could say it went to the dogs."

"We knew youse'd be back." Glynis wandered in, half asleep. "Besides, we missed the dawn chorus!" She waved her fork in the air and commenced singing:

Oh, what A beautiful morning,
Oh, what a beautiful day,
I got a beautiful feeling,
Everything's going my way...

Little privacy existed for Martha and me in that no-man's-land between laundry and bathroom in the house on Gipps Street (although Martha did not seem to mind) so I arranged a short break in Canberra, ostensibly for Martha to meet Noel, Enid and Lindy, but with my expert planning skills I forgot to inform them we were coming.

A taxi dropped us at the end of the dirt driveway leading to Cambrey Farm, the place where my Australian odyssey had begun almost three years earlier.

I knocked on the door of the white weatherboard farmhouse but this time Enid did not come running out, arms spread in welcome. In fact, no one came out. We walked around the back and saw a man in the hen house collecting eggs; a neighbor, he informed us that the Eliots had gone away for the week.

Disappointed, we made the most of things. We cruised on Lake Burley Griffin, cooled off under the sprinklers on the lawn of Parliament House, rode a bus to the Snowy Mountains, climbed Mt. Kosciusko and walked through acres of wildflowers across the highlands to the Thredbo chairlift. It was there that I asked Martha if she would like to return to England with me.

"You see, I really want you to meet my family. I know they would love you as much as I do."

Sitting in a Swiss-style ski lodge supping on tea and vegemite sandwiches, she replied. "Yes, I would love to come with you."

That was it. No argument.

Before boarding our bus back to Sydney, we wandered through pretty rose gardens to the Australian House of Representatives, where we witnessed the dénouement of Australia's involvement in the Vietnam War. The Australian House of Representatives, equivalent to the House of Commons in Britain or Congress in the United States is in reality closer to a bar room slanging match than the highest forum of debate in the land. The venerable man of Sussex, Hillaire Belloc, once said: *The standard of intellect in politics is so low that men of moderate mental capacity have to stoop in order to reach it.*

Gough Whitlam's standard of intellect stood somewhat higher than that of most politicians. At the same time as we were easing our posteriors onto the hard seats of the visitors' gallery, the leader of the opposition was raising his posterior from one of the soft green leather seats in the House of Reps. He shot a verbal broadside at Prime Minister Billy McMahon over his unwillingness to withdraw troops from Vietnam, his negative attitude toward China, and his mishandling of the South African rugby tour. McMahon did not respond to any of the criticism; instead, he walked out of the chamber without saying a word. McMahon is remembered as a bench warmer between John Gorton and Whitlam (somewhat like Gerald Ford between Nixon and Carter) but his glamorous young wife Sonia will always be remembered for the dress she wore to a state dinner at the Nixon White House. It had a slit up the side, exposing flesh from the waist to the ankle and made the front page of all the newspapers in the land.

Soon, the front page of all the newspapers in the land would report that in a no-confidence motion, the house voted 57 to 52 against McMahon, a serious event in a parliamentary democracy, which forced his government to call an election. Whitlam felt the pulse of the people and ran on a populist agenda, easily defeating his opponent. His first act was to withdraw Australian forces from Vietnam and abolish conscription, thus saving the lives of countless National Servicemen in a pointless war:

We now enter a new and more hopeful era in our region. Let us not foul it up this time. Australia has been given a second chance. The settlement agreed upon by Washington and Hanoi is the settlement easily obtainable in 1954. The settlement now in reach – the settlement that 30,000 Australian troops were sent to prevent, the settlement which Mr. McMahon described in November 1967 as treachery – was obtainable on a dozen occasions since 1954. Behind it all, behind those 18 years of bombing, butchering and global blundering, was the Dulles policy of containing China.

Heading back to Sydney, my thoughts were far removed from containing China; they were focused on the girl sitting next to me.

"There's just one thing about me coming to England with you," she said.

"Oh! What's that?"

"I'd like to see some of Australia first. You know Lennie and Glynis are heading north to Cairns and the Reef?"

"Yeah. I was there last year. It's a fantastic place!"

"Well, I kinda said I would go with them, but I was hoping you would come."

I was taken off-guard, but the sudden prospect of touring the Great Barrier Reef with three gorgeous women was just too good to pass up.

On my return to work, the cavern, normally buzzing with conversation and banter was dead quiet, the drivers loading in slow motion. It seemed a little odd to see Ken Harrison stacking bread in my neighbor's van. Ken was the best manager I worked for in Australia, always friendly and helpful; nothing was too much trouble for him. I approached him with some trepidation because I had not figured out how I was going to tell him I was quitting.

Upon seeing me, he jumped from the van, put an arm around my shoulder and bade me sit down on an upturned blue plastic bread crate. He sat down on another and faced me.

"Are you ready for this, mate?"

"Ready for what?"

"Speedy's in jail."

Speedy had always seemed a quiet, pleasant chap with a competitive edge. He liked to be the first out and the first back each day and having him parked next to me, added a bit of spice to an otherwise boring task as I raced to fill my van first. Usually he won the race, but I liked the competition, and if I did happen to beat him, I got a rather self-indulgent satisfaction from being the first out of the starting gates.

"What? Why?" I said.

Ken's cheeks puffed out like a hamster storing nuts, then he expended the air very slowly.

"Why? Because he shot his wife – she's dead."

"Oh my God." I did not know what to feel or say. I really knew very little about Speedy. I didn't even know he was married.

"Yep. He caught her in bed with another bloke. Crime of passion, mate."

I did not say a word about leaving. I did not say a word for two more weeks.

I drove down the hill into Rose Bay and pulled up outside Fleming's Supermarket, where a surprisingly large crowd was gathered on the pavement, their eyes looking skyward as if waiting for Manna from Heaven. A beautiful, elegant bird swooped low across the harbor.

Chatter spread among the crowd:

"What an amazing piece of engineering!"

"It's her maiden flight to Australia, you know."

"Yeah, the poms are trying to flog a few of 'em to Qantas."

"The bugger's too noisy, I say."

Watching the clean futuristic lines of the Concorde flash across the Sydney skyline, I decided it was time to do the honorable thing and come clean with Ken. But when I got back to the bakery I did the dishonorable thing and fabricated a story that to this day, I still feel guilty about. I thought Ken would empathize when I told him I had been called up for National Service. He did empathize, but it proved a big faux pas because on my final day the bread carters organized a party to wish me well in Vietnam. I felt badly but had neither the heart nor the courage to tell them the truth: that I was heading off on a jaunt to Queensland with my girlfriend.

"Come back any time, mate," said Ken. "There'll be a job for you here when you get out of the army."

I knew he meant it.

I looked forward to heading north to Cairns, but not the 36-hour bus journey that it required to get there, so we broke the journey for a hedonistic Easter weekend in Surfers Paradise.

The pre-colonial occupants of Surfers, the Banjalang people, called the area Kurrungul, referring to the endless supply of hardwood for boomerangs. The Surfers Paradise we saw was a suburb of the larger city of Gold Coast, consisting of endless rows of high-rise buildings, cheek-by-jowl with the beach catering exclusively to tourism. It reminded me of Miami. Not that I had ever been to Miami!

On our way to the main beach we observed pretty young women carrying bags of coins and wearing nothing but gold lamé bikinis and tiaras.

"The local government employs them to roam the streets and feed the expired parking meters of tourists," Martha informed us. "The meters were unpopular from the start, so when tourism began to drop the mayor came up with the idea of the bikini girls."

"Why don't they just get rid of the meters?"

"Because the publicity generated by the gold lamé bikini girls attracts thousands of tourists!"

They certainly made for a pleasant stroll to the beach, but when we got there, the cupboard was bare. A cyclone had hit and washed away all the sand, leaving Surfers looking like a space-age Brighton. It had also washed up hundreds of bluebottles, a small blue jellyfish with long entrails. Standing on or brushing up against one in the ocean could result in a nasty sting that left a trail of red welts across the body, a lot of pain, or in a worst-case scenario, death.

Lying on the rocks where sand should have been, Martha pulled a newspaper cutting from her purse. She unfolded it to reveal a picture of four glamorous girls in bikinis on the sandy beach. Two were sitting, one kneeling, and one standing behind them, forming a loose pyramid shape. One of the girls sitting at the bottom of the pyramid was Martha. The page three headline read: *International Pyramid of Glamour*.

Lennie read the caption aloud: *All the way from Santa Barbara, California, USA came shapely Martha Coony, who reveled in the surf and sand at Surfers Paradise.*

It made us laugh.

"It was taken right here in the sand – well," she looked around, "where the sand used to be, anyway!"

I tried to imagine my father's reaction when I told him that the "Beak" was bringing home a page three pin-up girl. I hardly believed it myself.

DEPARTURES

The show over, the curtains drawn, our little group of friends began to exit the stage to make an entrance somewhere else in the world. But before the exodus began I turned twenty-one, so we had a party at Gipps Street to celebrate this milestone and bid farewell to those departing.

"How did you manage to end up in another house full of women?" Graham asked.

"I have no idea. My mother always said it's better to be born lucky than rich!"

"Well, half your luck!"

I had to admit I had been lucky but on the other hand, it had required an awful lot of hard work and angst before that "luck" began to materialize. Gary Player, once famously said, "It's amazing – the more I practice, the luckier I get!" I did wonder how lucky Graham and Jonathan would be on the journey that lay ahead for them. Their body language suggested they had spent too much time in each other's company. They shared an apartment together, worked together and were clearly getting on each other's nerves.

"Hey, Johnno, youse need to light the barbie," yelled Glynis. Anticipating the mass exodus from Gipps Street, she had moved into an apartment with Denise for the short period of time before her own world travels began.

To actually find the BBQ, one had to hack a path with a machete through a backyard with grass so long it resembled a cross-section of the Argentinian Pampas. In the dusty storage area under the house Graham and I found a can of paraffin, which we used to douse the charcoal. When I dropped a match into the middle, the thing went off with a whoosh, sending blue-colored flames in all directions, some of it in the direction of the Pampas.

"Shit, somebody grab a hose," yelled Graham as the dry grass caught fire.

"It's under the house," shouted Lennie, who had quit her job at the Olympic pub and in a matter of days would depart on the *Northern Star* for the long cruise home to the UK.

Things were getting out of hand. I pulled a damp beach towel off the washing line and beat the flames with it. Glynis and Beth appeared with a hose that looked like it had last been used in a Keystone Cops movie. Brittle and full of holes, it was to all intents and purposes, useless, so en-masse we ran to the kitchen and grabbed saucepans, bottles, jugs and anything that held water and poured it on the blazing grass – somehow getting it under control before it became the conflagration that consumed the Eastern Suburbs. But, it didn't stop there. The Keystone Cops were out of control; buckets of water flew in every direction. No one escaped a drenching.

With the Pampas sufficiently singed and trampled, the BBQ fired up, and the tenants doused, the guests began to arrive. The first through the door was Donna with her new boyfriend Jamie, whom she met on the ship coming out to Australia and recently hooked up with again. Jamie looked every inch an Australian surfer with his long blond hair and suntan, but he actually hailed from rainy Manchester. "I want you and Martha to be the first to know that Jamie and me are engaged!"

That was a surprise. Donna's two years as a ten-quid-tourist had passed and now she prepared to head home to Sussex with Jamie. I am sure she had thought twice about marrying the US Marine. Her mother Joan had a similar liaison with a Canadian serviceman in World War II, and the result had been Donna, who never saw her father until her twenties, when she travelled to the United States to seek him out. Jamie was several years Donna's junior. I had an uneasy feeling that the two were not well matched, but who was I to judge? Lou, who had dropped out of university to become a Volvo mechanic, arrived early to organize the disco, which featured a plethora of Elvis Presley records. He climbed a ladder to thread colored lights through the jungle like trees in the back yard. I harked back to Griffith, where children had plucked similar colored lights from the trees that illuminated the goings-on at the weird *Canalival*. Since then Lou had become conventional and I'm sure Mrs. Maher would have said, *He's such a nice boy too, especially now he's decided to settle down and marry Pamela.*

Beth, perpetually broke from sending much of her pay packet home to the family in Parkes, smoked more than ever. She had invited Yehud, a tall, rugged Jewish lawyer whom she was secretly dating, but he was officially engaged to a chosen Jewish girl and if his parents found out, there would be hell to pay.

After downing his last home-cooked meal for some months, Graham turned the key in the ignition of his beat-up VW combi-van, which promptly spluttered and died.

"How far do you think you will get in this thing?" I asked. He turned the key again. Same result.

"I don't know, John. It needs a new engine."

"Not to mention a panel job," Jonathan interjected, referring to the damage done when the van flipped on a trip to the outback.

"Ah, don't worry about that!" Graham responded. He turned the key again...*Puuutt...putt... phutt...* "We'll keep going until it breaks down then we'll dump it and hitchhike."

"You might as well dump it here then!" Lennie shouted.

"Can someone give us a shove?" Jonathan pleaded.

Shoulders leaned into the back of the van and pushed it all the way to the bottom of the street, where it spluttered into life, then roared out onto Bronte Road and downhill toward the beach.

A few minutes later, it came roaring back toward us.

"Good luck, see you in England next year." Martha shouted. As if to punctuate the end of her sentence the old banger juddered, backfired and took off like a rocket up the steep incline of Bronte Road and headed for Perth.

Back at the party, the night wore on. Around midnight we heard a knocking on the front door.

Beth opened it to expose two fresh-faced uniformed policemen.

"We've had a few complaints from your neighbors about the noise. Do you mind keeping it down a bit?"

Holding tightly to Yehud's arm, a half-smoked cigarette poking from the corner of her mouth, Beth said, "Sure. No worries, boys. Do you wanna beer?"

The taller of the two looked at his mate, who nodded back as if there was some secret understanding between the two of them.

"Not now, but do yuz mind if we come back later?"

"Course not, mate. The more the merrier," responded Beth, sucking on what remained of the stub.

Jam-packed with wall-to-wall people, some invited, some not, the house cleared a bit after the visitation of the long arm of the law.

The two cops returned at 2:00 am and plonked themselves down on the threadbare carpet in the living room, dressed in blue uniforms and checkered peak caps, drinking cans of Tooheys Draught till the sun came up over the yardarm. That's Australia for you – everyone out to have a good time at all costs, even the police.

A month before the clock began ticking toward our own imminent departure two things happened: First, I shipped home the Boer War suitcase on its final voyage before being permanently retired to my parents' attic. Second, cousin John left for a two-month tour of Europe to visit his relatives for the first time, including my family in Sussex and my auntie Doreen in London. I felt some pride in having been the catalyst to bring them together. At Kingsford-Smith, we gathered with great aunt Mary and friends to bid cousin John farewell but the realization dawned that we would be gone ourselves before he returned, so it was a sad farewell. John had been good to me over the three years I had been in Australia and Martha had grown fond of him in the short time she had known him.

Two weeks prior to D-Day, we received a card postmarked Perth:

Thanks again for the wonderful send-off you gave us. Haven't had a decent meal since! Well, the old girl made it all the way up to Cairns, across the top end to Darwin and all the way round the Kimberley coast to Perth – about 6,000 miles, we estimate. The oil leaked badly towards the end, but we hobbled into Perth and sold the van for more than we paid for it in Melbourne. Next stop: India, Pakistan, Iran, Iraq and Turkey – all on public transport. See you in England in a few months...we hope! Graham and Jonathan

Now, there's a story with a happy ending and a fine advertisement for the good old 1960s vintage VW campervan. The next story did not have such a happy ending. I received another card, this time from great aunt Mary.

My Dears,

I'm in the Prince of Wales Hospital. I don't want you to worry now, but I took sick on the way to Melbourne to stay with friends. I became delirious and collapsed at the airport. Next thing I know, I'm in the hospital! The doctors say I have bronchial pneumonia. Until now I haven't been well or conscious enough to let you and Martha know,

Love, Auntie.

We hastened to Mary's bedside. She seemed in low spirits. She was missing John, still in Europe but adamant that she did not want the doctors to contact him.

"What good would it do bringing him all the way back here? He worked hard for this holiday. He couldn't do anything anyway and besides, I'm in good hands."

Our last visit to great aunt Mary came the day before our departure. Tears rolled down her cheeks as soon as we walked into her room.

"I'm so sorry, my dears – don't usually get like this, but I've grown so fond of you and Martha. I'm afraid I'll never see you again."

I started to cry too. "You'll see us again, Auntie."

"We'll be back, don't worry, and we'll write you from wherever we are," Martha said.

"I hope so, dear, I hope so. Be off with you now… before I start blubbering again."

I hugged her. We waved a final goodbye from the corridor. The image of her lying alone in that hospital ward, looking frail and sad, remains one of the most painful moments of my life.

The emotions pervaded the farewell dinner with friends at the Woolloomooloo Wool Shed, a jolly restaurant whose theme harked back to old shearing sheds, bullock trains and bush tucker. I did not feel so jolly, sitting on a bench at a communal table supping on kangaroo tail soup and damper, my sadness compounded by the knowledge that this would be the last night we would spend with Glynis, Beth, Denise, Noeline, Barry and Lou. Thoughts of absent friends flooded in – great aunt Mary, cousin John, Lindy, Elisabeth, Noel and Enid, Joy and Rudi, Georgie, Gary, Graham and Jonathan – all who had made my stay in Australia so memorable. I gazed out the window. I had arrived in Australia at this very spot three years earlier and sat on the curb across the street, waiting with two nurses and the Boer War suitcase, wondering what would happen next. Now I was about to make the reverse journey – but still wondering what would happen next! What happened next is another tale for another day.

Before leaving the house on Gipps Street, Waverley, I looked into the bathroom mirror. I placed my hands over my face and slowly lowered them. The face was still the same, but the person behind it had changed a little. I smiled and headed out the door, leaving the house filled only with memories and ready for the next group of tenants.

Thirty thousand feet above the Pacific in a Pan Am 707 bound for Los Angeles, I looked at Martha.

"What was it she whispered to you?" I asked.

"Who?"

"Great aunt Mary. What did she say, you know, when you first met her. You said you'd tell me one day."

Martha dabbed her eyes with a Kleenex.

"Oh my gaash…" She took a deep breath. "She said she could never understand why you left your family to come to Australia and go through all the things you did but…" She dabbed her eyes again and smiled, "… when she met me, she knew."

"She knew what?"

"She knew that you were meant to come here – to meet me."

AFTERWORDS

John and Martha married in 1974 before returning to Australia for a further nine years. They now reside in California and have two children.

Made in the USA
San Bernardino, CA
24 March 2017